OUT OF THE DELTA

The Anthology

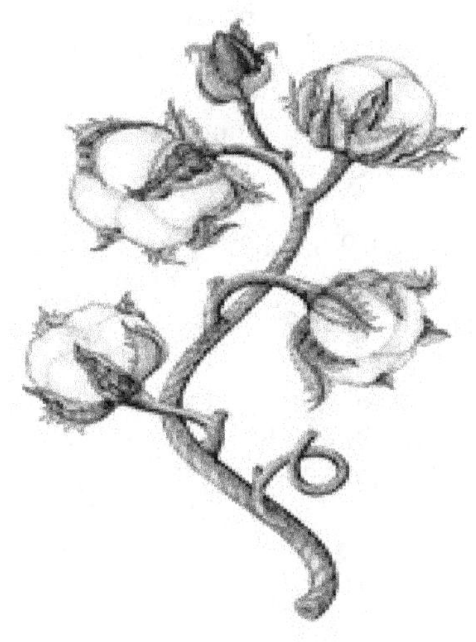

ZEEK TAYLOR

OUT OF THE DELTA
The Anthology
by
Zeek Taylor

Published by Sandy Springs Press
Sandy Springs, Ga.
www.sandyspringspress.com

Printed in the United States of America
First Printing 2022
First Edition 2022

ISBN: 979-8-9862877-2-0 (eBook)
ISBN:979-8-9862877-3-7 (Paperback)
ISBN:979-8-9862877-4-4 (Hardcover)

Editor: Lila LaBine
Cover Design by GetCovers.com
Follow Zeek Taylor online http://www.zeektaylor.com

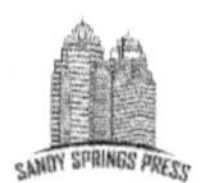

DEDICATION

Dedicated to my life partner, Dick Titus
and to the memory of my parents
Allene and Z.W. Taylor

Table of Contents

INTRODUCTION

I began writing short stories as a way to record my memories and to hone my writing skills. The stories in this book were originally written as "Throw Back Thursday" posts on Facebook. I received positive feedback and requests to compile the stories into a book.

These stories are autobiographical tales that begin in the Northeast Arkansas Delta town of Marmaduke. They continue with my journeys through other locations, professions, and encounters that have shaped my life.

The stories are loosely arranged in chronological order. Times and situations may sometimes overlap. My intent and hope is that each tale stands alone as a short story that makes you laugh or cry, and perhaps inspires you. At the least, I hope you are entertained.

CHAPTER 1 — BOYHOOD

Protectors

Until I was four years old, my parents, two sisters, and I slept in a large, narrow room. I would scoot my green metal youth bed up against my parents' bed and nestle down between our mattresses. I felt protected. When my sisters and I got a little older, my parents decided it was time that we have separate bedrooms. A wall was built that divided the big room into two rooms. My parents moved into what had been a guest bedroom, and my sisters were given the front part of the newly walled room. I was given the back section. I had my very own room. I was alone at night for the first time. It was dark and I was scared.

I had seen the movie Pinocchio, and I was terrified by the villains in the film, Honest John and Gideon the Cat. I thought they were hiding underneath my bed at night. I didn't dare look. For my fourth birthday, I was given a sailor doll. He was dressed in navy blue, and he had a composite head. He was my friend, and I took him everywhere with me. My sailor doll was my protector during dark, lonely nights. I was no longer afraid of the dark and the creatures who I thought were under my bed. One day I dropped my sailor doll and his head shattered. I was distraught. After he was broken, I was once again terrified at night until my grandmother made me a sock monkey as a "protector." My fears abated.

I would cover my head at night and snuggle with my sock-monkey friend. I felt safe and secure. Soon the sock monkey was joined by a new stuffed animal—a hound dog—and then by a real dog, Jiggs.

One Christmas while looking through the Sears Christmas catalog, I spotted a Sad Willie clown doll. I asked Santa to bring me Willie. He did. After that Christmas, I would snuggle underneath the covers with the hound, the clown, and the sock monkey every night. Jiggs would lie on top of the bedspread, against my legs. I had protection.

At times, our guardian angels are who we make them.

Christmas Memories

When I was a very young boy, I claimed Reverend Fern Cook as my girlfriend. Miss Fern was the minister of the Methodist church we attended. The church and the parsonage were across the alley from my family home. That location allowed me to have frequent visits with the good reverend. If I saw Miss Fern in her yard, I would run across the alley to get a hug.

During the Christmas of my fourth year, I was excited to take Miss Fern a present—an assortment of candies and cookies that my mother had made. I walked across the alley, carefully balancing the platter of sweets. My little dog, Jiggs, was close behind. I knocked and knocked on Miss Fern's door. No answer. The door was unlocked. I decided I would go in and leave the gift as a surprise for my girlfriend.

Jiggs and I entered the parsonage and placed the platter on the dining table. It was then that I saw Miss Fern's beautiful Christmas tree. It was lit with bubble lights and decorated with lovely ornaments and sparkly icicles. I spotted real candy canes on the tree. I took one off the tree and ate it. I took another one and gave it to Jiggs. I ate another one. Jiggs ate another one. I decided I might as well take the rest of the candy canes home with me. The tree was tall, but I was able to reach quite a few to take back across the alley. I went straight to my room and laid the candy on my dresser. My mother came to my room and spotted the candy canes. She wanted to know if Miss Fern had given them to me. I told my mother the truth. My mother sternly informed me that I would return the candy, and I would apologize for my misdeed.

My mother kept going back and forth across the alley to see if the reverend's car was back in the parsonage's carport. I sat on the couch and waited. Finally, Miss Fern returned home, and mother escorted me across the alley with candy canes in hand. Jiggs stayed home this time. I was concerned that Miss Fern would be mad at me and no longer want to be my girlfriend. That would have meant no more hugs. I was so relieved when the kind reverend said, "I knew you were coming, and Santa and I placed the candy canes on the tree just for you." She then took the rest of the candy off the tree and gave the canes to me. On that day Miss Fern taught me about love, forgiveness, and the true meaning of Christmas.

Santa Claus Is Coming to Town

The Sears Christmas Wish Book came out in early fall during the 50s. My younger sister and I would spend hours looking at the pictures in the colorful catalog. We would read each item's description and carefully make the important decision about what we wanted Santa to bring us for Christmas.

One year I made a decision in short order. There was a farm set in the Wish Book, complete with a tin barn, fencing, and plastic animals. I had to have it. There was one problem. I was beginning to doubt the existence of Santa. I was afraid if I didn't "believe" then I would not receive the farm set.

It was confusing for me when we would go Christmas shopping, and I would see Santa in more than one store, and all on the same day. I was beginning to doubt my mother's explanation, "They are Santa's helpers." I thought, "Well, then why are they all dressed like Santa?"

I didn't dare mention my doubts to my younger sister. She was unwavering in her belief in the Jolly Ol' Elf. I was afraid to discuss my doubts with my mother for fear that by just questioning out loud Santa's existence, I would eliminate my chance of receiving my dream gift, the farm set.

Every year in December my family attended the nighttime Christmas parade in Paragould, Arkansas. The year of my doubt, as was customary, we bundled up, and drove to the nearby town for the parade. We parked and walked up the street to where the parade would pass, and we secured a good viewing spot. It was then that my mother realized she had lost her purse. Not only had she lost her wallet and the money that was in the purse, but she had also lost her favorite handbag. It was a hand-tooled tan and red leather bag that my aunt Betty had brought to her from Casablanca,

Morocco. My mother muttered a cuss word and then said, "That's that. It's gone. Just enjoy the parade."

Standing on the curb with my father, two sisters, and my grandmother while waiting for the parade to begin, I felt sorry for my mother. After the parade was under way, I soon was lost in the grandeur of the floats and the precision of the marching bands. I was mesmerized by the twirlers who were bedecked in skimpy holiday outfits and wearing white majorette boots with tassels. I forgot about the lost purse.

The last float was occupied by Santa, who was sitting on a sleigh pulled by large, illuminated plastic reindeer. As it neared, my mother gasped when she spotted her purse sitting on the front of the float. A Good Samaritan had found it and placed the purse on the front of the float, knowing that whoever had lost it would certainly see it. We followed the float to the end of the parade. My mother kept proclaiming, "Santa found my purse." She retrieved her prized handbag while happily thanking Santa Claus. He patted me on the head. My doubt about Santa's existence then went away. He had to be real and have magic to pull off such a feat.

On Christmas morning I found the farm set that Santa had left for me. Believe.

Love and Life Lessons

When I turned four years old, my parents decided I was old enough to have my very own dog, and on my birthday they took me to a kennel in nearby Paragould, Arkansas. After looking at all the puppies in the cages, I selected a small reddish-brown puppy. The kennel owner said that he was a toy terrier. He soon became my best friend.

My father and I took the dog to the vet for his shots. I thought the vet was about the nicest person I had ever met, and I wanted to be like him. I decided that I would become a vet when I grew up, and I would work with animals. I also decided in the first grade that I would like to be an artist. I was happy when my mother said I could be both.

I named my little birthday pup "Jiggs." He went with me everywhere that dogs were allowed to go. In the little town where I grew up, that was anywhere and everywhere, including the little grocery stores and cafés. He slept with me, and he tolerated being wagged around and, at times, being dressed in some of my younger sister's doll clothes.

A couple of years after Jiggs came into my life, a beauty shop client of my mother's had a dog with a litter of puppies. The lady asked if I wanted to see them, and I excitedly replied, "Oh yes." When I saw the little spotted pups, I immediately asked her if I could have one.

She said, "You will have to ask your parents."

I ran home and begged my parents to let me have another dog. I promised I would take care of it.

Knowing that the dog was going to be rather large, they did consent but with the stipulation that the dog would live outside. I ran back to the home of the lady who had the dogs, told her the good news, and picked out a fluffy black-and-white pup. I named her "Angel." In my family's backyard there was a nice doghouse that none of my father's bird dogs seemed to like. I asked my daddy if Angel could have it for her house. He thought that was a good idea. I found some old paint, and with one of my art brushes, I wrote Angel's name in big black letters above the doghouse door. No one told me that I had misspelled it. It was much later I learned that I had written the word *Angle*.

The day my father and I picked up the pup and before we brought her home, we drove to the vet's office to get her looked over and get the first round of her required inoculations. I held her and kissed her many times on our fifteen-minute drive to the vet's office. When we arrived, I sat in the waiting room while my father took her back for the inoculations.

When he came back, Angel was not with him. He said, "Let's go to the car."

When we got into the car, I asked why my dog wasn't with us. He said, "Angel was sick, and the vet had to put her to sleep." She had parvo. I asked him what it meant that the vet had put her to sleep, and he gently explained it to me. Not wanting my daddy to see me cry, I climbed over the front seat of the car, and I lay in back sobbing. He left me alone to grieve.

When I got home, my father had me scrub my hands, and my mother had a change of clothes for me. I then ran to my room and there was Jiggs, tail wagging, and waiting for me. I hugged him tightly. At a young age I learned about love and loss. Jiggs lived to the ripe old age of sixteen.

Smart Dog and Art

At age five, I wanted to go to school. We did not have kindergarten where I lived. My father was good friends with the superintendent of schools, and as a favor to my daddy, he let me start first grade a year early. My father drove me to school every morning. During the first week, every time he dropped me off, I would run down alleyways and beat him home. My parents couldn't figure out why; I had begged to go to school. I confessed that I didn't want to be away from my dog. I had a sympathetic first-grade teacher, Miss Versa Butler, and she let me take my dog, Jiggs, to school. He sat in a little seat beside me. From then on, I loved school. I told everyone that Jiggs had learned his ABCs but couldn't say the alphabet out loud because he hadn't yet learned to talk.

I decided to become an artist during the first year in school. I won the grand prize in the first-grade art contest with a crayon portrait that I did of my mother. I drew her hair in fabulous circles with a crayon called mahogany, and I gave her almost perfectly round cheeks with a carnation-pink crayon. As the winner, I had my choice of either a big ol' peppermint stick or a Chick-O-Stick—a toasted, coconut-coated peanut butter stick. I chose the Chick-O-Stick and devoured my prize during the next recess. After winning the contest, there was never any doubt in my mind that I wanted to become an artist. I stuck with my plan.

Dressing Like a Man

A couple of weeks after starting the first grade, I noticed with interest and envy that a boy in my class was not wearing suspenders or overalls. Max was wearing a belt. I didn't know that they made belts for little boys. Then I saw other little boys wearing belts that were just like the ones that grown men wore. By gosh, I wanted one too. I begged and begged my parents for a belt. They finally consented. However, I had to wait until the next weekend when we could go to Graber's, a department store in nearby Paragould, Arkansas.

My mother was a hairdresser. Every Saturday after she finished working, my family would load into my father's car and go to Paragould to grocery shop at Kroger. If my mother got through working early enough, we would get there in time to shop in one of the town's department stores before ending up at the grocery store. On the Saturday when I was to get my belt, I was worried she wouldn't get through in time to go to Graber's. I kept running into the beauty shop to see if she was almost done working. I was hoping that her last customer wouldn't take too long under the hairdryer. My mother did get through in time that Saturday, and we made it to the department store to buy the belt. I'm not sure I could have waited another week. The first night I had the belt, I fastened it around my pajama bottoms, and I slept in it. I felt grown up.

Cookies and Kool-Aid

I grew up in the Northeast Arkansas Delta town of Marmaduke. It had a population of 650 people. Within the city limits there were five churches. If attended equally, each church would have averaged 130 residents. Although most folks did attend, not everyone was a churchgoer, at least not on a regular basis. I don't think I ever went to any one church back then that had 130 people in attendance. The town had one Church of Christ and one Methodist church. The three other churches were all various branches of Baptist: General Baptist, Missionary Baptist, and Southern Baptist. Outside the city limits there were many country churches, including a few more Baptist congregations.

My two sisters and I attended the Methodist Church regularly with our mother. When small, we mainly went to Sunday school. I liked Sunday school because there was always a good chance that some kid in the class would have a birthday celebration. When that happened, the teacher would run down to Crouch's grocery store and buy vanilla wafers and little tubs of vanilla ice cream that we ate with wooden spoons.

Another perk of Sunday school is that we got to color mimeographed pictures of Biblical scenes. I didn't care what the subject matter was as long as I could take advantage of the dozens of crayons available to me. There were colors in the Sunday school classroom that I didn't have at home.

When I got a little older, I opted to stay home and watch African American church services that were broadcast on television via Memphis stations. I watched only for the music, and I turned off the TV when the preaching came on. My mother didn't mind if I stayed home. It was my choice. However, I was not to go out of the house on Sunday morning because some good churchgoer might see me and wonder why I wasn't in church.

During summer, my church hosted a week-long vacation Bible school. I loved going, mainly for the cookies, the Kool-Aid, and the crafts. One of the Baptist churches was directly across the alley from our house, and they also hosted a vacation Bible school. One year the Baptist preacher came a-calling and invited my sisters and me to attend. My older sister told him that we couldn't because "We are Methodists." That didn't stop me. I knew that the Baptists also had cookies, Kool-Aid, and crafts.

I started going to both vacation Bible schools when I was five years old. When I was in the first-grade class at the Baptist Bible school, each student was given a line of scripture to learn. The line was to be recited at a program performed at the end of the Bible school. Each year the program was held at night in the church sanctuary, and it was heavily attended by beaming parents, grandparents, and family friends.

The line that I was given was "The Lord is my Shepherd." I was to recite only the one line. I misunderstood and thought that I was to memorize the entire 23rd Psalm. I practiced and practiced until I had it down pat. The night of the program, my entire family was in attendance. Each of my classmates recited their one line. I recited all of the 23rd Psalm, and I received a large round of applause.

When we got home, my older sister wagged her finger at me and said, "You were just trying to show off in front of the Baptists. You are nothing but a show-off."

My mother stepped in and said, "No, he is just an overachiever." I asked her if that was a good thing. She said, "Yes."

Thereafter the term *overachiever* stuck in my mind. At least she didn't call me *adorably precocious* or a *ham*. Bless my mother's heart.

When I was six years old, my teacher during that summer's Baptist Bible school was Miss Betty. There were ten students in my class. Miss Betty had a baby boy who was a few months old, and she brought him to class with her. One morning the baby was fussy, and to stop his crying, Miss Betty opened her blouse and pulled out a very large breast and proceeded to nurse the baby. I was fascinated. I had never seen an uncovered breast.

When I returned home from Bible school that day, my mother was somewhat shocked when I answered her question, "What did you learn today?" with "Miss Betty's booby is bigger than my head."

It took a lot of begging on my part before my mother consented to let me return to the school the next day. I felt lucky to be there. Half the kids were absent due to the "exposure." It was difficult for me to pay attention that morning. I kept looking at the sleeping baby boy and hoping that he would wake up and cry. However, no such luck.

The Hottest of Dogs

In Marmaduke there was a grocery store, Crouch's, a few doors down and across the street from our home.

The grocery store was a gathering place for locals, and it was located directly across the street from the town's city hall and jail. The jail had been featured in the *Arkansas Gazette* as the only jail in the state with a cell that had a picture window adorned with homemade curtains. Crouch's grocery, owned by Viola and Bus Crouch, was the perfect place to watch the comings and goings from city hall and the jail.

Viola was one of my mother's best friends, and she always treated the Taylors as family. She and Bus lived in a nice large house that was kitty-corner from the store. Every week Viola walked the block to my mother's beauty shop to get her weekly shampoo and set. She had a standing appointment for several decades.

Connected to the grocery store on one end was a service station. Connected to the store on the other end was a café, complete with a jukebox and a pinball machine. The food was home cooked, the menu included open-faced beef or pork sandwiches complete with mashed potatoes, gravy, and slaw. The meal cost fifty cents. I spent a lot of time and many nickels playing the pinball machine and the jukebox. For several decades, my family went to Crouch's to buy groceries, eat in the café, get gas for the car, or just to visit.

When I was four years old, my aunt Betty, uncle Leroy, and cousins came to visit my family. While they were there, my six-year-old sister Cheryl, my five-year-old cousin LeJean, and I decided to have a wiener roast.

We took some hot dogs from my mother's refrigerator, and we brought them to the backyard. We decided the best place to make a fire for the wiener roast was in a doghouse that my daddy had built for his bird dog, Old Tip. The doghouse was built inside a shed that was connected to the garage that housed the family car. Tip's house was filled with easily ignited, highly combustible straw.

My cousin and I had a penny. We went across the street to Crouch's and purchased a one cent box of matches. Viola was suspicious of our purchase. She kept an eye on us and contacted the fire department when she saw smoke billowing from the shed and garage. The fire truck was Johnny-on-the-spot, and the damage was minimal.

Due to our young ages, my sister, cousin, and I were forgiven and had our hot dogs in the house that night for supper.

My mother was forever grateful to Viola for saving the shed, garage, and family car. There were benefits to growing up in a small town. We watched out for each other. I no longer eat hot dogs.

Learning New Words

One Halloween my younger sister, one of our friends, and I went trick-or-treating. Our friend, Stevie, was the middle son of our new-to-town Methodist preacher. He and his family lived across the alley from our house in the parsonage next door to the church. I was eight years old on that Halloween, the oldest in the group, and therefore, I felt responsible for the safety of the others. After two hours of trick-or-treating, we each had a large grocery sack full of candy. On our way home, we were confronted by the preacher's oldest son, Buddy, who was twelve years old and a bully. He stole all our candy. We immediately ran home, crying all the way, to tell my mother. She was furious, and she went in search of Buddy with the three of us hot on her heels.

She found him, retrieved our candy, and cussed Buddy out. I didn't know she knew such words, some that I had never heard. She held on to Buddy's arm, and we all proceeded to walk the couple of blocks to the parsonage. When my mother rang the doorbell she was still furious, and she continued to use the offensive words in front of the preacher. He was so mad at Buddy that he didn't seem to notice my mother's salty language. Perhaps he knew better than to mess with a mad mama bear.

The next Sunday my mother put on a nice dress, her gloves, and her favorite hat. She held her head high and crossed the alley to the Methodist church, where she sat in her usual seat on the pew in the last row.

The preacher never mentioned the incident, Buddy never bothered us again, and I learned several new words that Halloween night.

Not My Monkey

As a child I had many pets. I had dogs, cats, a pony, mallard ducks, geese, pigeons, hamsters, turtles, and a rabbit. I also had aquariums, and I had parakeets.

The one pet that I desperately wanted was a monkey. I would see ads for squirrel monkeys in the back of comic books. No matter how much I begged my parents to let me order one, the answer was always "No, monkeys are too nasty."

In the fall during cotton harvest when folks had money, there was an auction held each Saturday night in downtown Marmaduke. The auction gave folks an opportunity to socialize and to spend some of their "cotton-pickin' money." I loved going to the auctions to watch people bid, and I liked viewing the ever-changing merchandise.

At one of the auctions, there was a live monkey that was going up for bid. I arrived at the auction early, saw the monkey, and immediately ran the couple of blocks back home to get my daddy. I wanted him to go to the auction and bid on the monkey.

He did go back to the auction with me, but he refused to bid on the monkey. Hoping to appease me, he bid on and bought for me a fairly good-sized chalk deer complete with antlers. That helped a little, but it wasn't a monkey. More than sixty years later, I still have the chalk deer. It has an aged patina, the antlers are long gone, and I've had to glue one of its ears back on a couple of times. Every time I look at the deer, I think, *You should have been a monkey.*

Fowl Play

Some of my favorite pets were feathered friends. The first feathered pet I remember was a black-and-white speckled hen. She was a gift to me from my first-grade teacher, Miss Versa Butler. I named the chicken "Polka Dot." She lived a long time, running around our large yard and sleeping at night in a nesting box in the garage. She fit in just fine with my menagerie, and she seemed to enjoy the company of the other animals, including my cats. Eventually she was joined by six ducks and some geese.

My ducks were mallards, two drakes and four hens. Mallard drakes are commonly known as "greenheads," and the hens are called "suzies." I thought it odd that all the girls had the same name. My daddy brought them home to me when they were ducklings. They were sweet, fuzzy yellow and brown babies. Until they got feathers, they lived in a cardboard box in my bedroom, with a lightbulb hanging above them for warmth. When they were big enough, they moved to the yard, and they never strayed off our property. I never saw them fly. I don't think they realized that they could take to the air. My daddy's bird dog was very protective of the ducks and kept any and all predators at bay. Our house was on concrete pillars, and the ducks slept under the house at night. Every now and then, one of the suzies would make a nest and sit on eggs. The eggs never hatched. My daddy said it was because it had thundered and that prevented the eggs from hatching. I never understood why he thought that could be the reason.

I also had parakeets. Except for one, I named each of them "Timmy" after my favorite TV star, the young boy on *Lassie.* The one exception was a solid white 'keet that I named "Angel." Angel enjoyed riding on top of the cars on my electric train. My older sister was terrified of birds. Although it was very naughty of me, I thought it was fun to hear her scream when I let one of my parakeets fly free in the house. My parents didn't think it was funny. I couldn't help myself.

For several years, I had a large walk-in coop that housed several fantail pigeons. My uncle Buster gave them to me. Unfortunately, he tagged the ones that were to be mine with rubber bands on one of their legs. He left the bands on too long, and by the time I got them, two of the birds had lost a foot. It didn't bother me. I called them my pirate pigeons.

Two of my favorite feathered pets were geese. Early one spring I walked down to the feed store and purchased a pair of goslings. My mother allowed me to keep them. The geese, Mutt and Jeff, quickly imprinted on me and considered me to be their mother. I enjoyed walking the couple of blocks to our downtown with the goslings following me in single file. The goslings would often leave a mess on the sidewalk. It didn't matter much, as there were always messes on the sidewalk left by the old men sitting on benches and spitting tobacco. During warm weather, I was always barefoot. When I walked downtown during the summer, I kept my eyes focused on the sidewalks to avoid stepping in the tobacco juice. During the summer that I had the goslings, they instinctively weaved through the obstacle course with me.

When the goslings grew into geese, they became territorial. They patrolled our unfenced yard and kept away every creature that they thought didn't belong on the property. Unfortunately, that included the women that came to my mother's beauty shop. Mutt and Jeff would nip at the ladies' legs and chase them to the door of the shop.

My mother said, "They have to go." One of my father's good friends had a cotton patch, and he used geese to weed the cotton. Geese do not like the taste of cotton, but they will eat young Bermuda grass, Johnson grass, sedge and nut grass, puncture vine, clover, chickweed, horsetail, and many other weeds. Even though I was sad to see them go, I thought that the cotton farm would be a good place for them to live. I knew they wouldn't be eaten because they would provide a valuable service as weed eaters in the cotton field. The first night that they were gone, I cried while worrying that they were missing their "mother."

Children do not always look like their mother. Not at all.

Caw of the Wild

When I was a child in the Arkansas Delta, I spent as much time outdoors as possible. I loved our large yard in the middle of town, and I enjoyed watching visiting birds feasting on the fruit from my mother's cherry tree and the grapes from her vines.

I was twelve years old when I was surprised and delighted by a feathered visitor who showed up in the backyard. It was early spring that year when I went outside and, shortly after exiting the screen door, was startled when a crow landed on my shoulder. Although I flinched, the crow stayed put. I reached up with my hand and gently placed the large bird onto my forearm. The tame crow obviously had been someone's pet.

During the summer that year, nearly every time I went out the back door, the crow was there to greet me. I had snacks for him from my mother's icebox. He loved bologna. I named him Benny.

Benny would land on my shoulder, my head, or my arm. He did not do the same for other members of my family. The crow and I had a special bond. A few times, the brave bird perched on my shoulder while I rode my pony. There were moments when I thought about taking Benny inside my house and putting him in a cage. I just could not do it. I realized that it was important for him to be free.

In the fall of that year, Benny's visits became fewer, and eventually he quit coming. I was sad, but I hoped that he was safe and sound, and happy. Most of all, I hoped he was still flying free.

Since that time, I've had a fondness for crows, and I often use them as subject matter in my paintings.

Thank you, Benny, for the inspiration.

No Need for Shoes

In Marmaduke during the 50s and 60s, school was not in session during September and October. Those were the months of cotton harvest, and we were in the fields "a pickin'." Instead, we went to school in July and August. During the summer months, students had the option of going to class barefoot. Students in the first three grades were required to have a note from home saying it was permissible to be barefoot. A note was not required to be shoeless for students in grades four through twelve.

I loved to be barefoot, and that's how I went to school during the summer. I started toughening my feet as early as possible, and if weather permitted, as early as March. One of my childhood friends had to abide by his mother's rule, "No bare feet before May 1." I felt a guilty pleasure when I pranced around without shoes in front of him prior to his permissible barefoot date. By May, my feet were very tough. I enjoyed showing off, and I would tell friends, "Watch me run down a gravel road without shoes." The soles of my feet were like leather.

During the warm months there were two requirements at bedtime: check for mosquitoes in the house and wash feet before getting into bed. By bedtime, my feet were black with dirt and required vigorous scrubbing.

There were hazards to being shoeless. The greatest peril was stepping on honeybees that were feasting on clover. Our yard was filled with the blooms, and I often stepped on a bee. Most of the time the pain was bearable, but it hurt enough that if my parents were in earshot, I would get in trouble for yelling out a cuss word. One spring I was stung multiple times, and my swollen foot required me to use a cane for a week or two.

The worst barefoot trauma did not happen to me but to my younger sister. When I was eleven and she was nine, we were bicycling shoeless one night. When her bike pedal went up under a car bumper, the bumper almost cut off four of her toes. I fainted for the first time ever when I saw what had happened. Fortunately, doctors were able to reattach her toes. Although we still went barefoot, we never again rode our bikes without shoes.

I am still a proud barefoot Arkie. No matter the season, when I walk into my house, I immediately kick off my shoes. No need to wait till May.

Building Castles

Fried fish is a staple food in the Arkansas Delta. My family had fish on the table three or four times a month. My daddy ran nets on the Saint Francis River, a swampy river that fed into the Mississippi. He would check the nets every weekend, and many times he brought home a catfish weighing over one hundred pounds.

We considered catfish to be fine eatin.' A fish meal would always include fried potatoes, slaw, onion, and hush puppies. When my daddy caught a really big catfish, he would cook it in a big iron kettle in the yard, and everyone in the neighborhood would enjoy the feast.

My family would often go fishing on a Sunday afternoon during the summer. My daddy had a flat-bottom boat, olive green in color and powered with an outboard Evinrude motor. The boat was big enough to accommodate my parents, my grandmother, my two sisters, and me.

Early on, it became evident that there was no way on earth that I was going to bait a hook. A family member, usually one of my sisters, would bait it for me. I thought, *How could they be so mean to those worms?* When my bait was hooked and in the water, I was bored to death sitting still, holding the bamboo pole, and watching the red and white float while waiting for a bite. I would last about five minutes before I started squirming, talking, and driving everyone crazy. I could not sit still in the boat and be quiet. I was far too fidgety and way too talkative.

When I was ten years old, my parents figured I was capable of taking care of myself, and they thought it would be best for me, and all family members, to leave me on the shore while they went out in the boat. That suited me just fine.

I would spend the afternoons building castles with the muddy sand, collecting driftwood and mussel shells, catching crawdads and minnows, and exploring. I was a good swimmer. There were no worries about me drowning if I should fall into the river. One would never get in the Saint Francis River on purpose. The water was coffee colored, and the muddy brine was home to water moccasins, snapping turtles, and gar.

At times during the fishing trips, my family would float out of sight and go around a bend in the river. I liked when they couldn't see me. I felt free from supervision, I felt responsible, and I felt grown up. I also felt free to turn cartwheels, dance, sing, and just be silly. I could do whatever I wanted to do without fear of being ridiculed by my sisters.

The fishing trip would end well before dark so there would be enough time to clean the caught fish after we got home. My sisters liked to clean the fish. My daddy had built a fish cleaning table in the backyard.

My sisters, Cheryl and Rhonda, would get the metal handheld grater-like fish scalers, and they would vigorously and rhythmically start removing the scales. No way could I do that. When they slit the fish open to remove whatever was inside, I would gag.

I decided that while they were cleaning the fish, I was better off staying in the house. I would sit in my room, think about my day, and remember how much fun I had while playing on the riverbank.

I am very fortunate and thankful to have had understanding parents who let me build castles in the sand.

Let's Pretend

When I was a child, I spent many hours playing outside and pretending. I was often joined in playtime by my friends and sisters. In my little Delta town, there were no after-school programs or public facilities available to children. We amused ourselves.

I didn't have a playhouse, but when my mother got a new appliance, I turned the large item's shipping container into my own little house. I would carefully cut a door and some windows into the heavy-cardboard box with a butcher knife. I would spend hours drawing on the walls with crayons. I would draw and color curtains around the windows, furniture, and paintings for the walls. On the cardboard floor, I would draw linoleum. After I finished with the decorating, I would spend many hours in the house. My little home was often visited by my younger sister, my dog Jiggs, and a cat or two. The cardboard playhouses didn't last. They were outside, and they eventually collapsed after a few rains.

I also did not have an elephant. I was a big fan of Johnny Weissmuller's Tarzan movies. The films often played in the late afternoons as a "Million Dollar Movie" broadcast from a Memphis television station. I saw each one several times. I wanted to be Tarzan, but I needed an elephant. The closest thing to an elephant that I had was the propane tank in our backyard. I spent many an hour riding it. If my little cat Mitzi was nearby, she became a ferocious lion.

One time my elephant almost did me in. I was a growing boy and eventually became tall enough to reach the electric wires that were above the propane tank. The lines ran from the house to an outbuilding. One day I decided they were vines for me to swing on just like Tarzan did in the movies. I jumped up and grabbed the wires. The wires stretched down far enough that my bare feet were back on the metal tank. I received a tremendous jolt of electricity, about a hundred times stronger than the shock I had received after sticking a bobby pin into an electric outlet.

My mother was in the kitchen and heard me screaming. She saw what was happening, ran out with a broom, and knocked me off the tank. The electric wires were still in my hand when I hit the ground. They were pulled completely off the house. I was "shook up" from my near fatal jungle ride, and I stayed off my elephant . . . for a while. Pretending to be Tarzan, I craved excitement and danger. Imagination sometimes becomes reality.

Jump Down, Turn Around, Pick a Bail of Cotton

During the fall in the Delta, cotton gins operated around the clock, and the economy boomed. I started picking cotton in 1951 at the age of five. My grandmother Eva Belle Harvey had picked cotton all her life. I loved my grandma and wanted to work in the field just to be with her. She made a little cotton-pick sack out of a pillowcase for me, and she attached a colorful shoulder strap to it. The sack was just the right size for a little boy.

Along with my grandmother and me, my younger sister picked. My older sister did not. She claimed to be allergic to cotton. I never questioned her excuse for not picking, but I did wonder how she was able to wear cotton clothing? My mother and father too never questioned her reason for not working in the cotton field. My parents did not make us work. My younger sister and I wanted to work.

When I got older, I went to the fields with friends, and I graduated to using much larger pick sacks. The sacks were made of heavy-duty canvas duck with rubber or tar reinforcement on the bottom side to keep them from wearing out as they were being dragged on the ground. Sacks were available in six-foot, seven-foot, and nine-foot lengths. Pickers placed a rock or cotton boll in one of the inside corners of the sack at the bottom and secured it with a wire made into a loop on the exterior. The wire loop allowed for the cotton-filled sack to be hung on a scale and weighed.

At the beginning of the season, the cotton husks were hard on the hands. Some pickers wore cotton jersey gloves with the ends of the fingers cut from the gloves. I picked bare-handed. It didn't take long for my fingers to toughen and become calloused.

When poke berries were ripe, we would decorate our sacks with the bright purple juice from the berries. We would draw pictures and write our names on them. That was our form of graffiti.

Cotton farmers didn't want to pay for wet cotton. It weighed more at the scales. Therefore, workdays in the cotton patch started the minute the dew was off the plants. We were paid three cents a pound, three dollars a hundred. Older pickers would work two rows at a time, one on each side. It was grueling, backbreaking work. We would alternate between bending over and crawling along on our knees while we picked. Tall cotton not only yielded more but also meant a person didn't have to work as hard because they didn't have to bend over so far. In the South, the term "walking in tall cotton" also means that times are good and that a person is successful.

When a pick sack was filled, it was hoisted across the picker's shoulder and carried to the cotton wagon to be weighed and emptied. Lifting that filled sack was at times the hardest task of the day. A nine-foot sack could hold seventy pounds or more. Emptying the sack in the cotton wagon was also difficult. At each weighing, the farmer would record the pounds picked by each worker. He would use a pencil to write the numbers down in a notebook. Even though I was a scrawny teen weighing about 110 pounds, I could pick between three and four hundred pounds of cotton a day. We were paid in cash at the end of each workday.

Pickers would break for lunch midday, find shade, and eat with dirty hands. Each worker brought their own lunch. Many of the workers had lunch pails that were recycled small metal lard cans with handles. My mother didn't cook with lard, and I didn't have one of the red and white pails. I proudly carried a store-bought lunch box.

We called the noon meal "dinner." It usually consisted of sandwiches, chips, or the ever-popular canned Vienna sausage. Oftentimes my mother would make me a sandwich from a leftover breakfast sausage and biscuit wrapped in tin foil. In the heat, the sausage and biscuit sandwich would stay nice and warm.

If the cotton farmer had crushed ice available in a tub, we were able to keep our Coca-Colas nice and cold. We also kept our drinks cooled in thermos bottles. The cotton farmers did have cold water available for drinking that was cooled by a big chunk of ice. We all shared one metal long-handled dipper to drink from, and no one thought anything about sharing that dipper.

Fields were picked three times. Workers preferred fields that offered "first picking" because the yield was higher. When the fields were picked the second time through, there was less cotton to harvest. By the time of the last picking, the third time through, there wasn't much left, and most of the cotton bolls were rotten. That picking was called "pulling." When we "pulled cotton," we could strip the stalk and put the cotton along with the attached hulls into the sack.

For the first and second pickings, the cotton farmers wanted the cotton to be clean with no trash in the pick sack. Because trashy cotton weighed more, when we pulled, we received only two cents a pound. I could pull about four hundred pounds a day. Pulling was done in the late fall. It was often chilly, and we worked while wearing flannel shirts.

I liked working in the fields and making money. I used my cotton-picking money to buy new school clothes, paperback novels, records, and school supplies. At the age of twelve, I made enough money to buy a small horse. At fourteen, I purchased a small Allstate motorcycle for $125 from the Sears catalogue, and at sixteen, I was able to buy a 1952 Ford for $300. I continued picking cotton each fall, until I graduated from high school at the age of seventeen.

Back then I thought life was good and that I was truly "walking in tall cotton." I am grateful for my early work experience. It taught me "incentive." I learned that the harder I worked and applied myself, the greater the rewards. It was a valuable lesson that I still try to apply to my life today. I'm still "walking in tall cotton."

No, I Don't Speak Spanish

During the 50s and 60s, cotton harvests in the fall brought interesting visitors to my little town. One of the local cotton growers, who farmed hundreds of acres, brought in migrant pickers from Mexico. The cotton farmer owned a couple of old school buses that transported the workers from south of the border to Arkansas to work during the eight weeks of harvest.

The Mexicans, all men, worked for lower wages than we did. They picked for two cents a pound, two dollars for a hundred pounds. We were getting three cents a pound, and that equaled three dollars for a hundred pounds. The Mexican pickers were extremely hard workers. Often on the way to work, I would pass by a field where they were working. I could see from the amount of cotton in their sacks, they had been picking since daybreak.

The Mexican workers had a different method of picking than we did. We dragged our pick sacks draped across one shoulder, and we picked to the side. Many of the pickers from Mexico would straddle their pick sacks and drag the heavy bags of cotton between their legs.

The Mexicans lived in shotgun shacks on the cotton farm. Housing was provided by the cotton grower. Ten or more men would live in one of the two-bedroom houses. The houses were called shotgun shacks because they were long and narrow with one room directly behind the next. The doors were lined up in such a way that it was said you could shoot a shotgun through the front door, and the shot would travel all the way through the house and out the back door. Most of the shacks were without indoor plumbing and had hand-drawn wells and outhouses.

When I was a child, I was curious about the workers from another country. They were very different from the folks living in my area. After working in the fields all week, the Mexicans enjoyed coming into town on Saturday nights. They ate in the local cafés, and they bought food in the grocery stores to take back to their shotgun shack homes.

When I was around ten, I befriended one of the workers, Juan. I sought him out every Saturday night during the fall of that year when the workers came into town. Juan was in his twenties. Despite our language barrier, we had a good time together. Juan taught me words in Spanish, and I taught him some English words. He would point to an object, and I would tell him the word for it in English, and he likewise would tell me the word in Spanish.

On the last Saturday spent with Juan before he was to go home to Mexico, we continued our language lessons. Juan pointed to a piece of wood that was placed across a ditch as a walkway. I said, "Plank. It's a plank." He told me the Spanish word.

After he had left that evening, I worried almost to the point of obsessing that I should have said "board" instead of "plank." I worried about my conceived mistake for weeks. I hoped that Juan would return for the next cotton harvest so that I could make the needed correction.

I never saw him again. However, I doubt if he remembered the English word "plank" any more than I remember the Spanish word for the object. I still don't know.

Little Zeek Wanted a Pony

One of my favorite childhood books was *Little Benny Wanted a Pony*. After reading the book, I too wanted a pony. When I was twelve years old, my parents said that if I made enough money picking cotton to purchase a pony, then I could have one. From the minute they told me that, I couldn't wait for cotton-picking season to begin.

I didn't want just any pony; I wanted a pinto. I had Native American blood in my heritage from both of my maternal grandparents. From watching Westerns on television, I came to the conclusion that most Native Americans had pintos. I would settle for no less. I felt that it was my obligation to ride a multicolored horse in honor of my heritage.

A few weeks before the cotton season, my daddy and I made plans to build a stable and to fence the very large lot next to our house. We were in the middle of a little Delta town, and there were no zoning restrictions concerning livestock and fowl. A friend of mine in town had a cow that he rode on occasion, and many folks inside the city limits had chicken pens. Bunk Tuberville, who lived in town, had a team of horses. Humans and beasts lived in harmony in Marmaduke.

Daddy could see how determined I was to buy a pony, and he knew that we should have the stable and fence ready before the beginning of the cotton harvest. We enjoyed working together to build the stable. However, at times he did get tired of my constant babbling about my future equine purchase.

My great-uncle Floyd was a wheeler-dealer and a gambler. He always had odds and ends to sell, including merchandise he won while playing cards. About that time, he won a small pinto gelding in a poker game. It was larger than a Shetland but not as big as most horses. It was the perfect size for a twelve-year-old, and it was a pinto. He offered to sell the small horse to me complete with saddle for $125. He said that he would hold it for me until I could come up with the money.

I quickly estimated that for three cents a pound of cotton, I would need to pick over 4,200 pounds in two months. I had to average picking 525 pounds a week. When I was twelve years old, I could pick between 125 and 150 pounds a day. I was confident that I could reach my goal during the eight weeks of harvest. I did, and I got my little horse. I even made some extra money, enough to buy a currycomb and other accessories necessary for equine care.

The little horse's name was Prince. I didn't like the name very much, but I was advised to keep it. I did keep the name, but I added "Albert." "Prince Albert" was the name of a popular pipe tobacco. What I didn't know when I purchased him, is that Prince hadn't been broke. I tried to ride him, but being inexperienced, I kept getting bucked off. My parents were proud of the hard work I had put in that fall while picking cotton. They decided to reward me by paying to have Prince trained by a professional. When he came back to me from the horse trainer, Prince was rideable.

Despite being trained by the pro, the horse still had a stubborn streak. It was a constant struggle between us as to who was the boss. I could handle him most of the time. However, he was always kicking and leaving bruises on my sister and my friends. He bucked off one of my friends, and that friend suffered a broken arm. If I had the saddle on Prince, even when he bucked, I could stay astride. If I was on him bareback, I was thrown off.

Sometimes when he decided he didn't want me on him, he would lie down and roll over. I had no choice but to get off him.

Although we were often at odds, Prince Albert and I did love and respect each other. I think we understood each other. I was stubborn myself. I also knew that he would do anything I wanted him to do if I kept apples handy as treats. I enjoyed that wonderful creature for the many years that I had him. He was worth every pound of cotton that I picked to purchase him.

Hard work paid off, and I still love the smell of a horse.

Playtime

In the Northeast Arkansas Delta town of Marmaduke, where I attended school during the 50s and 60s, there were few activities for young people outside of school and church. We didn't have a band, choir, or a drama department at our school, and the only competitive sport was basketball. We attended school in July and August, and we were out of school in September and October during cotton harvest. While kids from larger schools were playing or attending football games, we were in the fields picking cotton.

Marmaduke did not have a skating rink or a swimming pool, and we didn't have little league baseball. The town's only movie theater had closed in the early 50s. We did have a Boy Scout troop, and I enjoyed scouting activities. Despite the lack of youth facilities and activities, we were never bored. We entertained ourselves.

Summer nights were spent outdoors, and kids could safely venture anywhere within the city limits. My friends and I caught lightning bugs and played yard games, like Red Rover and tag. We walked or rode our bicycles all over town. We stayed outside until dark when the mosquitoes came out in full force and made playing outdoors miserable. We then reluctantly went into the house, often with lightning bugs in jars, and we scrubbed our dirty bare feet before getting into bed.

Before turning out the lights at bedtime, I would check for mosquitoes in my bedroom. Nothing was more irritating than to have one of the pesky bugs buzzing and circling my head while I was lying in bed in the dark.

During summer months there was a fly swatter on my dresser, and it was used to squash the bloodsucking insects.

My parents owned three big lots in town. Our house sat on one of the lots. The lot next to the house had fruit trees growing on it along with my father's very large vegetable garden. The third lot was overgrown with Johnson grass. My father would let it grow tall so that I could play in the head-high grass. He showed me how to use a sling blade to carve a pathway into the center of the grass-covered lot where I would clear a huge circular-like room in the middle of the tall growth. I would leave the cut grass on the ground. When dried, it made a thick pad that kept additional grass from sprouting. My friends and I spent many summer hours in the grass room. Sometimes my male friends and I pretended it was a fort on the Western frontier. Other times while playing with my younger sister and her dolls, it became a cozy home.

When I turned twelve, I bought a small horse with money that I had earned from picking cotton. The third lot was then fenced, and a stable was built for the horse. The grass was never tall again because Prince, the horse, found the grass to be quite tasty.

I didn't have a treehouse, but I did have a tree nest. There was a twenty-foot-tall tree next to one of the outbuildings in our backyard. The tree was partially covered with honeysuckle vines. I would climb high up into its branches and form the vines into a large bird's nest. It was big enough and strong enough to accommodate four kids. It was the perfect hideaway and a good place to smoke dried grapevines and not get caught.

Parents in Marmaduke did not worry about their children going out and about in town, and we were allowed to roam freely. There was little if any crime, and doors were left unlocked. Everybody knew each other and looked out for each other. One place I was not allowed to go was the sawmill. We were warned to stay off the huge mounds of sawdust because they could collapse, burying and suffocating us. We didn't listen. After the sawmill workers went home for the day, we would climb to the top of the mounds and surf down on our butts. Before heading home, I would carefully shake the sawdust out of my hair, pants, and shirt.

We knew we were not to climb the water tank that was located on the north end of town. It went without saying that going up the ladder of the one-hundred-twenty-foot water tower was forbidden. However, we did climb it, but only under the cloak of darkness. Because Marmaduke was sitting on flat ground and no building in town was more than two stories tall, the water tank was the only place to see an aerial view of the town. Teenagers would climb up the tall tank with a can of black spray paint to tag the cylinder at the top with "The class of" followed with the numerals of the year they would graduate. I never did write on the tank with spray paint. That was vandalism, and if I had been caught, I would have disappointed and embarrassed my family.

Only once did my parents become concerned when I didn't return home for supper. On that day, a friend and I had decided to play at his father's cotton gin. We were ten years old. It was summertime, and because it was not ginning time, there were very few workers on site. We climbed a ladder to the top of a metal silo that was more than three stories tall. The bin was empty, and we climbed down the interior ladder to the bottom of the large cylinder. The sunlight coming in through the entrance hole allowed us to see.

Once inside we couldn't talk loudly for fear of being heard, but we could talk loud enough to enjoy the echo-like reverberation of our voices. We ran in circles inside the huge cylinder until we were exhausted. We then sat down and continued echo talking. When a train roared by on the nearby Cotton Belt Railroad track, we screamed, and then we laughed.

Two or three hours after we had climbed into the bin, we heard people calling our names. We gave each other the *Oh crap, we're in trouble* look. Our parents had become worried because we were more than an hour late returning home for supper. Half the town had been out looking for us. We yelled back, and we carefully climbed to the top of the bin. When I poked my head out the opening, I was surprised to see both sets of parents and twenty or more townsfolk standing down below. They applauded. I looked at my friend, and I could see relief on his face. We were not in trouble. Our folks were just glad to find us alive and unharmed. We received hugs, and we were made to promise to never go into the bin again. We promised.

I did keep my promise and never went back into the bin at the cotton gin. I did continue to go back to the sawmill.

Television and the Moon over the Mountain

I was four years old the first time I saw a television. My family was visiting relatives in Detroit, and they had a TV set in their basement rec room. I didn't want to do anything the week we were there but sit in front of the black-and-white screen. I particularly liked the *Howdy Doody Show* that was broadcast daily. My favorite character on the show was Flub-a-Dub, an amalgamation of eight different animals. When the time came to leave Detroit, I watched my relatives' television until the car was loaded. I didn't want to leave, and my father had to pick me up and carry me out of the basement.

A few weeks after we had returned home, Lester Wycoff opened a television store in my hometown. My entire family walked down to his store, and my parents picked out a nice console. It was the very one that I wanted. When Mr. Wycoff turned it on, the program on the screen was a variety show featuring dancing girls. I thought that each time I turned the set on I would see the Rockette-style dancers.

On the day when my father picked up the television set, he also came home with a very tall antenna that he had bought from Mr. Wycoff. He attached it to the house. It went way above the rooftop. My father fiddled with the antenna and eventually had it turned to sharply pick up the only available stations in the area. They originated from Memphis, and they were NBC, CBS, and ABC affiliates, the only networks available in 1950.

The antenna was like a lightning rod, and my father would disconnect the TV the minute he heard distant thunder. He removed the plastic clothespin connection from the back of the set and placed it in a glass fruit jar so that it wouldn't touch the floor. One time he neglected to disconnect the set before bedtime even though a storm had been forecast. Half asleep and oblivious to nearby thunderous booms, he was on the way to the bathroom in the middle of the night when lightning hit the antenna. The bolt traveled into the television, and it exploded as my father, in his underwear, walked by the set. The explosion and Daddy's cussing woke up the household. We all rushed into the living room and saw the acrid smoke that poured from the set. It was the first time my two sisters had seen my father in his underwear. He quickly retreated to the bedroom, donned a pair of pants, and he and my mother carried the set into the yard in case it caught on fire. We got a new Zenith the next day.

Lester Wycoff only sold Zenith brand televisions. He convinced my parents that there were no finer sets on the market. Until the day my mother passed away, she remained loyal to the Zenith brand. When I purchased a small set for my mother's kitchen counter one Christmas, I made darn sure it was a Zenith. She was pleased that she could sit at the table, eat supper, and watch *Wheel of Fortune* on the best brand of television that was on the market.

When I was a child, I loved to watch *Captain Kangaroo*, *Pinky Lee*, *Soupy Sales*, *Roy Rogers*, and *Ding Dong School*. I had a childhood crush on Miss Francis, the host of the *Ding Dong School*. During one segment, Miss Francis held up a stuffed rabbit and asked, "What should we name the rabbit?"

I replied, "Carrot."

Miss Francis said, "I think Carrot would be a good name."

I was convinced that she had heard me. I ran into my mother's beauty shop to excitedly proclaim, "Miss Francis talked to me through the television."

My mother laughed and said, "That was nice of her." Although not a children's show, I also enjoyed *The Kate Smith Hour*. I could barely wait until the show's end when Miss Smith would sing "When the Moon Comes over the Mountain." It was my favorite song.

When I got older, I watched *American Bandstand* each afternoon. Weekend nights, I stayed up and watched black-and-white movies on the *Late Show*. I watched until all channels went off the air at midnight, and the image of a Native American's head appeared on the screen.

I still talk to the television, especially while watching the news channels. I don't think they hear me the way Miss Francis did the day I named Carrot. I sure do miss Kate Smith and Miss Francis.

Poke Sallet and Purple Stains

Poke grows wild in the South. While most parts of the plant are toxic, if prepared properly, poke leaves and stems are safe to eat. However, it is advised that gloves be worn while picking and preparing the leaves. The greens should be boiled in water, drained, and rinsed with cold water. The process should be repeated two more times before the greens are considered nontoxic. Because poke is strong in flavor, it is often mixed with turnip, mustard, or collard greens. When served, a little pepper vinegar should be poured over them. Cornbread is traditionally served with all greens and should be cooked the Southern way, without sugar. The bread is tasty when dipped in the pot likker, the juice left in the pot after cooking the leaves.

When my mother cooked poke, everyone knew what we were having for supper. The strong odor from boiling the greens filled every room in the house. They tasted better than they smelled.

The young, tender stems of the poke plant may be harvested in early spring and cooked using the same method of boiling and rinsing that is used when preparing the leaves. The cooked tender stems are known in the South as "country asparagus" and often served with hollandaise sauce.

Although tempting, the beautiful aubergine-colored berries should not be eaten, but the juice from the berries may be used for dyeing fabric. My friends and I would use the berry juice to write our names on canvas sacks that we used when picking cotton. Along with our names, we often adorned the pick sacks with crudely finger-painted designs. The purple stain from the juice would remain on our fingers for several days.

One summer three of my boyhood friends and I decided it would be fun to have a water-gun shoot-out. Instead of water, we decided to use pokeberry juice. We spent days gathering bucketfuls of the dark purple berries. My grandmother let us use her metal, coned-shaped juicer that she used for making grape juice and tomato juice. My friends and I put the pokeberries inside the cone, and we pulverized them with a wooden pestle. The deep purple juice fell into a pan below.

After a few hours of berry straining, we had enough juice to use for our planned water-gun war. We each donned old jeans and white T-shirts and prepared for battle. We filled our water guns with the juice, and we enjoyed a fun-filled afternoon spraying each other with the purple liquid.

By day's end our clothing and skin were stained with purple blotches. Even though we tried to avoid shooting each other in the face, I did end up with a purple ear and a purple stripe in my hair. For several days we proudly sported our battle scars.

Going Across the Alley to Find Jesus

The Methodist church and parsonage were across the alley from my parent's home. It was convenient and too convenient at the same time. Most Sundays my mother would don one of her best dresses, a hat, and a pair of gloves, and go across the alley to make an appearance. She rarely missed, but she always sat on the back pew so that she could hurriedly exit the church following the last "amen." She didn't want to spend time in the receiving line shaking hands with the good reverend, so she made sure to beat the preacher to the door. She was anxious to get Sunday dinner on the table, and therefore, her idea of a good preacher was one that gave a short sermon.

I followed my mother's lead. During my exit, I unfastened my clip-on tie and undid my shirt collar. If the weather was warm, by the time I got to our back door, I was barefoot. I was bored while at church. When I was old enough to wear a watch, I constantly glanced at my Timex. I tried to stay awake, but I wasn't always successful.

I usually sat beside my younger sister and occasionally we would get tickled. I would try not to look at her for fear of laughing. I did enjoy making her giggle by letting out a silent fart, a church creeper. She would hold her nose and try not to laugh out loud.

The choir at our little church was fairly good with one exception. One member, Miss Dee, could not carry a tune, and she sang louder than the other choir members. I could not help but grimace when she hit a sour note. When Miss Dee wore her favorite pearl necklace to church, my sister and I could not help but get tickled. When the lady belted out a hymn, the tight necklace would rhythmically move up and down on her throat.

The Methodist preachers that served our parish were not only our ministers but our neighbors. Many of the preachers' kids became close friends of mine. It has been said that the children of ministers are among the naughtiest of kids. I can attest to the fact that they can be naughty, a lot of fun, and rebellious. That's why I liked being friends with them.

When I entered the seventh grade, I was finally old enough to attend the Methodist Youth Fellowship. I had longed for that day. A couple of years prior to joining the MYF, I would sit in a lawn chair in my backyard and watch the older kids in the group play tetherball on the church lawn. I wanted to play. I also knew that the MYF sponsored teen dances. Dancing was not allowed at my public school, and the only place in town to dance was in the Methodist Fellowship Hall at the MYF-sponsored dances. I loved to dance, and I was glad to be a Methodist.

Because it was a small church, the bishop would often assign a newbie to be the minister. The small parish served as a good place for them to get their first experience as clergy. One young minister who came to town tried to introduce new methods of worship to the congregation. He wanted parishioners to clap their hands while singing hymns. Many of the staid members of the church were taken aback at his efforts to make them be lively during the musical interludes. No one clapped. The young preacher didn't stay long before he was moved to another parish.

My older sister, Cheryl, was a gifted pianist. She accompanied several soloists and groups who performed in our church. The group she played for the most were three young siblings, the Day Sisters, who also attended our church. They rehearsed in our living room. If they sang "Always," then I knew someone was getting married. If they sang "Beyond the Sunset," then I knew that someone had died. They sang many a "special" in our little church.

Although I was not the best churchgoer, I cherish the memories that were made in that little church. My sisters were married there, my nieces and my nephews were christened there, and the funerals of my grandmother, my parents, and my older sister were held there.

I still get teary-eyed when I hear "Beyond the Sunset."

Haunted, Who You Gonna Call?

Like most kids, I was terrified and fascinated at the same time by the possible existence of ghosts. There were times at night alone in my dark room when I would refuse to open my eyes for fear of seeing a spirit. As an added protection to avoid a sighting, I slept with a pillow on top of my head.

The scariest room in the house that I grew up in was far from my bedroom. The room was my mother's beauty shop. Originally it had been the front parlor of the old house that was built in 1900. A few years before my parents bought the house, a distant relative took her life in that room. The night of her suicide, the young lady coifed her hair, put on makeup, and donned her finest dress before putting a pistol to her temple and pulling the trigger. She wanted to look good when her body was discovered.

My grandmother had a photograph of the deceased. She had been a lovely young woman, and the image of her beautifully posed in the picture was imprinted in my mind. I knew I would recognize her if sighted, but I did not want to see her. I wished that I had not seen her photo and that my parents had not told me about the suicide. I would not enter the beauty shop at night without turning on the light and giving the spirit of the young lady ample time to leave the room.

My grandmother, who lived a few blocks from my family, had a possibly haunted room in her home. The front bedroom of the house was where her father, my great-grandfather, had died. I was thirteen at the time. Along with other family members, I spent time sitting in the room during his passing. I have vivid memories of the morning a raspy sound came from the old gentleman's throat. The old-timers said it was the "death rattle," and that he would soon be gone. He died later that day in his bed.

Following his death, my grandmother laid out his body in the very room where he had passed. The body remained there for two days prior to the burial. All furniture in the room had been removed, mirrors were covered with black fabric, and folding chairs lined the walls for the mourners to sit in. The casket was left open for viewing of the deceased. A steady stream of visitors came through the front door of the house. Every woman who entered carried prepared food. The dining table, kitchen table, and all countertops were covered with pies, cakes, and casseroles.

The viewing room was constantly occupied. Volunteers "sat wake" during the night. It was disrespectful to leave the body unattended. The only time the room cleared of mourners was during the daily visits of the undertakers who freshened my great-grandfather's makeup.

Long after his body had left the room, I had the feeling that my great-grandfather's spirit was still in there. I never again went into the room at night even when the light was on. I had loved my great-grandfather, but I didn't want to experience an after-death visit with him.

It was many years later before I again thought about the possibility of seeing a ghost. I had bought a house in Eureka Springs, Arkansas. The town's reputation as a location with a sizable spirit population is part of its attraction. I enjoyed hearing stories from locals who told of eerie encounters. Even after hearing the ghost stories, I wasn't particularly worried that the home I had purchased could be haunted. However, one night while I was sound asleep, I felt someone on top of me. I was underneath the covers and barely able to move while a spirit being held me down. I was not afraid. I was furious. I forced my way up while screaming, "Get out of here. This is my house!" And that was that. There were no further encounters.

I don't know whether the experience was real or a dream. In my mind, the event did happen. Since that time, I no longer fear ghosts, imagined or real. I can shout them away.

I still believe in ghosts, but *I ain't skeered.*

Canine Chatter

From the moment I was old enough to open the kitchen door, I would let myself out and go into the backyard to visit with the dogs and cats. The cats lived in the yard and slept in one of several outbuildings during warm weather.

Like many homes in the Delta, our house sat on concrete piers and was underpinned with corrugated metal skirting. My daddy left one small opening in the skirting so that the cats could go under the house during the winter and keep warm by lying next to the lower part of our floor furnace.

My family had small house dogs, and we also had a couple of large dogs that lived in the backyard. Even though the yard was not fenced, they rarely ventured far and were always excited to see me when I came out the back door. They knew not to jump on me. Instead to show affection, they would lick my face, and I would giggle. More than once my mother caught me bending down over the dogs' food bowl and sharing their meal.

When I got older, it was my job to carry food out to the dogs. Around the age of four, I went outside to feed them, and I asked my daddy's bird dog, "Tip, do you want the red bowl or the green bowl?"

Tip answered, "The green bowl."

I threw the dog bowls into the air, and I ran into the house to tell my mother that Ol' Tip could talk. Every day for several weeks, I would ask Tip which bowl he wanted. Even though I tried, I could not get the bird dog to speak again.

A couple of years later, my father confessed that he had been in the backyard outhouse that morning, and he had answered for Tip.

I wish he hadn't told me.

The Most Important Room

The kitchen in my boyhood home was very small. From end to end it was eighteen feet long and only eight feet wide from side to side. The walls were covered with red linoleum that was supposed to look like ceramic tile. It didn't. The countertops were covered with thick red linoleum and were edged with a metal strip.

After many years of use, the metal strip became tarnished and would leave a black metallic stain on the clothes of the person standing at the sink washing dishes. To prevent the staining, the metal was eventually covered with duct tape. The sink slowly turned black in places where the enamel had worn away. There was a small Warm Morning gas stove near the back door that kept the room toasty in the winter months. Nothing ever changed in the kitchen except for appliances that quit working and the linoleum floor when it had worn through.

There was very little counter space. Most of it was covered with needed items: breadbox, coffee maker, canisters, and can opener. In later years space was made for a microwave and a tiny television. My mother never missed *Wheel of Fortune*, and when the little television took its place on the counter, she no longer had to leave her kitchen at 6:30 p.m. to watch the show on the television in the living room.

The little counter space available was covered with pies and cakes. My mother thought a meal was not complete without dessert. Sweets were always available in her kitchen.

Above the kitchen table hung a print of an Asian man. My mother had purchased the print in the 50s. Even though I was a kid at the time, I had ideas about the proper way to decorate. I thought the frame on the painting should be red and match the kitchen's color scheme. I painted the frame red with my mother's nail polish. It remained on the wall with its red nail polish–painted frame for the next forty-five years.

Much of the food prep was done on the kitchen table. That space was shared with several items that never left the table, including salt and pepper shakers and an AM/FM radio. My parents bought the radio while I was in college doing a weekly radio show from the Arkansas State University campus. With the exception of listening to me on the only FM station in the area, my mother kept the radio tuned to a Paragould, Arkansas, AM station. Not only did Paragould station KDRS broadcast daily the area's obituaries, but it also told listeners who was in the local hospital. Those were things my mother thought she needed to know.

When folks came to visit the Taylor residence, they always came to the rear of the house and knocked on the kitchen door. Sometimes they just came right on in. Until the time my mother was living alone in the large house, the door was never locked. If someone knocked on the living room door at the front of the house, we were all startled and we would wonder, "What stranger is at the door?"

The kitchen was the heart of the house. As an adult, when I returned "home," I entered through the back door. I often found my mother sitting in her usual spot at the kitchen table. She had my supper on the stove, and the television was blaring. She spent more than sixty years in that house, and if not working in her beauty shop, she spent the better part of her time in the kitchen. Thousands of meals were prepared in that crowded space.

The morning I received the call that my mother had suddenly passed away, I immediately drove the six hours to that old house in the little Arkansas Delta town. It was a sad day when I walked into that little kitchen and saw my mother's empty chair. The kitchen in my boyhood home was very small. The memories created there were very large.

Yucky Foods

When I was a small child, I ate pretty much everything that was put on my plate. I wasn't a picky eater. When I got older and I realized the source of some food items, I would say, "Yuck, I can't eat that." I was sympathetic to the often-mentioned starving children in China, but I didn't see how eating everything on my plate could provide them nourishment.

The only wild game I would eat was mallard ducks that my father had shot. He was an avid duck hunter. In time, I quit eating duck as well. I didn't like biting down on the small metal shots, the residue from my father's double-barreled shotgun, which could be found in the duck meat.

Even though I grew pickier as I got older, my lunch often consisted of what I would have considered gross food items if I had known what the ingredients were. Next to the fried pies and the bag of chips in my lunch box, there was a fried bologna sandwich or a pickle loaf sandwich. The processed lunch meat was slathered with mustard and placed between two pieces of "light bread," which is what we called white bread.

Occasionally my mother would fix a fried Spam sandwich for me to take for the noon meal. When I wanted something other than sandwiches, I would take a couple of cans of Vienna sausage to the cotton patch. Lightly glued to the can was a slotted key that was attached to a metal strip on the can. When attached and wound around the can, it removed the top and revealed the contents. When I took the cans of sausage, I would take saltine crackers to eat as a side. Unlike the fried quail or a pile of fried brains, the Vienna sausage, Spam, and luncheon meats didn't look like anything that had ever lived. Therefore, I could eat the questionable meat products that lacked a visual that would have bothered my "weak stomach."

It's been decades since I've eaten canned meat, but I do miss the times when I used a key to open my lunch. That made "dinner" fun.

A Time to Dance and a Time to Not Dance

My younger sister and I were active kids, and we were encouraged by my mother to engage in creative play. We were rarely told to "calm down." When that did happen, it was usually a request from my father because he couldn't hear the Cardinals baseball game playing on the living room radio. He would say, "Take it outside," and we did. The only times my mother would strongly and repetitively request that we be quiet and still were during visits to my father's parents, Grandmother and Grandfather Taylor.

Grandfather Taylor was a Methodist minister. He began his preaching career as a circuit rider on horseback in Lawrence and Sharp counties in Arkansas. He was able to advance in his career, and in time he became the pastor of large parishes up and down the Arkansas Delta. His assigned churches were always within a couple of hours' drive from where my family lived. Every two or three months we would go for a Sunday visit. We would arrive in time to attend church and to hear my grandfather preach. With the exception of funerals and weddings, it was the only time my father attended church. He would say, "I had enough of church while growing up."

On the way to my grandparents' home, my mother would remind us several times to behave, to be still, and to be quiet once we got there. My grandparents had four grandchildren, and that included my two sisters and me. My mother told us, "Grandmother Taylor is not used to being around kids. You will make her nervous if you are too loud."

Following the church service and Sunday dinner, my father and grandfather would retire to the study for a father-son visit. My mother and older sister would sit in the parlor with my grandmother and aunt Bettye Sue. My younger sister, Rhonda, and I would ask to be excused, and then we would exit the house to play outside or inside the nearby church. While playing, we had to be careful to not mess up our clothes. We wore our Sunday go-to-meeting clothes all day long while there. I wasn't allowed to wear blue jeans in my grandparents' home.

During one winter visit, it was too cold for us to play outside. Not wanting to be stuck inside the house and required to sit quietly on the couch, we went next door to the unlocked church. The church building was old, beautiful, and historic. Rhonda and I enjoyed talking and singing while alone in the large sanctuary. The acoustics were amazing.

Although I could barely carry a tune, my sister didn't seem to mind. She was always my best audience. I loved performing for her, and I decided to put on a show for her while in the sanctuary. I didn't think that I was being sacrilegious. I probably didn't know what that meant. I jumped up on the altar and began singing and dancing. My balance was perfect as I strutted back and forth. My sister was clapping and laughing.

To enhance my performance, I decided to add a little costuming. I picked up the baptismal font, a beautiful, shiny, and footed bowl, to wear on my head like a hat. I raised the font high and turned it over. The glass liner fell to the floor and shattered into hundreds of tiny pieces. The performance ended.

My sister and I spent the rest of the afternoon picking up every trace of glass from the carpet. We hid the chards inside a heat grate located in one of the sanctuary walls. We were able to clean up the mess, hide the evidence, and return to the parsonage just in time to say goodbye before leaving for home. My mother remarked how unusually quiet my sister and I were while riding in the car. We were afraid to talk too much for fear that we would accidentally reveal our misdeed, make my father mad, and upset my mother. She would have been mortified, and she would have worried herself sick.

That night while in bed, I did my "Now I lay me down to sleep" prayer, and I added a request for Jesus to forgive me for breaking the liner to his font. I think he did, but I don't think my grandmother would have if she had known. I've often wondered if the glass is still in the grate.

Sears and Roebuck

I was a child in the 50s, and my first memory of Sears was looking through the retail company's Christmas catalog, known as the "Wish Book." It always arrived several weeks before the holiday. Text and photographs in the catalog described every toy currently made that a child could possibly want from Santa. My sisters and I searched through the toy section to pick out our "wants." We took turns looking through the catalog.

We didn't argue over it in case Santa was watching and taking notes about impolite behavior. The wait for my turn sometimes seemed to be excruciatingly long. I thought, *How long does it take for my sister to look at an ol' baby doll?*

After days of studying the pages, we would write our names on the items we wanted. Because our list of desired gifts always got out of hand, my mother requested that we number the items with descending numerals to denote our favorites. I made certain the number 1 that I placed by my favorite toy was large and heavily circled. When finished, we gave the catalog to my mother, who turned it over to Santa. He then decided which toys to bring us on Christmas morning.

The regular Sears catalog that came through the mail was much larger than the company's Christmas catalog. Sears used to offer mail-order kit houses for sale through the catalog. Even though the company stopped selling the kits in 1940, it still offered nearly every item an American household needed to furnish a home. Besides the usual clothing items offered, one could also buy appliances, curtains, rugs, furniture, tools, and more. The earlier catalogs offered many items that would seem odd to purchase through the mail in today's market. At one time, Sears sold ponies, donkeys, bees, and chickens. I longed to order one of the purebred animals shown in the catalog. Several popular breeds of dogs were listed along with Siamese and Persian cats. No matter how badly I wanted a poodle from Sears, my parents said, "No, you have enough pets."

When a new catalog arrived in the mail, my younger sister and I were allowed to cut up the old one and make paper dolls out of the photographs. We glued the cut-out figures onto heavy construction paper with Elmer's glue. When the glue dried, we carefully cut around the figures. While my sister cut out paper dolls of girls and women, I cut out photographs of animals.

The first time I ordered from the catalog using money I had made from picking cotton; I ordered a stereo that could play both 45s and albums.

When I was fourteen, I used some of my cotton-picking money to buy a red Allstate 125 motorbike straight out of the Sears catalog. It arrived in two large cardboard boxes. With my father's help, I put the bike together, poured gas into the tank, hopped on, and immediately ran into a ditch.

Many of the items in my parents' home came from Sears. My father bought Sears Craftsman tools, and my mother had Coldspot and Kenmore appliances. We wore clothes from Sears. Some of the items were bought directly from the company's brick and mortar stores rather than the catalog.

My family made frequent shopping trips to Memphis and our first stop before heading to the city's downtown area was the Crosstown Sears store. The building that housed the store was huge and served as a company catalog merchandise distribution center as well as a retail store. The shopping area occupied the first few floors, and access from floor to floor was via an escalator. My younger sister and I spent our time there riding up and down on the moving stairs.

The Memphis Sears stores were favorite shopping outlets for Gladys Presley, and where she picked out some of the furnishings for Graceland, the home of her son Elvis. She considered Sears to be upscale. My family did too.

Years later, shopping in the Memphis Sears stores with my mother became a tradition on the day after Thanksgiving. At the time, writing a check required two IDs. A credit card served as one. My mother had a driver's license, and because she needed an additional ID, she reluctantly applied for and received a Sears credit card. When we went to Sears during our annual holiday shopping trip, she would use her one and only credit card. She used it on that day and only on that day to keep the card active. She paid her Sears bill immediately the day it came in the mail. She didn't believe in credit cards, but she did believe in Sears.

I eventually got a poodle, but it didn't come from Sears.

Hot Times

I was born and raised in the Arkansas Delta, where the summers are hot and humid. No one I knew had air conditioning, including my family. With the exception of the often-asked question, "Is it hot enough for you?" folks pretty much ignored the heat. We were used to being hot during the summer months.

My childhood home was built in 1900. Like many of the early homes built in the Delta, our house had high ceilings. The higher the ceiling, the further warm air would move upward and keep the lower parts of the house cooler. The ceilings in my boyhood home were thirteen feet high.

My parents purchased the house in 1940 for six hundred dollars. Following a cash purchase, they had enough money left to install an indoor bathroom and an attic fan. The fan was in the living room ceiling, and it was powerful enough to move air throughout the house. Even though the air was warm when pulled through open windows, the moving air did make it feel cooler.

When I was a child, I worried about mice or other critters falling from the large hole in the living room ceiling where air was sucked upward to the fan. My older sister had said it could happen, and I believed everything she told me. Despite my fear of falling critters, I would stand under the fan opening while holding a balloon tied on a string. I would watch the balloon rise due to the suction of the fan, and I'd pretend it was filled with helium. Occasionally a balloon would get away from me and get popped by the fan blades. In early winter, my father would cover the opening with plywood. I worried that he would notice the dead balloons in the attic and scold me. He never did.

Delta folks spent time outdoors sitting under shade trees when the weather was hot. The outside was more comfortable than being inside. My father was one who enjoyed a good shade tree. He'd sit in the shade for long spells while smoking cigarettes and drinking Old Crow whiskey.

I never saw my father use a hand fan. The hand fans were pieces of colored cardboard that were stapled to a flat wooden stick. They were popular cooling devices in the South, and most often used by the ladies. Most of the fans had advertising on them. Politicians and funeral homes were frequent fan advertisers, and they distributed the fans for free. Many of the fans had pictures of Jesus on them and were available alongside the hymnals in churches. Air was moved in torrents by fan-waving churchgoers during summer worship services. All the fans, even ones with secular advertising on them, were known as "church fans."

My mother's beauty shop was connected to our house. Even though the shop had the thirteen-foot ceilings and many windows, it would get very hot when the hairdryers were on. My mother had an old-fashion permanent wave machine that emitted a lot of heat. In the summertime, women connected to the machine would have the church fans moving at rapid speeds. Other customers in the beauty shop would help fan them. My mother kept smelling salts available for the ladies who were overcome by the heat. My younger sister and I would often slip into the beauty shop at night, sniff the smelling salts, and enjoy the dizzying effects from the vapor. I suspect the liquid was nothing more than pure ammonia poured over the packed cotton inside the small vial.

One of the hottest places to be during Delta summers was inside automobiles. The only way to keep reasonably cool while driving was to have all the car windows rolled down. My mother and grandmother wore headscarves inside the car to keep their hair from getting messed up by the fast-moving air. My father kept our car in a garage and during the warm months, the windows were always down even when the car was parked.

Because school was not in session during fall cotton harvest, we attended classes during July and August. Both the elementary school and the high school buildings had been built with lots of windows to help with airflow. Industrial-sized floor fans ran constantly, blowing hot air. The fans created noise that made hearing difficult. To avoid the warmest part of the day during the summer session, school began at 7 a.m. and ended at 1 p.m. Schools during the 50s and 60s had dress codes. Marmaduke schools were fairly lenient when it came to dress during the summer. Boys could wear shorts to class. Girls could not, but they were allowed to wear "knee knockers," pants that came to the middle of the knee. To not arouse the boys sexually, half the girl's sexy knees had to be covered. Both sexes were allowed to go barefoot.

The first air-conditioned buildings I remember were movie theaters. Many Delta folk went to the movies just to get cool. In time, my father did purchase window units for our home and my mother's beauty shop. Even though we were much more comfortable with air conditioning, I did miss the big opening in the living room ceiling and the thrilling possibility of critters falling on my head.

I missed floating balloons.

Naughty Boy

Like most boys, I was curious about sex and naked bodies. I liked hearing off-color stories and jokes. When away from adults and with my boyhood friends, I thought it was fun to hear and to use naughty words. I could not control my laughter when a friend would say "tallywacker."

When the situation called for it, my mother would let slip an expletive. She would cover her mouth and tell my sisters and me to not say the word that she had used. Each time she said a bad word out loud that I had not heard before, I would make a mental note of the word for future use.

I was very careful to not blurt out a naughty word in front of my grandma. She never cussed, and I doubt if she had ever heard most of the curse words that I had stored in my repertoire. The only near-naughty word I ever heard her say was in her favorite riddle: Born without skin, speaks once, and never speaks again? The answer was "A poot." She would say the word, turn a little red, and then giggle. I asked her often to tell me the riddle just so I could hear her say "A poot."

My father did cuss a lot but not in front of my mother, my sisters, or any female. With male friends, he didn't hold back. Because I was his male child, I was privileged to hear and learn many swear words from him. The only curse word he would not say was the one that "took the Lord's name in vain." It was forbidden in the Ten Commandments. His upbringing as a preacher's son prevented him from saying that curse word.

When I was with my boyhood male pals, we said every cuss word we knew and as often as we could. *Damn* was a favorite adjective. When we learned a new bad word, we shared it among our group. When I was in the fourth grade, a friend taught me a new word he had heard his mother say. The word was *pregnant*. He said it was even in the dictionary. During the next recess, we stayed in our classroom long enough to get the dictionary off the shelf to see the word in print. Sure enough it was there. After spotting the word *libido* in a magazine in my mother's beauty shop, I also found that word in the dictionary. I felt sophisticated when I first used *libido* in front of my friends. I doubt that I used it correctly.

My friends and I were curious about the human body. We anxiously awaited the newest issue of each month's *National Geographic* magazine.

Occasionally there were photos of unclad people in it. When the magazine was placed on the periodical shelf in the school's library, we would grab it and quickly turn the pages to look for bare-breasted women.

Even before I had seen unclad women in the *National Geographic* magazine, I was familiar with the female anatomy. In my family's living room there hung a fairly large mirrorlike piece of art that depicted two beautiful nude women. My uncle Vernon had purchased it in Detroit. When he took it home, his wife wouldn't let him hang it. He called my mother and asked if she would like to have it, and she said yes. She thought it was beautiful and didn't hesitate to display it in our home.

My uncle Lowell gave me a small naughty booklet called a Flip-Teez that he had picked up in a burlesque bar. When opened, the booklet showed the image of a lovely showgirl. In front of the woman's image were layers of clear celluloid, and each layer had hand-painted clothing items on it. As each layer was lifted, some of her clothing was removed, until the final image revealed a beautiful nude woman. I almost wore it out.

My father never had "the talk" with me. I learned about sex from friends. While still in grade school a pal explained to me how babies were made. He got the information from his older brother. I told him that his brother had to be lying. There was no way that could ever happen. "Why would anyone do such a thing?" In time, I learned that he was correct.

I miss being naive and learning something new and naughty. It was fun and exciting. I still giggle a little when I think of my grandma saying "A poot."

Till the Cows Come Home

My younger sister and I sometimes stayed overnight at my grandmother's home. She lived in a two-bedroom house that she shared with her father, my great-grandfather, on the edge of town.

Rhonda and I looked forward to the overnighters. We knew we would play the card games Old Maid, Go Fish, and Authors. We looked forward to having popcorn that had been popped on a wood cookstove in the kitchen or on the potbelly stove in the living room when the weather was cold.

My great-grandfather thought playing cards was possibly a sin. He didn't want to take a chance. He sat watching us play while he smoked a pipe and listened to religious shows on the radio that were broadcast from faraway Mexico. He would retire early to his bedroom at the rear of the house, while we stayed up sometimes as late as 10 p.m.

The house did not have indoor plumbing. Before going to bed we took one last turn going to the outhouse. My sister and I slept with my grandmother. She slept in the middle, and I always claimed the right side of the bed as mine. I felt safe and secure lying next to her. The fluffy feather mattress embraced me, and during the winter months, a pile of quilts kept us warm.

The first time I stayed the night at a place that was not my own or my grandmother's was at my friend Tommy's house. I was a third grader when my mother decided I was old enough to do an overnighter after my friend's mother invited me to spend the night. Tommy's mother was one of my mother's best friends, and I was often around her. I felt comfortable and safe staying overnight at her house. She saw to it that Tommy and I had a good time and plenty to eat. Tommy's mother loved to cook, and when I left their home after sleepovers, I was stuffed.

When my mother told me that one of her beauty shop customers wanted me to spend the weekend at her house, I said that I didn't want to spend a whole weekend with strangers. The customer, Maggie, only came to the beauty shop every few months to have her long hair trimmed. I wasn't around her much, and I didn't know her husband Jim at all. I had seen him sitting in front of the beauty shop in his truck while waiting for his wife to get her hair fixed. Maggie didn't know how to drive.

She would leave the shop with freshly trimmed hair that my mother had twisted into figure-eight braids on the back of her head, and she would climb into the truck. If I was in the yard, I would wave to them when they left. That's about the only interaction I had with them before receiving the invitation to stay in their home for the weekend.

Jim and Maggie were an elderly couple and childless. She told my mother, "We would love to have a young person around even if only for a day or two."

My mother told me that I would hurt their feelings if I didn't accept their invitation. I didn't want to hurt Maggie's feelings. I consented to spend the weekend at their house.

They picked me up the following Friday when I got home from school. Jim drove slowly on the gravel roads in the hills west of town, and it took about thirty minutes to get to their home. The couple owned a small dairy farm that was far away from any neighbors. As we approached their property, I saw a herd of fawn-colored jersey cattle grazing in the field.

Their home was a quaint farmhouse with an old wooden barn out back. Maggie showed me to my room. It had an iron bedstead and a wooden plank floor; it was quite different from my room at home. I liked it.

While Maggie fixed supper, Jim took me with him to put the cows into the barn. We went into the field, where he attached a harness and leash to the lead cow and started walking with her. The other cows followed.

After supper, Jim said that it was now time to milk. He asked, "Do you want to help?"

I said, "I don't know how to milk cows, but I'll go watch."

He said, "Nothing to it. I'll teach you."

I went to the barn with Jim and Maggie, and we each got a milk bucket and a stool to sit on. It didn't take me long to get the hang of milking, but my small hands and inexperience kept me from keeping up with Maggie and Jim.

They filled several buckets while I worked trying to fill one. I didn't get it filled before all the cows were milked, but the couple thanked me over and over for being a good helper. While lying in bed that night before dozing off, I felt a sense of accomplishment and could not wait until the next morning when I could again help with the milking.

On Sunday afternoon, the couple took me home. I told my mother that I had a swell time and that I had helped on the farm. That evening my mother was surprised when I asked for a glass of milk at supper.

I didn't like milk.

Saturday Night Footlong

I was a healthy baby, and I was downright fat. My mother told me that after I learned to walk, the fat went away, and I morphed into a scrawny kid. I stayed small well into adulthood.

When I started first grade at the age of five, I became aware that I was not as large as most of the boys in my class. I wanted to be bigger, and I wanted to be stronger. I couldn't understand why I wasn't because I had a hearty appetite and an insatiable sweet tooth. Many times I had heard my mother and her friends say that eating sweets made a person gain weight. I intentionally ate lots of sugar-laden food in an effort to get bigger.

My mother loved to cook, and like most Southern cooks, she fried everything that could be battered and put into a skillet of Crisco. We had more than one choice of dessert at the end of every meal. There were always several pies and cakes on the kitchen counter, ice cream in the freezer, and cookies in the cookie jar. I was able to, even encouraged to, snack between meals. My mother loved to see people eat.

Even though there were plenty of sweets to eat in our kitchen, every afternoon my sister Rhonda and I would each get a dime from my mother and go across the street to Crouch's grocery store to buy a Coca-Cola and a candy bar. We took two empty Coke bottles with us to trade for the new full bottles. Without the returned bottles, the Cokes would have cost seven cents each instead of a nickel each.

My sister and I always bought the same kind of candy bar, a Butterfinger. When we got to the store, I would ask my sister what kind of candy bar that she wanted even though I knew the answer. She would reply, "A Butterthinger." I found her mispronunciation amusing. The nice lady at the store never snickered or corrected my sister when she said "Butterthinger." I didn't either. I knew my sister would have whomped me on the head.

Every Saturday, my family would pile into our station wagon and drive ten miles to the nearest Kroger store. My mother and my older sister, Cheryl, would go into the store to do the weekly shopping. With each purchase, my mother collected Top Value stamps that she carefully licked and glued into books to later redeem for merchandise.

Before my mother went into the store, she would give Rhonda and me each thirty-five cents. My mother barely entered the store before we got out of the car and ran to buy a ten-cent toy at Ben Franklin's, x-ray our feet at the Red Goose shoe store, stop at a little food stand for a footlong hot dog, and return to the car to devour the hot dogs.

When we got home, and my mother had put the groceries away, she cooked hamburgers and French fries, our traditional Saturday night supper. That was my favorite meal of the week, and even though I had already eaten a big hot dog, I ate again. I would eat the burger and fries, and then I would have dessert.

No matter how much I ate, I didn't get bigger. I didn't turn into a strong he-man, and I never attained the size or strength one needed to excel in sports. I stayed small. As an adult, I've wished to be smaller, and I often think, *Oh, to be able to eat like a kid again. I want a Butterthinger.*

Homesick in a Hurry

The first time that I was away from home for any length of time was during a week-long stay at Boy Scout camp. Until that time, I had only spent an occasional overnighter at my grandmother's house or a friend's house, and one weekend with a couple who had a dairy farm.

Those visits were for only one or two nights, and I was never more than five miles from my family. I knew that my parents could pick me up in a matter of minutes if I wanted to go home. My grandmother's house and my friend's house were within walking distance to my house, unlike the Boy Scout camp that was an hour-and-a-half drive from my hometown.

I was eager to join the Boy Scouts. Months before I had turned ten years old, the age required to join, I had memorized the scout oath and subscribed to the scouting magazine *Boy's Life.* I wanted to "be prepared" and be ready to go the minute I took the scout oath.

The weekend before my first meeting, my mother took me to Belk department store to buy my uniform. I had begged to get the uniform months before joining, but my mother wanted to wait to purchase it in case I had grown some. I had not.

After joining, I looked forward to each meeting, and I especially liked the day hikes in nearby Crowley's Ridge. With money that I had saved, I purchased outdoor gear, including a telescoping drinking cup and a metal canteen housed in a canvas carrier.

During my first summer as a member, I signed up to attend the week-long stay at Camp Cedar Valley in Hardy, Arkansas. I spent many hours deciding what clothes to pack into a long, round khaki-colored duffel bag. The duffel bag had been given to me by my father, who had used it during his stint in the army during the 40s.

The morning my troop was to leave for camp, I walked across the alley to the Methodist church, the gathering place for our departure. There were twelve scouts and two adult chaperones all waiting, packed and ready to go. The scout leader, who went by the name "Curley," loaded us into three cars while assuring us that we were going to have "the time of our lives."

The panic set in as I took my seat in one of the cars. I didn't want to go, but I didn't get out of the vehicle. I didn't want the guys to think that I was a "mama's boy." I was.

After the hour-and-a-half drive, we arrived at our destination. The camp was in the Ozark foothills, a lovely setting, with the Spring River running through it. We were assigned a rustic cabin that contained several bunk beds. I chose a top bunk. I worried as I made my bed. Were the sheets and blankets I had brought up to standard? Was I making the bed right? While at the supper table that first evening in the mess hall, I began agonizing about going to bed. Lights out was at 10 p.m. Even though I was in a cabin with other guys, I was afraid. It was pitch-black dark, and through the screened windows I could hear the night sounds coming from the woods. I held back my tears. Because I was bone tired, I soon fell asleep.

During the daytime, I enjoyed the camp. I signed up for several classes, including archery and crafts. I enjoyed swimming in the river despite hearing the urban legend that there was *something* in the water that occasionally drowned a scout. The tale was made more believable because a week earlier, a scout had drowned in the river at nearby Camp Kia Kima, a Boy Scout camp for Memphis-area troops.

From the first day of camp, a Sunday, I looked forward to Wednesday. That was the day a scout's parents could visit their son. I had prepared a desperate plea to my parents to take me home. When they arrived and told me the pregnant dog that I had taken in had her puppies that morning, I was even more determined to leave camp.

My father gave me a pep talk, told me that Saturday was only three days away, and I would be going home then. He told me that if I stayed, he would be very proud of me. Because I wanted nothing more than to make him proud, I made the decision to stick it out.

I returned home the following Saturday with my head held high and feeling proud as punch. I forgot my earlier angst as I received parental praise and smelled sweet puppy breath from the newborn litter. I had spent a week away from home for the first time. I was a survivor.

Dying to Know Who Will Show

Death rituals and customs in the Arkansas Delta are set in stone. When I was a child, I attended an occasional funeral, and I often accompanied my parents when they went to visitations. The visitations took place the evening before a funeral when people gathered to pay their respects and to view the body of the deceased. The event was usually held in a funeral home, but at times it took place in a private home.

When I did attend a visitation, I was amazed at the floral displays. Large metal screens and wire stands were filled with wreaths of colorful, fragrant flowers. The sticky-sweet smell was overwhelming. I would marvel at the broad satin ribbons, and I wondered how the florist had written in glitter on the ribbons. On the day following a visitation, I often overheard women talking in my mother's beauty shop about the number of flowers that were at the deceased person's visitation. They thought that the more flowers that surrounded the body, the more popular had been the departed. My mother's customers would remark, "There were sure a lot of flowers there. She sure was loved."

I had a morbid curiosity about the body laid out in the casket. Were they stiff? Although I would sometimes see a bereaved person kiss a corpse or touch the hands of the deceased, I didn't dare touch a body to find out.

Did the dead person have on socks and shoes? I thought it odd when folks would look at a dead body and say, "Don't they look natural?" I never thought they did. They looked dead.

At the age of eleven, I developed a lump under my arm. I was certain it was a cancerous tumor. I didn't tell anyone I was dying. I didn't want to upset my parents.

I checked the lump several times a day to see if it was getting larger. I couldn't tell for sure, but I figured cancer had already spread and it was too late to do anything about it.

I envisioned my funeral and visitation. I mentally planned the event by taking ideas from the funerals and visitations that I had attended. I created fantasy scenes borrowed from romanticized tragic movies when the bereaved would either faint or throw themselves onto the casket of their beloved. Would anyone faint at my funeral or plop atop my coffin? Would there be wailing?

At night before falling asleep, I would create a list of folks that might attend my visitation. Would Tommy be there? Would he cry? I knew that if I did die there would be some people who felt guilty about my passing and say, "I'm sorry that I wasn't better to Zeek." Then I would think, *It's too late you mean ol' idiot.*

I imagined having more flowers at my funeral than would fit inside the Methodist church sanctuary where my service would be held. I spent time thinking about what I should wear while lying in the casket. I wondered whether I should pick something out or leave that decision to my mother.

The lump went away. I suspect that it was nothing more than a swollen lymph gland. Even though I had spent many hours planning my funeral and visitation, I didn't die. While I was happy to be alive, I did think, *The town sure missed a good funeral.*

CHAPTER 2 — TEEN YEARS AND THE TURBULENT 60s

Teenage Angst

I looked forward to becoming a teenager, and weeks before my thirteenth birthday, I started preparing for the transition. I sent five dollars to *Teen* magazine for a one-year subscription. I walked downtown to Bradsher's Drugstore and stocked up on Clearasil acne medication even though I didn't have pimples, and I purchased Aqua Velva aftershave lotion even though I did not shave.

To fulfill another of my teenage obligations, I bought a stereo. I ordered it from the Sears catalog. It arrived days before my parents could take me to the record store in Paragould, a larger town nearby. I was desperate to play a record on my new stereo. I needed an album.

I walked downtown to Bradsher's and found the only record in the drugstore. It was a Connie Francis album that was attached to a tube of Brylcreem. The record was free if I bought the Brylcreem, an oily crème men's hair ointment that was advertised on the album cover. I purchased it and hurried home to play the record. I played it over and over again. I was amazed at the brilliance of Connie Francis as she sang folk songs.

My parents could not wait for Saturday and our shopping trip to Paragould when I could purchase new records. They had heard Miss Francis sing "Down in the Valley" way too many times. After I purchased several new records, the Connie Francis album disappeared and did not resurface for many years. I did keep the Brylcreem handy and used it proudly until the tube was empty.

My sister Cheryl was three years my senior, and I envied her freedom. She got to ride in cars with her friends, and she could stay out until 11 p.m.

on weekend nights. When she had friends over, I was not allowed to hang out with them.

When I finally turned thirteen, to my disappointment, nothing much had changed. My voice had not deepened, pimples did not suddenly appear on my face, and I was still not allowed to hang out with my sister and her friends.

I was a late bloomer. While several of my male classmates were maturing, developing deep voices, and beginning to shave, I was still checking and hoping daily to find my first body hair. I wanted to be manly, and tall enough to play basketball. I wanted someone to tell me that I was handsome. I had teenage angst, and I had an inferiority complex.

My younger sister did pay me a compliment. She said, "You have a neck like a movie star." I thought, *That's the nicest thing anyone has ever said to me.* In reality, which was not the case. My parents and grandmother constantly praised me and said they were proud of me, but their praise wasn't enough. I wanted praise and compliments from my peers. For several months following my sister's movie star–neck comment, I spent a lot of time peering into my dresser mirror, posing, and looking at my neck.

Even though I was small and skinny, I was never bullied, although my own comparison to my male classmates did turn into a form of self-bullying. I put myself down. I had many friends, and I was fairly popular, but that wasn't enough. I still wanted to be admired for being strong and manly.

One thing I could do that did set me apart from other guys at school was dance. Most of them couldn't, and rarely would they make an effort to dance. *American Bandstand* was a popular show at the time, and teen girls loved the show. Because I could "bop," the girls sought me out at parties. I eventually learned to appreciate the talents I did have, and I quit bullying myself.

One thing I learned during that time is that good words and praise do encourage people. Compliments can make them feel good about themselves even if it is just a mention of their "movie-star neck."

One Short, One Long

I was a young teen when telephone service came to my hometown of Marmaduke, Arkansas. Prior to the arrival of phones, news and gossip traveled by word of mouth from neighbor to neighbor.

My mother's beauty shop was attached to our house, and because they couldn't call, women would stop by the house to make their hair appointments. The beauty shop was a prime location for hearing and reporting news. The men communicated each morning over coffee at a local café, in the pool hall, or in the barber shop. If there was news of prime importance, word traveled by mouth like wildfire in the small town with a population of 650 people. Within an hour's time, every citizen had received the news. Before we had phone service, townsfolk received some of their information by listening to the noon radio show that was broadcast on KDRS from Paragould. Special attention was paid to the obituaries that were read on air.

If there was a fire in town, everyone knew. We heard the siren of our one fire truck, and we would leave our houses and head to the scene of the blaze. Watching burning structures was a community activity.

My daddy was mayor when phone service came to town. Securing the service had been one of his main goals while he was in office. I was very excited about the idea of communicating via the telephone. I had learned from movies and television that talking on the phone was an essential part of being a teenager. When we finally did get our phone, our number was LY7-2221. The LY stood for Lyric.

Unfortunately, we were on a party line with an elderly woman, Miss Goforth, who lived down the street. Her ring was two shorts. Ours was one short and one long. I gritted my teeth every time I heard two shorts because I knew the line would be tied up and friends could not call me.

To check if the line was open, I would pick up the receiver. Often, I would hear Miss Goforth talking. Usually, she was talking about her health. I thought her conversations were boring. That changed when Miss Goforth, who was in her eighties, found a boyfriend. Then, if I "accidentally" picked up the phone and she was on the line, I found her conversations to be rather interesting. I didn't hear a proposal via the phone line, but when Miss Goforth became engaged, word spread like crazy. The pending nuptials became topic number one in my mother's beauty shop.

Miss Goforth married, sold her home, moved in with her husband, and gave up her phone. I was very happy that she had found love, and I was exceptionally happy for me. I was a teenager living in a home with a private line. However, even though we were no longer on a party line, I still had a problem. I had two teenage sisters who constantly wanted to chat with their friends. Also, my mother wanted to keep the line open so her beauty shop clients could call and make appointments.

Several times a day for several years, "Get off the phone!" could be heard in the Taylor home. I still got most of my news by word of mouth.

Dents and Bruises

When I turned fourteen, I wanted wheels. I was two years away from getting my driver's license, but in the state of Arkansas, a person could operate certain small, motorized vehicles without a license. Included in the category were mopeds and very small motorbikes.

I turned to my go-to source, the Sears catalog, and I found a small Allstate motorbike that fit the bill. The bike was bright red, small, and perfect for a scrawny fourteen-year-old. The price was $125. I used money that I had saved from picking cotton and ordered the bike.

I was surprised when the bike arrived in two large cardboard boxes. After unpacking it, my father helped me put the pieces together. I took a quick glance at the manual to read how to mix the proper proportion of oil and gasoline and then put the mixture in the tank. I was so anxious to take the bike for a spin, I didn't bother to read the rest of the manual and learn the proper operating procedures.

I kick-started the bike and took off at a jaunty pace. The controls were rather touchy, and I accelerated at a breakneck speed. A half block into my journey, I tried to locate the brake. Before I could stop the bike, I ran into a ditch and was thrown over the handlebars. I escaped serious injury. However, I did have a bruise that ran from my knee up to my waist.

I was proud of my injury. I described the wreck to my friends as "my near brush with death." My little bike suffered a dented fender. That hurt worse than my bruised leg. The night of my wreck, I read the rest of the operating manual.

Tan My Hide

In the 60s, not only was it fashionable to have a tan, but it was also thought to be good for one's health. Beach movies starring Annette Funicello and Frankie Avalon, along with the surfing-themed music of the Beach Boys, convinced me and my friends that in order to be "with it," we should be bronze colored.

It didn't matter that we lived in the Arkansas Delta and very far from any ocean.

In the summer, my friends and I lay in the sun on quilts in our backyards. We slathered our bodies with a concoction of baby oil and staining iodine. We did not wear sunscreen. That would have slowed down the tanning process. We applied lemon juice to our hair, thinking it would speed up the sun's bleaching of our locks.

School was not in session during September and October so that students could pick cotton at harvest time. Therefore, we were in school in July and August. School during the summer months let out at 1 p.m., which left plenty of time in the afternoon to devote to tanning.

Although the temperature was very hot and the humidity was stifling during summer in the Delta, nothing would stop us from achieving our quest for a Hollywood tan. A nearby hose connected to an outdoor faucet was available for an occasional misting. When the temps became unbearable, I would run an extension cord from the kitchen and hook up an electric fan.

Proper sunbathing also required listening to a transistor radio. In the Delta, the radio was always tuned to our favorite Memphis AM rock station, WHBQ, a station famous for being the first ever to air an Elvis song, which was "That's All Right."

My best tan did not come from the sun. While at school I noticed dark stains on the arms and hands of some of the students. The dark stains were caused by rubbing walnut husks on the skin in order to kill ringworm. Using walnut husk juice was a folk cure. I don't know whether or not the cure was effective. However, I did know that it made the skin a beautiful brown color.

My friend Donnie lived on the north edge of town. There was a huge walnut tree behind his family's barn. I told him that I knew a way to get a quick, dark tan by using the walnut husks. He agreed to give my plan a try.

Late that summer we went behind his barn and found a bumper crop of walnuts on the ground. There were no nearby neighbors, so we stripped down, husked some walnuts, and began "staining" each other. We wore gloves so that we wouldn't overly stain our hands. Although the husks were somewhat abrasive and it took a while to evenly cover each other's bodies, the final result would have made Frankie Avalon jealous.

We made plans to attend a late afternoon softball game that evening. To create the best contrast with our bronzed skin, we wore white shorts and white tank-style T-shirts. We arrived at the ball field shortly before dusk, knowing that the soft light of sunset was the best time to show off a tan. Everyone at the game raved about our tanned bodies. We never gave away our bronzing secret.

I had never surfed and had never seen the ocean, but that summer evening I became a beach bum with my walnut-toned skin.

We can go anywhere our minds take us. Surfs up.

Bejeweled

Across the street from my high school in Marmaduke, Arkansas, was a small café named Nettie's. It was considered an honor to work at Nettie's, and I was lucky enough to work there during lunch and after school. I received fifty cents an hour and free food.

The little diner had a jukebox and served sandwiches. A hot dog cost a dime, a chili dog was fifteen cents, a hamburger cost twenty cents, and a barbecue sandwich was a quarter. The owner, Nettie Lambert, cooked a roast each morning, which she used for making the barbecue. We also sold cokes, milk, candy, chips, and some school supplies.

Nettie always wore long, dangly earrings in her pierced ears at a time when only carnival workers and "gypsies" had pierced ears. When she was young, she had pierced her ears with an ice pick. Inspired by Nettie's dangly earrings, my sister decided that she, too, wanted pierced ears.

I volunteered to do the piercing. I numbed her ear with an ice cube, put a bar of soap behind her lobe, and pushed a sewing needle complete with thread through her ear lobe. It did hurt, but she was brave enough to let me do the other one. Immediately after the piercing, I removed the thread and placed a gold earring in each ear. We used lots of rubbing alcohol to prevent infection.

The next day at school, my sister received lots of attention, and I received lots of requests from her friends for me to pierce their ears. Over the course of a few weeks, I pierced the ears of forty or more of our friends. I did the "operations" at night in my mother's beauty shop. I'm proud to say, inspired by Nettie, that I helped bejewel Marmaduke High.

I Work Hard for My Money

My parents were both hard workers. During the 40s, my father flipped hamburgers in a small café, and he taught math and etiquette in a one-room schoolhouse. In the 50s and 60s, he managed a branch bank. It was a one-man operation, and he was everything from the manager to the janitor. He did have banker's hours. The bank closed at 2 p.m., and by the time he did the tally, dusted the furniture, and swept the floor, he was home by 3:30 p.m. He finished working long before my mother was through with her workday. When he got home from the bank, he continued to work around the house or in the yard. Because my mother kept long hours, he would often cook supper for the family.

My mother worked in her beauty shop six days a week. Many days she started at 7 a.m. and didn't finish until 5 or 6 p.m. During the seventeen years that I lived at home, I only remember her taking a week off work three different times. During two of those weeks, the family went to Detroit to visit my mother's brother and his family, and my mother's great-aunt. They had moved north during the 40s to work in automobile plants.

My mother loved to work, and she loved making her own money. My parents had lived through the Great Depression of the 30s, and they knew what it was like to not have enough. They worked hard to earn enough money to make sure their children didn't do without.

Influenced by my parents, I, too, liked making money. I started picking cotton at the age of five, and I picked until I graduated from high school. Because working in the cotton patch was seasonal and only occurred for six weeks during the fall, I was always looking for other ways to make money. During the winter, I would spend time in my mother's beauty shop drawing pictures for her clients. I charged them five cents for each piece of art. There were several fruit trees on my parents' property. When the fruit ripened, I would set up a stand by the front sidewalk, and I would sell cherries, plums, apples, pears, or whatever fruit was in season. In the late fall, I sold pecans from the trees in our yard. That was not an easy item to sell because many folks in town had pecan trees. When I was a teen, I made hand-painted earrings that my mother sold for me in her shop.

When I got old enough to push a lawnmower, my father offered to pay me fifty cents to take over his task of mowing during the summer. I jumped at the chance. I had a large piggy bank where I kept my money. I hid it in my bedroom closet just in case a burglar might get wind of my savings and take it. That was highly unlikely to happen in the small crime-free town of Marmaduke.

One day, with my savings in a brown paper bag, I walked the three blocks to the bank where my father worked. I plopped the money down onto the counter in front of Daddy and proclaimed, "I'm ready to open a savings account." I left the bank with a small savings book. Every time I made a deposit, it was recorded in the little book. I enjoyed looking at it every day or two, and I relished the fact that I was making money while collecting interest. I made that money without lifting a finger.

In high school, I worked at the lunch counter at Nettie's, a small store that was across the street from the high school. I earned fifty cents an hour. My lunch and snacks were free, and Nettie would give me a few free Salem cigarettes each day.

During my sophomore year, I saved part of my earnings to make what I considered to be an elaborate purchase. I withdrew some of the money from my savings account, went to a jewelry store in nearby Paragould, and bought a diamond ring. It had one fairly good-sized diamond in it that was set in a white gold mounting. The ring set me back fifty dollars, an extravagant purchase for me at the time. The only time I took it off my hand was when I was picking cotton. I felt like a rich man when the diamond ring was on my finger.

The diamond is no longer in a ring. I had it made into an ear stud, and it is always in my ear. For many decades, the diamond has served as a visual reminder of the values my parents instilled in me, and it is a symbol that hard work has its rewards.

Racing in Slow Time

When I was a child, I couldn't wait for my mother to finish work on Saturday afternoons. When she got through, my family would get in the family car, and my father would drive us the ten miles to the nearest Kroger's in Paragould, Arkansas, for the weekly grocery shopping.

While she shopped, my younger sister and I would go spend the money she gave us and then rejoin my father, who never left the car. I knew he was nipping on the Old Crow whiskey that he kept hidden under his seat. I could smell it on his breath when my sister and I returned.

I enjoyed sitting in the car with my daddy because I thought he was the smartest man in the world. I believed that he knew just about everything because he could identify each automobile that passed by us on Pruett Street. He would say, "Here comes a Chevy," or "That's a Ford." Every now and then I would blurt out, "That one's a Pontiac." It was the only car I could identify because of the car's distinctive hood ornament that depicted a stylized head of the Ottawa chief, Pontiac.

My daddy was not brand loyal when it came to purchasing cars. However, he was "color loyal" and bought autos in his favorite color of pink. When I was in grade school, our family car was a 1952 Ford sedan that was pink with a cream-colored top and a fancy Hollywood tire on the rear bumper. The next car that my father bought was a pink 1957 Chevy station wagon that once again had a cream-colored top. By the time I was ready to drive, my father had purchased a coral pink 1959 Chevrolet Impala with a cream top. When he bought the car, it was far too wide and too long to park in our 30s garage, so he built a large carport to house the new vehicle.

Driver's education classes were not available when I was a high school student. Many of my friends learned to drive out of necessity. They lived on farms where they drove work trucks and tractors as soon as their feet could touch the pedals.

One time a friend let me try my hand at driving his father's John Deere. I smashed part of a row of cotton. My friend and I both decided it would be best to wait until I learned to drive a car before I attempted to drive a tractor. Fortunately, his father wasn't mad at me for destroying some of the cotton plants, and he didn't ban me from riding on the tractor with his son.

A year before I turned sixteen, I picked up a driver's manual from the DMV office and began studying for the driver's exam. Six months before I turned sixteen, my father began teaching me to drive on the hilly roads of Crowley's Ridge that bordered the west side of town.

I was a rather small teen, and I could barely see over the steering wheel of the Impala. I had to sit on a couple of pillows so I could see the road through the windshield. The car was as long as a "whore's dream" (one of my father's favorite expressions), which made it difficult for me to parallel park. I was glad the car was an automatic, and that managing a clutch pedal was one less thing I had to do with my feet. The car had power steering, but I still found it difficult to make the vehicle turn. The first time I tried to turn a corner I ended up in a shallow ditch. My father was calm and patient with me. He seemed to enjoy our one-on-one time together while I learned to drive his beloved pink Impala.

The day I turned sixteen, I took my driver's test. I had memorized the test booklet from cover to cover and made a perfect score on the written exam. The state trooper who administered the test was a large man who somewhat intimidated me with his size and authoritarian demeanor. He sat fairly close to me in the front seat of the Impala. I think he wanted to be able to grab the steering wheel if necessary. Even though I was nervous, I did fine on the driving part of the test until it came time to parallel park. I knocked over the flags that defined the parking area. The trooper said, "Close enough. You are trying to park a very long car." I passed and was the proud owner of a driver's license.

In anticipation of receiving my license, I had managed to save three hundred dollars of my cotton-picking money to buy a car. Unlike my father, I didn't pick a pink one. I bought a baby blue, six-cylinder automatic 1952 Ford.

I received my first speeding ticket two weeks after I had bought the automobile. One Saturday after my sister and I had been shopping in a nearby town, we hurried home to watch the Miss America pageant on television. We didn't want to miss the opening parade of contestants representing each state, and we particularly wanted to see Miss Arkansas, who would be near the front of the lineup. I drove ninety to nothing to get home. Just as I pulled into my parents' driveway, a state trooper pulled in behind me with his patrol car lights flashing. I tried to explain the urgent need for me to hurry home, but the trooper did not accept my excuse.

By the time I tuned into the pageant, Miss Wyoming had already left the stage. From the kitchen window, my father had watched me receive the ticket. He told me that it was my problem and that I would be the one to pay the fine. He also told me that he hoped I had learned my lesson, and I would no longer speed. I did not learn my lesson, and I've received many tickets for speeding since that first time.

While many of my friends drove eight-cylinder hot rods, I was very content cruising around in my little Ford. For a six-cylinder, it was fairly peppy. Guys from my school often went down the highway to the mile crossing to drag race. The mile crossing was the first place on the highway where the road crossed over the Cotton Belt Railroad tracks. If someone said, "Meet me at the mile crossing," they were going to race. I didn't stand a chance racing my car against hot rods. However, I knew that I stood a chance of winning at George Ray's Drag Strip in Paragould.

George Ray's was a legal racing venue that was heavily attended Sunday afternoons by folks from several surrounding Delta counties. Admission was charged to attend the half-day event. The paved race track was a quarter mile long. Two cars raced at a time when given the "start signal" by George Ray, who served as the flagman.

There were several classifications for the competing cars depending on horsepower and whether a car had been altered or was "stock." Stock meant the cars were exactly as they were when they had left the factory and had not been altered or "souped-up." Letters denoted classifications, with AA assigned to the fastest and most powerful. AA/Stock was for the highest factory-rated horsepower cars. My little Ford was in the slowest stock category—N/Stock Automatic.

I didn't care that my car was in the slowest classification. It was in mint condition, and it was the fastest vehicle in its class. The little Ford never lost a race at the drag strip. The trophies were wooden with "George Ray's Drag Strip" engraved on the metal logo attached to the front of each one. There was a shiny silver metal automobile on the top. I displayed the trophies in my bedroom, and I couldn't have been more proud of them if they had been won while driving a Corvette in the AA Class.

Despite limitations, there are times we can use what we got and still come out a winner.

In 2006, George Ray's Drag Strip was listed on the National Register of Historic Places. George Ray passed away in 2009.

I Could Dance Like Nobody Else

My parents loved to dance. Once a month on a Saturday night, they dressed up and drove to the Kingsway Supper Club in Paragould, Arkansas, where they danced the night away. I thought my mother looked like a movie star when she donned her fancy dance clothes.

My sisters and I inherited my parents' love of dance. My mother taught me the dances that she knew, including the Charleston. Other ballroom dances were learned when my sisters and I attended weekly classes at the Westbrook School of Dance in Paragould. We learned the waltz, bop, cha-cha, rumba, samba, and more. To keep up with the latest dance fads, I watched the American Bandstand television show. I was the first in town to do the twist. I had twist shoes with rotating discs on the soles.

There was little opportunity to dance in the tiny town where I lived. Several of the town's elders considered dancing to be sinful, and because of their influence, the school board would not allow dances to take place. We had a banquet in place of a prom.

To get around the ban on dances, my friends and I would turn my mother's beauty shop into a dance hall on Saturday evenings. The only other place in town to dance was at the Methodist Church Fellowship Hall, at dances sponsored by the Methodist Youth Fellowship. I came from a long line of Methodists, so I felt right at home at the dance parties, while my Baptist friends who attended seemed to be a little nervous. We kept their attendance secret from their parents.

One of the best days of my teen life was when I got my driver's license, which enabled me to drive to nearby towns to attend teenage dances. On the very first Saturday after turning sixteen, friends piled into my newly purchased car. We went to Jonesboro, Arkansas, where we attended our first real teen dance with music performed by a live band.

One of our favorite places to dance was in an enclosed pavilion at Reynolds Park in Paragould, Arkansas. It was there where I met James Mangrum and his friends who lived in nearby Black Oak, Arkansas. They were in the process of forming a band that became The Knowbody Else.

They quickly became my favorite band, and I became a groupie. If they were playing anywhere within driving distance, I would be at their gig.

Their fan base grew as did their fame. The band signed a record deal with Stax records in 1969 and moved to Memphis. In 1970, they moved to Los Angeles, signed a contract with ATCO records, and changed the band's name to Black Oak Arkansas. In 1971, they released an album by the same name, *Black Oak Arkansas*. James Mangrum became known as Jim Dandy. In the 70s, the band released ten albums that "charted." BOA became known as one of the leading Southern rock bands and a pioneer in that genre. The group earned three gold records. In 1975, I saw Black Oak Arkansas in concert at the Mid-South Coliseum in Memphis. They played to a sold-out crowd of ten thousand.

I stood in the aisle and danced.

Tenderhearted Chicken Farmer

During my freshman year in high school, I took a year of agriculture class. I wasn't interested in farming, but I needed to take the course to get enough credits to graduate. The little school that I attended did not have art, music, or language courses, and in the 60s, boys did not take home economics. I had no other option but to study agriculture.

While in ag class, I watched films that taught activities I knew I would never practice, including a film that graphically explained how to castrate a hog. I did learn one thing during agriculture class that came in handy later. I learned to weld. I used that knowledge while in sculpture class in art school.

Every boy in my ag class had to have a year-long project. Most of the students chose to raise an acre of cotton. I lived in town, and I didn't have an acre of cotton. I decided I would raise chickens. My daddy and I put up a fence and built a chicken house in our backyard. Then I went to the local feed store and bought twenty baby Rhode Island Red chicks. The clerk placed the little fowl into a cardboard box. While walking the three blocks back home, I petted the chicks to comfort them. I thought, *These babies are adorable.*

I kept a record book about my project, recorded the cost of chicken food, hours of labor spent, and other expenses incurred. At the end of the school year, I was to kill the chickens, dress them, and weigh them. Following that gruesome task, I was to go to the grocery store, check the price per pound of dressed chicken, multiply the price by the pounds of my dressed birds, deduct my expenses, and determine whether I had made a profit.

There was no way I was going to kill my chickens. Many of them had names and all were pets. The lady who had been my first-grade teacher, Miss Versa Butler, had a "fun farm" out in the country, and she came to my rescue. She let me move my chickens to her place. They lived out the rest of their lives on her farm. I had visitation rights.

After the relocation, I had no choice but to lie to my ag teacher. I turned in my record book showing that I made a slight profit. I received a passing grade. I knew then that chicken farming was not going to be my calling. I chose instead to go into the arts, a profession where I can honestly declare, "No animals were harmed during the creation of this painting."

This Fragile Life

While I was a young man, death came a-calling. I was sitting in history class in high school one spring morning when the principal came in and asked to speak to one of my classmates.

Soon we heard screaming. The weather was warm, and all the windows were open. Everyone in class rushed to the open windows when we heard my classmate Willie Mae and her sister screaming and crying while being led away from campus. Their father had accidentally run over their four-year-old sister, Jackie, with a plow after she had fallen from a tractor while riding behind him.

Our class had only thirty-three members, and we were a very close-knit group. We didn't know how to react to the tragedy. Some of us just sat and cried. Many of us had lost elderly family members, but we were not prepared to lose someone in our community who was young.

A few short years later while I was a freshman in college, death came calling once again and took another young person. I was just beginning my life's journey as a young adult when one of my dear friends ended her journey. Sonya, a beautiful, sweet woman who I had once dated, passed away as a result of a terrible accident.

One Saturday night she received an engagement ring from a young man. The next morning on their way to church, engagement ring on her finger, the couple was involved in a head-on collision.

Sonya's fiancé had suffered minor injuries. She had suffered severe head injuries. Due to the severity of her injuries, she was transported to a hospital in Memphis and placed on life support. Sonya did not survive.

Her body was sent to the local funeral home. Her family decided to have her laid out in an open casket so that her friends could see her one more time. Her head had been shaved while in the hospital. The funeral home had put a wig on her. When I viewed her body, all I could see in my mind's eye was how she once had looked.

The custom at the time was that the deceased was not to be left unattended. The night before the funeral, a few friends and I sat up all night with Sonya's body. During the wake, we cried, we laughed, we loved, and we realized how fleeting life was for all of us. I realized that I was no longer immortal. Every day counts.

Taking It Off for the Fourth of July

For many years, Marmaduke, Arkansas, has celebrated the Fourth of July with an annual picnic. The celebration features bands, political speeches, barbecue, and beauty contests. The picnic was established as a benefit event to raise money for the upkeep of the area's cemeteries. Proper maintenance of the final resting places of loved ones is very important to the folks in the Delta.

During the 60s, one method of raising money for the picnic and for the cemeteries was to sell "chances" to win a new car that had been donated by a local dealership. The winning "chance" would be drawn as the finale of the picnic. I spent part of one summer driving the car here and there in the Delta. My sister, one of our friends, and I would take the car to nearby towns and go door-to-door and from business to business selling the chances. The law considered selling chances to be an illegal gambling activity, so we asked for "donations." For each "donation" of one dollar, the donor received a free chance to win the car. For each book of forty chances that we sold, we earned four dollars for ourselves.

The annual picnic was a much-anticipated event, and when I was a kid, the holiday was one of my favorite days of the year. Even after graduating from high school and moving away, when possible, I returned to Marmaduke on the Fourth of July. In 1966 while home from college, I was asked to be the escort to the reigning Miss Arkansas. She was making a guest appearance, and because my father was chair of the picnic committee that year, I was chosen to be her escort. It's always "who you know."

The best years at the picnic were the ones when the town was able to secure a carnival that would set up a few days prior to the Fourth. When I was sixteen years old, a carnival was at the picnic. Along with the usual rides, games, and sideshows, there was also a girlie show. Many of the townsfolk were outraged. I was excited and chomping at the bit to go to the show.

The Mid-South Fair was held each fall in Memphis. I attended several times. My favorite part of the fair was the sideshows. I was particularly intrigued by the girlie shows. Often the beautiful burlesque dancers were paraded in front of their tents for a teaser preview. One year the barker had two pitches. He said, "This beautiful girl does the splits over a watermelon, and it completely disappears." Turning to another dancer, he said, "And this lovely girl wears a costume that is made from fabric that costs fifty dollars a yard. However, she only wears fifty cents worth." Oh, how I wanted to see that, but alas, I was too young to buy a ticket. Even though I was only sixteen the year the girlie show came to the Marmaduke picnic, I thought, *This is my best chance to see some strippers.*

The picnic ended at 10 p.m. with the drawing for the car and a fireworks display. The carnival was still open, but most folks went home. I walked the few blocks to my house with my parents, told them I was tired, and went to my bedroom. After I knew everyone in the household was asleep, I got out of bed and dressed. My bedroom was at the rear of the house. A couple of years earlier, I secretly had moved the hinges on one of the window screens so that it opened like a screen door. I would often crawl out through my window and go for late night strolls.

That night, around 11:30, I went out through the window and walked back to the carnival. The girlie show had advertised a "Midnight Rambling Show" that would be the best show of the day. I paid my two dollars, lied about my age, walked in, and took my seat. I certainly didn't look eighteen, the age for admittance. Even though I was sixteen, I looked about fourteen. The ticket seller didn't care. He just wanted my money.

There were quite a few men in the audience. I knew several of them, but I trusted that they wouldn't snitch on me for being there. To do so would have also incriminated them. The dancers were all African American ladies. Three were svelte, lovely women who skillfully danced while they moved scarves and feathers so that nothing illegal and forbidden was revealed. I was amazed and appreciative of their talents. They each danced a couple of times before the star dancer came on stage to do her number.

Her name was Shirley. She weighed about three hundred pounds and was billed as "Shirley in the Temple, a performer who can jiggle things that other dancers don't have." And she did. I was mesmerized by her skillful performance. I left the tent happy that my curiosity about burlesque had finally been satisfied.

I learned three things: anticipating the forbidden is often more exciting than experiencing the real thing; where there's a will, there's a way; and from Shirley, use what you got.

Punching a Clock

I graduated from high school at the age of seventeen. I was a scrawny 115 pounds, a small guy with big plans that included college in the fall. Prior to graduating, I had picked cotton each fall while in school. That year, I would be in college during the harvest season, and for the first time to help pay school expenses, I needed a steady, forty-hour-a-week job, where I had to punch a time clock.

My daddy had a friend who was a foreman in an aircraft plant located in a nearby town. Through that connection, Daddy got me a summer job at the factory. I started at $1.47 an hour and when I got my paycheck, I was very disappointed that after taxes I had only cleared $47 per week. I made much more than that while picking cotton, a job where no taxes were withheld, and everyone was paid in cash.

I hated my job. Work in the plant started at 7 a.m. Each worker had to be standing by their appointed machines at 6:55 a.m. so that when the whistle sounded, there was not one second of work missed. The plant was not air-conditioned, and it was extremely hot during that summer in the Arkansas Delta. Hot as it was, I had to wear long sleeve shirts to keep my arms from being burned by flying sparks. I operated a machine that drilled a long, narrow groove into an aluminum frame that was part of a helicopter motor mount. I guided the drill with one hand while squirting kerosene on the drill to keep it from balling up.

The fumes were horrific. It took about five minutes to do each one, followed quickly by the next one.

I went to work day after day, and I detested every minute of it. Not wanting to be a quitter and not wanting to disappoint my father, I kept the job for the entire summer. I learned two things from working there: I was determined to stay in college and never have to work in a factory ever again, and from then on, I would find my own job.

Dark and Handsome

Following active duty in World War II, my mother's two brothers returned to Arkansas and a bleak economy. They could not find employment. Like many young men from the region, they moved to Michigan and worked in the automobile plants. They each married women from Michigan, had children, and made a life up north. Each summer, they returned to Arkansas for yearly visits with their Southern family.

One of my mother's brothers, Uncle Lowell, married an Arab American woman. Her name was Betty. She was a wonderful woman and a beloved member of our extended family. Aunt Betty and Uncle Lowell lived in the Detroit suburb of Warren. The Arab American neighborhood where they lived extended for blocks and blocks.

Uncle Lowell and Aunt Betty had three children. Their oldest son, Jimmy, was near my age, and we became close friends. My female classmates looked forward to his yearly summer visits. My friends, like me, were very Waspish. Jimmy had black hair and a dark complexion. He looked very different from the rest of us boys. The Arkie girls compared him to Frankie Avalon and Sal Mineo, and they vied for his attention. Sometimes, it is good to be different. Also, it is good for me to come clean and confess: I have half-Yankee cousins. There, I feel better.

Minor Legend for a Day or Two

When I was a teenager, I weighed 110 pounds, and I stood five foot six. Although I didn't look strong, I was wiry, and I had enough strength to hoist a seventy-pound sack of picked cotton across my shoulder and walk to the weighing wagon.

The only sport available to play in the high school that I attended was basketball. I was short, and I was not focused or interested enough to take the time to become a good shot. Although my mother was only four foot eleven, she had been a basketball star while in school. She loved the game, but she never pushed me to participate.

I didn't take after my father physically. He was a large man, five foot eleven, and he weighed more than twice what I weighed. When he attended Arkansas State College, he was a star football player. I never asked him questions about his time on the college team. I didn't know enough about football to ask, and I was glad my high school did not have football. It was another sport I could not have successfully played.

The first time I attended a football game was during my first semester at Arkansas State University. I decided to attend the homecoming game. All the guys in my dorm were excited about it. I wanted to fit in, join in sports conversations, and be a "with it" college student. I attended the game, had no clue what was happening, and only stayed through the halftime show.

I never went to another college game. Many years later I did attend one of my nephew's junior high school games. I couldn't keep up with the ball, and I still didn't know what was happening.

I was never bullied in high school. That didn't happen in my small town, a place where everyone knew each other, and kindness prevailed. I still thought it was important to prove myself as a man if for no other reason but for my self-esteem. When my PE teacher, Coach Ray, brought two pairs of boxing gloves to class and asked who wanted to learn to box, I was the first to step forward. The coach demonstrated a few moves, and the fight was on.

The gloves looked huge on my hands as I danced around, dodging his attempted hits. I was small, but agile enough to avoid his jabs. I found an opening, and I landed a hard right blow to the side of his head. I was shocked at my action, and I forgot to dodge. The coach's immediate reflex was to strike back. He hit me hard. He knocked me out and I fell to the floor. It took a few minutes for me to come to.

For a few days, I was a minor legend. I was the guy who had punched Coach Ray in the head. Sometimes one good lick is all a person needs to prove themselves. Since that day, I have not put on boxing gloves, and I have not fought with another person. There are other ways to prove one's worth. However, that one time, it sure felt good.

Hair Everywhere

I grew up with a beauty shop attached to my boyhood home in Northeast Arkansas. My mother's shop was one door away from our living room. Her customers would often stroll through our living room on the way to the family bathroom. The women would interrupt our TV viewing with their small talk, and they tracked hair onto the living room floor. Hair seemed to be everywhere. As a kid, I played on the linoleum floor in the beauty shop, rolling my toy cars through the hair clippings. We would burn the swept-up hair along with other combustibles in a burn barrel in the backyard. The hair would sizzle and pop while burning, and it released a horrid stench.

I liked having the beauty shop attached to the family home. It gave me ample opportunity to play with hair color, not only on myself but on the hair of my friends. When my sister was in the seventh grade, I bleached her hair to a platinum shade. She kept it that color for many years. My sister's boyfriend was kicked off the basketball team after I bleached his hair. It was permissible for girls to be bleached blonde, but it was not permissible for basketball players.

Another one of my friends was sent home from school after I colored his hair cardinal red. I had to quickly fix it before he was allowed to go back to class.

I had friends who were identical twins. They lived in the nearby town of Rector. They were very good-looking blond-headed boys, and they were next to impossible to tell apart. I thought I was doing them a favor by dyeing the hair of one of the boys jet black so that he would be different from his brother. Their mother didn't agree. The morning after the dye job, she woke the boys for school, saw the black-haired twin, and scared her entire neighborhood with her screams.

My father went to Irby's Barber Shop to have his hair cut. He said it was only fair since the barber's wife, Cricket, had my mother do her weekly shampoo and set. I think my father actually went to the barber shop for the gossip and because it was "the manly thing to do." I didn't go to the barber shop. My mother cut my hair. The first time I had someone else cut my hair was when I visited relatives in Amarillo. My uncle was in the air force, and I had my hair cut on base. I was scalped and vowed to never again let anyone but my mother touch my hair.

Unfortunately, I forgot that vow the next summer when a Native Alaskan came to Arkansas to visit friends. He told me he knew how to cut hair. He asked if I wanted him to trim mine. I said, "Sure." I was very trusting and thought, *How often does one have the chance to get their hair cut by an Eskimo?* He took the electric clippers to my head, cut a swath down the center, laughed, and said he was only kidding. I had to have the rest of my hair buzzed off to even it up.

After the two bad haircut experiences, I learned my lesson and would allow only my mother to cut my hair. I knew that my mother would do exactly what I wanted to have done, no more and no less. When I grew my hair halfway down my back, she would, as requested, barely trim the ends.

While I was enrolled as a student in the Memphis College of Art, I had a friend who went to New York City on vacation and returned to school sporting a shag haircut. The heavily layered look was the latest hairstyle of the day. I wanted one. I found a photo of pop star David Cassidy, who sported the cut. I drove to my mother's house in Marmaduke the next weekend, showed her the picture of Cassidy, and had her cut my hair to look like his. It was perfect. I was definitely "styling my shag."

I could always trust my mother to trim my hair just right, and she did up until the day that she died at the age of eighty-eight.

Trust is everything.

Not Too Much Trouble

It wasn't easy to make trouble and get away with it while living in a small town of 650 people in the Arkansas Delta. Everyone in town knew each other, and most of the residents had lived there for their entire lives.

They were descended from settlers that had arrived in the 1800s long before the town was incorporated in 1909. Everyone knew each other and their business.

When I was a teenager, I knew that if I was caught doing anything bad, everyone in town would know about it. At school, many of my teachers had been classmates of my mother. I had to behave in class, or my mother would have known before I even got home from school. I don't remember too much trouble occurring at school, nor do I remember anyone getting expelled. I'm not saying that my friends and I were perfect; we were not. But we learned to be sneaky.

When I was a preteen, I liked to sneak puffs from my great-grandpa's pipe. He would leave it lit, and when he was not around, my sisters, cousins, and I would take a quick draw from the pipe. I would try my best not to cough and get caught by my great-grandpa. I also knew where my father hid his bottles of whiskey, and I would take a nip from one of his bottles while he was at work.

My bedroom was at the rear of the house, and I secretly changed the hinges on one of the room's window screens so that it would open like a screen door. I used the window to escape from the house at night and to meet up with friends. If one of us had access to a vehicle, we would ride out into the country and steal a watermelon from a farmer's melon patch. We dropped the watermelon onto the road or a sidewalk where it would burst open. We ate the contents with our bare hands.

My friends and I didn't do anything really bad, and we probably did pretty much the same things our parents had done when they were young. Rolling a house with toilet paper at Halloween or stealing a watermelon were just things you did while growing up in a small Delta town.

Nettie's was a small store and lunch counter across the street from the high school. Students were allowed to go there during lunch, and it was an after-school hangout for local teens. The few kids that lived in town stayed there for an hour or so after school. Some of the kids that rode the "second bus" hung out there until time to board their bus to go home.

The school district did not have the funds to afford enough school buses for every student to be taken home immediately after classes. Some kids rode the "first bus" and were taken home immediately after school let out. After the first run, the buses would then return to take home the remaining students. I thought the "second bus" students were the lucky ones because they got to hang out at Nettie's.

I worked at Nettie's. Because I worked there, I was able to leave class five minutes before the lunch bell rang and five minutes before the last bell rang at the end of the school day. That gave me time to get to the store and get ready for work before the other students arrived. It also gave me time to pop a quarter into the jukebox and get first dibs on playing my six favorite songs. That quarter was half my hourly salary of fifty cents, but I did get a free lunch.

Nettie's was a safe place for us to let our hair down. Although Nettie was a friend and a beauty shop client of my mother, she was protective of her teen customers, and she never snitched on us. If we played hooky, we would hide at Nettie's. When someone from the school came looking for us, she would hide us underneath the counter.

Nettie's was also the place where we could safely smoke and not get caught. Adults never ventured into the store, so we were comfortable puffing away on our Salems. Cigarettes were twenty-five cents a pack. Although it was not legal, Nettie would break the seal on a pack, open it, and sell the cigarettes for two cents each. A pack held twenty smokes, and Nettie made an additional fifteen cents a pack. She didn't tell on us, and we didn't tell on her.

There were few places where we could get into trouble in our small town. Pool halls back then were reputed to be troublesome places for boys, but our local pool hall was overall a fairly tame hangout. I do know some wagering took place there. Most of the guys who hung out there were older than me, and I was not brave enough to venture into the building very often.

My father would get together with his friends and play poker for money. My friends and I played cards for fun but never for money. We weren't willing to wager and take a chance at losing any of the hard-earned money that we made from picking cotton.

The closest thing to gambling that my male friends and I did was to play strip poker. There was one sleepover with five or six of my guy friends that took place in a barn. We played strip poker, and when everyone finally lost and was naked, the loser of each additional hand had to climb hay bales and swing across the barn on a long rope. To us, the activities that night were terribly risqué. Our well-kept secret of the rope-swinging, naked night kept us giggling for several weeks.

We didn't consider it to be bad when my friends and I pulled a good prank. My sister, a couple of friends, and I decided to decorate the flagpole that was located in front of the high school. My mother kept a rag drawer in the kitchen. Among the rags in the drawer were numerous old worn-out brassieres and panties. Late one night in the cover of darkness, we tied the undergarments to the chain that was used to raise the flag. We spaced them every few feet, and we tied them good and tight with triple knots.

My sister and I left for school the next morning earlier than usual and got a good viewing spot from Nettie's. When students arrived on campus, they laughed and pointed at the flagpole. It took the poor student in charge of raising the flag a good while to get the undergarments off the chain so the flag could be raised. The culprits who tied the bras onto the flagpole were never caught. Thank goodness. My mother would have been terribly embarrassed.

Going to the Chapel

When I was a teenager, I went to several friends' weddings. People back then got married at an early age. While most students did wait to get married following graduation, there were students at my high school who got married while still in school. They could continue to attend but only after the girl signed an agreement stating that she would not get pregnant.

My neighbor, who was twelve years old, got married, signed the agreement, did not get pregnant, and graduated with honors. Two of my sister's unmarried classmates did get pregnant, and they were forced to leave school. My sister married while in the tenth grade, and she quit school. Gossip spread that she married because she was pregnant. With an "I'll show them" attitude, my stubborn sister did not get pregnant for a couple of years following her wedding.

Sally Ann, one of my classmates, married a suave California boy. Not too long after the wedding, the groom was killed when his vehicle was hit by a train. Sally Ann returned to school, and she may have been the youngest widow to ever attend Marmaduke High. Shortly after graduation, she married a young man who was one of our classmates.

Her second wedding was held a couple of miles up the highway from town in the very small Tokio Missionary Baptist Church. The building was located next to a Cotton Belt Railroad crossing. Weddings and funerals at churches near railroad tracks were timed so noise from a passing train would not interrupt the service.

While driving to the church to attend the wedding, I was thinking about a man who lived in Marmaduke. He had never in his life ventured out of the county of his birth until the day one of his friends decided the man needed to cross the county line. The friend drove him a few miles north from Greene County into Clay County. On their way, he saw the Tokio Missionary Baptist Church and said, "Hell, the bombing didn't hurt it much." He thought it was the "Tokyo" that had been bombed in World War II.

There were just a few cars in the parking lot of the small church when I arrived for Sally Ann's wedding. Because it was the second time around, the bride opted not to wear white. Instead, she wore the blue formal dress that she had worn to our junior-senior banquet. It was a large and fluffy formal with a hoop skirt underneath. The netting on the dress reminded me of puffed crepe paper that adorned floats in a parade.

The wedding ceremony was different from any I had previously witnessed. The officiating preacher shouted a fire-and-brimstone sermon intermingled with traditional wedding vows. I was afraid he was going to pass out. He hyperventilated, gasped, and turned bright red in the face while talking as fast as a Southern preacher could possibly talk. He was loud enough that I don't think fellow attendees heard me snort a time or two while I attempted to stifle my laughter.

Following the high-energy service, a reception line was formed, and guests congratulated the newlyweds. I tried to keep a straight face when I lied and told the bride that the ceremony was lovely. After everyone had offered their congrats to the couple, it was time for cake and punch. Instead of the traditional sweet, gooey, iced white cake, the bride and groom locked hands and sliced into a chocolate cake. Guests whispered to each other about the shocking departure from tradition. I thought it appropriate because it was the bride's second time to be married. I did regret that the punch was alcohol-free. I needed a drink.

Following the events at the church, an additional wedding celebration took place several miles away in a bowling alley in Paragould, Arkansas. Only the couple's closest friends attended, and I was among the lucky few. The bride, still wearing her blue formal dress, bowled several games. I didn't pay much attention to the pins when she slung the ball down the alley. My eyes were fixated on her dress, which occasionally flew up and revealed her matching blue panties.

Sally Ann bowled a good game, and the couple remained married for many years. Talk of the wedding lasted almost as long.

Empty Nest Except for a Chocolate Poodle

My two sisters and I moved from my parents' home during an eight-month period in 1964. My older sister married and moved into a farmhouse with her new husband. As planned, I started college that September and moved into a dorm at Arkansas State University. What was not planned was my sixteen-year-old sister's move out of the house that year.

My sister Rhonda never liked school, and she seemed restless living in our small town. When she received a proposal from a young man whom she had dated for only a short while, she said yes. The suitor had graduated from high school with my class and had moved to West Hollywood to work for his grandfather. I suspected that my sister saw marriage as a way to quit school and move to California. However, she said, "I want to marry him because I love him."

My parents threw a fit and refused to give their consent. I was upset as well, and I told her, "This is crazy and don't expect me to go to the wedding."

The family was in turmoil. My daddy sought guidance from his father, who was a Methodist minister. My wise grandfather told my parents, "If you don't give her your consent, she will likely run away to California, and you might not see her again." After much thought, my parents accepted his advice and gave the marriage their blessing. After my parents' change of heart, I softened and told my relieved sister, "I will go to your wedding."

My sister and I had always been very close, and I only wanted her to be happy. She planned a Christmas Day ceremony, a time when her fiancé would be back in Arkansas visiting his parents. I thought, *Damn, now she's going to ruin Christmas.* I gave the marriage six months.

The day after the wedding, the newlyweds headed for California. I was home for holiday break until after the New Year. That New Year's Eve, I stayed home with my mother. I knew that my father would be in bed long before midnight, and I didn't want Mama to be sitting alone when the New Year came in. On the big console TV in the living room, we watched the ball drop in Times Square. The next day we ate black-eyed peas and cabbage with hopes of a prosperous New Year. My mother was wishing she had her baby girl back home.

Six months later she got her wish. Things went bust in California, and the newlyweds returned to Arkansas. They arrived in my parents' driveway in a Buick that died on the spot. They had paid $95 for the car. My sister was holding a toy chocolate poodle that they had purchased while passing through Oklahoma. They had paid $100 for the puppy, and that expenditure had left them with $5 to their name.

For a while they lived in a trailer near my parents. After my brother-in-law got a job driving a milk truck, they moved to a nearby town. Their landlord didn't allow pets. They couldn't take the poodle with them. They left him with my mother. She loved the dog, and because of his presence, her house was no longer empty of a "child." She had a fur baby, a poodle named Cho Cho.

When my sister passed away in 2013, she had been married to the same man for forty-nine years. Together they had three children, and six grandchildren.

I had given their marriage six months. I learned that I wasn't so smart, I could not predict the future, and I didn't know what was in another's heart. True love has lasting power.

Fearful Peacenik Afraid to Come Out

I knew from an early age that I was gay. When I was a teen, I felt compelled to keep my orientation a secret. I wasn't ready for rejection, ridicule, and the probable bullying that would have awaited me. I would rather have died than come out. I lived a lie. I lived in fear of exposure.

When I turned eighteen, it was mandatory for all males to take their military physical. It was during the Vietnam War years, and the draft was in place. I was in my first year of college when I had to return to my hometown, board a bus with other eighteen-year-old males with whom I had grown up and go to Memphis for the military physical.

Facing the physical, I was very distraught. I had always considered myself to be a pacifist. Being in the military would have been foreign to my nature. My dream had been to serve in the Peace Corps. I really wanted to make a difference. However, that dream was not possible for me. Being in the Peace Corps was one way to get a deferment from the military. Only rich boys with pull could join the Corps. I was far from rich.

I had been told that if I ate lots of sugar, I would flunk the physical because my sugar level would show me to be diabetic. I ate a five-pound bag of sugar the night before the physical. The next morning, I boarded a yellow school bus for the journey to the old Veterans Administration Hospital on Getwell Road in Memphis. Hundreds of young men were there for physicals. I studied their faces, and I could sense that I was not the only one who was nervous. The physical took most of the day and was humiliating. We were herded naked from room to room and examined by numerous doctors.

I did have an option that would allow me to flunk the physical. I could check "the box." By checking "the box," one admitted that they were homosexual, and they would receive a 4F status: unfit for service. I had been told that guys who checked the box would be kept overnight for psychiatric evaluation. At the time, homosexuality was considered a mental disorder. I thought that the guys from home would find out that I was gay if I checked the box. They would have noticed I wasn't on the bus for the return trip. The sugar trick did not work. I passed the physical.

As long as I stayed in school, I had a student deferment. After graduation, I was able to obtain an occupational deferment because I was able to secure a teaching job. That's not what I had planned to do as a profession, but I gladly took the job in order to avoid the draft.

In 1969, the government decided that they would conduct a lottery to decide who would be drafted. On December 1st, 1969, I sat with many young men in a student lounge on the campus of Washington University in St. Louis, where I was attending night classes. We watched on TV as the lottery took place. During the broadcast, a military person drew from a container a birth date that was enclosed in a blue capsule. Each drawn birth date was then matched to a number that determined who would be drafted. That year, all birthdays that matched a number below 195 were eligible. Young men who received the lowest numbers were taken immediately. There were cheers and groans as the numbers were drawn. I won the lottery. I drew 281.

After watching the lottery, I left the lounge, and I went home alone to my apartment. My future once again belonged to me. I was elated. However, I cried while thinking about the young men who were not as fortunate as I had been during the drawing. Lying in my bed with eyes closed, I could still see the despair on their faces. I saw fear.

No longer subject to the draft, I was able to quit teaching and to return to school. I enrolled in the Memphis College of Art as a painting major. I was able to resume my goal to become a fine artist. I vowed to myself to never again "deny who I am," even in the face of death.

In reality, "That ain't living."

CHAPTER 3 — MARMADUKE

Turtles and Toilet Paper

When I was a kid, a good number of houses in Marmaduke did not have indoor plumbing. Those homes had outhouses in the backyards. The two churches that were across the alley from my family home had outhouses that received a great deal of use. My grandmother's house on the edge of town did not have indoor plumbing. When I visited her, I used the outhouse. It was not a pleasant experience sitting on a hard wooden seat. One had to be vigilant about wasps in the outhouses during warm weather and using an outhouse during cold weather was almost painful. Unlike most areas, we called outhouses "toilets," and the porcelain thing indoors was called a "commode."

My family home did have indoor plumbing. My parents put in a bathroom when they bought their home in the 40s. They left the outhouse in the backyard to be used as our second bathroom. Because I had two sisters who seemed to always be in the indoor bathroom, our outhouse often came in handy for me.

Marmaduke did not have a sewer system. When a toilet was flushed, the waste ran through pipes and emptied into one of a series of tunnels and into open ditches that crisscrossed the town. Citizens of the town were not allowed to flush toilet paper. The paper was placed in a covered trash can. In hot weather the smell from the ditches was unpleasant. Mosquito larvae could be seen wiggling in the stinky gray water.

Snapping turtles, some bigger than dinner plates, lived in the ditches. At times they would venture into our yard. I thought they were interesting creatures akin to dinosaurs. I did find them a little scary, but like most kids, I liked being scared. When a snapping turtle crawled out of a ditch, I enticed it to bite down on a stick, a natural instinct for the snapper. The turtle would not let go, and I would carry it and the stick back to the ditch. I had heard that when they did bite, they would not let go until it thundered. I was somewhat disappointed when I found it not to be true.

The ditches were fairly deep and ran under the streets through three-foot-wide rectangular concrete culverts. As a kid, I thought it was fun to get in, legs and arms splayed outward, and monkey walk through the tunnel under the street with my body well above the sewage. That "fun" did come to an end one day.

My great-aunt Beulah, who lived in Detroit, had sent me a flannel shirt for my birthday. It had a cream, brown, and green pattern of cowboys riding bucking broncos. I loved the shirt. One day while wearing it, I straddled the tunnel under the street. As usual I was very proud of my athletic skill as I made my way through the tunnel just two feet above the putrid water. But then my foot slipped and down I went. My favorite shirt was covered with nasty sewage. I ran to the house crying. My mother made me go to the back porch and undress. She had planned to throw away all my clothes, but after much begging on my part, she saved my flannel shirt. She washed it several times before she let me wear it again. I continued to rescue snapping turtles, but I never again ventured into the tunnel.

When I was in my early teens, my father was elected mayor of our town. He was responsible for getting a modern sewer system installed. The smell went away, and the snapping turtles moved on. I did miss the turtles.

Turkey Day, Duck Day

I was born on Thanksgiving Day. My Father joked that he was mad at me from the very beginning because I knocked him out of a day off. He worked in a bank, and he would have been off on Thanksgiving Day. He also would have been allowed to take a day off the day I was born to transport my mother to the hospital and be present for my birth. Due to my arrival date, both days off were combined into one.

I think the real reason that he was mad at me for being born on that day was that I knocked him out of a duck hunt. The first day of duck hunting season was Thanksgiving Day. On opening day, he would get up long before daybreak and go to his duck blind on the Saint Francis River.

The river was located in the Mississippi Flyway, a migratory route for mallards and other species of ducks. The Saint Francis was about five miles from our house. It was a swampy river filled with cypress trees and water moccasins. It was a nighttime resting place for the migrating waterfowl. Daddy always hunted duck on Thanksgiving morning, but he would make it back home in plenty of time for the midday holiday meal.

When I was ten years old, I was invited to go with him to duck hunt on opening day. Daddy woke me up at 3:30 a.m. I quickly dressed and climbed into his 1939 Chevy, a black car that he had named Ol' Betsy. The car had a removable rack on top that held a flat bottom boat that we were to take on our water journey to the duck blind. As we neared the Saint Francis levee, we stopped at a sharecropper's shotgun shack where we picked up my father's best friend, Lonzo. The minute Lonzo got into the car, the two men started drinking Old Crow whiskey. A few minutes later we were at the river. We took a fifteen-minute boat ride in the dark through swampy passages. As a ten-year-old boy, I found the ride exhilarating and very scary. I had heard tales of snakes falling out of trees into boats, and I was fearfully thinking about the fifteen-foot-long water moccasin that, according to legend, lived in the Saint Francis River.

The duck blind was a very small wooden shack that sat on stilts in the water. We exited the boat and climbed up the ladder into the blind. It was very cold, but the blind was soon warmed by a small fire built in a charcoal bucket. A galvanized coffee pot was placed on the blazing charcoal, and soon the air was filled with the smell of strong chicory coffee.

I drank the coffee from a metal cup. The two grown-ups drank the coffee and chased each sip with Old Crow. I was too young for whiskey and too afraid to ask for a swig, even though I had sampled my daddy's whiskey numerous times unbeknownst to him. We sat and we waited.

Just before dawn, I was told to be very quiet. As daylight crept in, we could hear ducks quacking. My father and his friend were poised at a window opening in the blind, guns in place, as they waited for the ducks to fly over. All of a sudden, dozens flew over, and shots were fired. No ducks were hit. I think all the whiskey might have affected the men's ability to aim properly.

We didn't see another duck. I was bored, chilly, and tired of drinking the strong, bitter coffee. On the way home, I slept in the car. Daddy shook me awake when we got home. I was very happy to enter my warm home, see my mother, and join my family for the Thanksgiving feast.

That was the one and only time that I went duck hunting. Although I loved my daddy, I knew that hunting was not my thing. Thereafter, I spent my Thanksgiving mornings at home with my mother, safe from snakes, and watching the Macy's Thanksgiving Day Parade.

I Almost Saw Kim Novak

In the small Delta town where I grew up there was a movie theater that seated fewer than 100 people. For a town with a population of 650, that was plenty large enough. For a special end-of-school-year treat, the town's elementary students were bused to the theater for a showing of *Black Beauty*. The feature film was the same each year, and it was preceded by a Little Rascals short film, "The Kid from Borneo." The short featured a crazed jungle native chasing the rascal kids while yelling, "Yum, yum, eat em' up!" It was both scary and funny.

The main attraction, *Black Beauty*, was about a horse, and the movie was wrought with drama and suspense. Fortunately for the young audience, the movie had a happy ending. I got to attend the special showing only two or three times before the theater closed.

A large, fancy movie house, the Capitol Theater, was ten miles down the road. The screen was much larger than the one that had been in my hometown's little theater. The seats were very plush. When Elvis started making movies, the Capitol Theater would premiere his holiday release on Thanksgiving afternoons. We always attended that premiere. Following a midday holiday dinner, my father would drive the family to the theater and be waiting to pick us up after the movie ended. With the exception of seeing *Gone with the Wind*, my father never attended an indoor movie.

However, he did see films when he took our family to the Sunset Drive-In in nearby Paragould. I think he was willing to go to the drive-in because he could take a bottle of whiskey to sip on. My mother made snacks for us to munch, but being kids, we also wanted to go to the concession stand for popcorn, cokes, and big dill pickles.

I loved the movies, but even more I enjoyed playing on the playground that was set up in front of the movie screen. The minute the car stopped, my sisters and I would make a beeline for the playground, knowing that we had a limited time to play before the movie started. We liked to whirl around on the spinning disc we called a merry-go-round. During the hot summer months, the car windows had to remain down. My father would buy a citronella incense swirled repellant. When lit, it kept the mosquitoes at bay. On the Fourth of July there was a special fireworks display between the double features at the Sunset Drive-In.

As a teen, I continued going to the drive-in with my friends. One weekend there was a scheduled showing of a double feature of Kim Novak movies. She was a popular actress at the time. The owner of the drive-in ran ads in the local paper that said Kim Novak would be there and would make a special appearance between the two movies. I was very excited as I had not seen anyone famous. My friends and I arrived early and got in a long line of cars. Soon the drive-in was filled to capacity. We anxiously awaited the end of the first feature and the appearance of Miss Novak. After the first movie ended, most folks left their cars and headed for the concession stand, where the star was to make her appearance on the roof.

The owner of the drive-in appeared on the roof, accompanied by his young daughter. His last name was Novak and his daughter's name was Kim. The crowd went berserk when they realized the little girl was the "Kim Novak" that had been advertised to appear. I feared that the man and the kid were not going to get off the roof alive.

People were screaming and yelling while throwing wadded up paper cups and popcorn boxes at the two Novaks. Folks got back into their cars and started honking their car horns. Everyone was mad as hell, and several cars peeled out. Quite a few speakers were torn from metal poles. Many of the moviegoers demanded refunds as they exited.

I learned one thing that night: if you promise folks Kim Novak, then it better be Kim Novak. The *real* Kim Novak.

Whatever you promise, it is best to deliver.

Bradsher's

Bradsher's Drugstore in Marmaduke was a typical small-town pharmacy with a soda fountain, assorted sundries, and gift items. The drugstore was owned by Don and Beulah Bradsher. Beulah, not liking her given name, went by "Bootie. The couple made a very good living. Each one had a Lincoln Continental car that they kept in a two-car garage attached to a blond brick home. They always had a Great Dane dog as a pet. I remember the sad day when one of their Great Danes, Tillie, was killed on the railroad tracks after being run over by a Cotton Belt Railroad train. Word spread like wildfire about poor Tillie.

I don't know how they got around health regulations, but the Bradshers kept an Amazon parrot named Pappy in the drugstore. He sat on top of his cage near the soda fountain. The parrot could talk, but only when he chose to do so. He would threaten to bite off the fingers of children when they got too close to him. I, too, teased Pappy with my finger. He would try to grab it. I would quickly pull it away. It was a game we both enjoyed, and fortunately for me, a game I never lost.

I did some of my Christmas shopping at Bradsher's. During the holidays, I would go there and purchase a perfume, Evening in Paris, as a gift for my schoolteacher. I thought there could be no finer scent.

Occasionally, I would sneak an adult magazine from the top of the store's magazine rack, place it inside a *Boy's Life* magazine, and look at "dirty" pictures.

An odd thing about the drugstore was that the far back corner was the liquor section, the only place in town to buy alcohol. There was a rear entrance to the liquor corner for clients who didn't want to be seen carrying booze out the front door. My parents called it the "Baptist door." I miss old timey drug stores with soda fountains.

Lucky in the Danger Zone

I did things as a child that today would be thought unwise to do, and perhaps some of the activities would even be banned. Often those choices involved the chewing and digesting of unsavory or toxic items. I loved the miniature wax soda bottles sold as candy and filled with colored, fruit-flavored liquid. Although I don't think toxins were involved, it made little nutritional sense to bite off the bottle top, drink the liquid, and then spend hours chewing the wax. But it was a cheap treat. The cost of a package of five of the little bottles was a nickel.

Then there were the plastic bubbles. A gooey, liquid plastic was squeezed from a tube and placed on the end of a straw. The goop turned into a bubble when you blew through the straw. The bubble lasted for a while, but when it deflated, I chewed the plastic. I enjoyed the chemical taste and the tough texture that made chewing a challenge, and I chewed until my jaw gave out.

During the spring, my friends and I enjoyed eating sheepshire from the yard. The plant was light green, looked like small clover, and had a yellow bloom. It had a sour, bitter taste. I didn't like it, but I ate it just because I could. Later I learned that it was a type of oxalis and was toxic if digested in large quantities. Apparently, I never ate that much because I never did get ill.

Other possibly harmful activities involved inhaling smoke and fumes. My mother had a grape arbor in our backyard, and it provided me an ample supply of dried grapevines to secretly smoke. I coughed with each drag and my lungs ached.

I enjoyed following the mosquito-fogging truck that drove through town during evenings in the summer. It was like playing in the clouds. I also spent many hours as a teen sitting in a car at the drive-in movie with a Pic mosquito coil burning. Later studies warned that prolonged exposure to Pic could be harmful.

Every Saturday my family would go to Paragould, Arkansas, to shop for groceries. While in Paragould, my sister and I would often run down to the Red Goose shoe store to x-ray our feet with the store's machine. It was fun to wiggle our toes and see the bones in our feet. We had no idea that overexposure to x-rays could be harmful.

My friends and I also enjoyed playing with mercury. It is the only metal that is liquid at room temperature. We would use the element to shine coins while being careful not to let the mercury separate into lots of little balls that scattered everywhere. We didn't know that it was very toxic.

While unaware that some of our childhood activities were harmful, there were things we avoided or did cautiously because we were warned by adults that they were harmful. They weren't. We worried that if we crossed our eyes, they would stay that way. We avoided swallowing watermelon seeds so that watermelons didn't grow in our stomachs. We believed that if we caught a toad, and it peed on our hand, we would get warts. Although I was told not to, I would throw caution to the wind and hang upside down from the monkey bars even though I had been warned that my liver would turn over. As far as I know, it did not.

In spite of unknown and even untrue hazards, most folks my age survived childhood and seem to be no worse for wear. What doesn't kill you makes you stronger . . . sometimes. Sometimes it does kill you. I was just lucky, I guess.

Doctored

While growing up in the Arkansas Delta, I knew many people, including family members, who practiced alternative forms of medicine based on old-time cures and folklore.

If I had a cold, my mother would plaster my neck and chest with Vicks VapoRub. The soothing touch of my mother's hands rubbing the Vicks onto me made up for the scratchy wool sock she would wrap around my neck. The Vicks treatment was accompanied by several doses of hot toddy: hot water, sugar, lemon, and whiskey all mixed together. For many years, I associated whiskey with medicine. A cure for a sore throat that my mother used was a warm saltwater gargle. I still do that today when my throat is sore.

I never did have a tetanus shot as a child. My grandmother knew what to do to prevent tetanus and other infections when a wound occurred. If the weather was warm, I was barefoot. I was constantly cutting my feet or stepping on rusty nails. When that happened, my grandmother would pour coal oil into a big, enameled metal pan, and I would soak my hurt foot in the coal oil for several minutes. Not once did my foot get infected from a cut or puncture. Another hazard to being barefoot was stepping on honeybees that dined on the clover in our yard. Every week or so, I would step on a bee and get a bad sting. My grandmother would remove the tobacco from one of my daddy's Camel cigarettes, and she would chew it until it was a paste. She applied the paste to the swollen spot on my foot. She told me that it drew out the poison. If one of my daddy's cigarettes wasn't available, she used baking soda that she had mixed with water to make a healing paste.

My mother and her friends eased the pain of arthritis by swallowing a poke berry every morning. They gathered the berries, washed them, and put a year's supply of berries into the freezer. Even though the seeds of the berries are thought to be toxic, the women never seemed to suffer ill effects, and they swore that the berries eased their pain. Poke berries and juice from the poke plant has been used for centuries, not only by early settlers, but by Native Americans who used the berries to treat any number of ailments. Scientists have studied and are still studying the medicinal uses of the poke plant. The women who swallowed the berries may have been onto something that really did lessen their aches.

Although I think there was validity to some of the folk cures that were used in the Delta, some applications made little sense and offered no logical explanation. There were two or three people in my town who were known to cure colic by blowing into a baby's mouth. The qualification of a person who could cure colic was to be one who had never seen his or her father. Mothers would call on these folks to cure babies of this common malady.

We mistakenly thought that toads caused warts. If one of the hoppy creatures urinated on a person, we believed that the person was destined to get a wart. I played with toads, but I was careful to avoid their pee. For those that did get a wart, they visited Mr. Parish, who could cure them of the unsightly blemish by rubbing the wart with a rag, saying something under his breath, and then telling the afflicted to bury the rag in their yard. The wart would disappear within a week. As unlikely as that wart removal method sounds, I saw it work more than once. I think it was a case of "mind over matter." The belief that the wart would be gone let the body get rid of it.

The cure that I most question was my grandmother's "surefire" way to get rid of chicken pox. When I came down with the childhood disease, she took me out to her chicken pen and threw a chicken over my head. I don't believe that cured me, but hey, the pox was gone in a week's time.

Some things in life defy logic, but if those things work, accept the gift, and go with it.

Eatin' Good, Eatin' Bad

My mother and grandmother loved to cook, but neither would have been labeled as gourmet chefs. Both were good ol' Southern cooks par excellence. This meant they could batter and fry any and all vegetables, collect Jell-O salad recipes, have Velveeta "at the ready," and have a grease can on the stove.

Growing up I ate most anything and everything that was put on my plate, including catfish; turnip, mustard, or collard greens; liver and onions; chocolate gravy with homemade biscuits; and fried bologna.

Although I would eat Vienna sausage straight out of the can and enjoyed fried Spam with scrambled eggs, there were a few things that I did refuse to eat. When my mother served fried brains for breakfast, I would retreat to the living room with a bowl of oatmeal. I could not look at fried quail because they looked like little cooked birds. They were no different to me than sparrows and mockingbirds. For obvious reasons, I never once ate chitlins. I didn't eat mountain oysters, gizzards, or tongue—most organs with the exception of liver.

I refused to eat deer, rabbit, and other wild game that many folks in my small Delta town considered "good eatin'." Disney movies did influence my food choices when it came to eating animals. I would not eat Bambi or Thumper.

My father was a duck hunter. My mother would cook the ducks with dressing or smother the fowl in a very soupy barbecue sauce. The duck when served with dressing was very dark and dry, but I did like it. Because of the liquid sauce, it was somewhat moist. I chewed cautiously, however, so that I didn't bite down on metal shots that were scattered throughout the meat.

With the exception of turtle doves, my grandmother would eat anything. She considered the dove "the bird of peace," and she thought that it should never be eaten. However, she cooked and devoured everything else: wild rabbit, squirrel, raccoon, and other game that I refused to eat. She also loved pickled pigs' feet.

When my great-grandfather was living, my grandmother would cook a hog's tail in a pot of boiled cabbage. My grandfather loved the hog's tail. I was nauseated by the sight of it, long and pink, and lying on his plate. Even though I loved boiled cabbage, if a hog's tail was cooked with it, I passed.

Two unusual desserts that my grandmother made were vinegar cobbler and green grape cobbler. She told me that when she was growing up fresh fruit was not often available, and at times canned fruit would not last the winter. Vinegar served as a substitute for fruit. Unripe green grapes were also a good substitute for fruits that didn't ripen until later in the season. I looked forward to visits from my great-uncle Floyd because I knew my grandmother would make him his favorite dish, a vinegar cobbler. It was delicious with a taste best described as sweet and sour.

It's not easy for me to pick out a favorite Southern dish, but near the top of my list would be cornbread and buttermilk. It was a favorite food of my mother and grandmother too. It is very filling and easy to prepare: crumble cornbread, place in a glass, pour in buttermilk, and eat with a spoon. The cornbread should be prepared Southern style, and that means without sugar in the recipe.

Even though I enjoy many kinds of food, both regional and ethnic, I still prefer good ol' Southern cooking. It tastes like home.

All the Gold Is in California

While growing up in the Northeast Arkansas Delta, I thought most rich folk lived in California. I also thought that all wealthy people drove

Cadillac cars, had palm trees in their yards, used cigarette holders, and owned French poodles who wore rhinestone collars. In the little town where I grew up, if anyone had money, I wasn't aware of it. I never saw anyone walking a poodle in Marmaduke, Arkansas.

With few exceptions, folks in my town did not have money. The upside of that was there was no separation due to class based on finances. We were all in the same boat, or at least in the same cotton patch. It was not unusual for our homecoming queen to live in a house without indoor plumbing. There was a line of townsfolk at city hall each month who were getting their government commodities, food supplements that included block cheese, tubs of peanut butter, rice, and beans. No one was looked down upon because they "didn't have," but they were helped and lifted up by those who did have a little more.

If anyone in the area had money, it was probably the owners of fertile farmland east of town. Their fields yielded good crops of soybeans and cotton. The dirt in that part of the county was rich black gumbo. Before the area was drained, it had once been swampland. The Northeast Delta has always yielded some of the best cotton crops in the state. If the owners of the land had money, they didn't make a show of it. Sharecroppers also worked the land. They worked just as hard if not harder than most, but unfortunately, they were among the poorest in our community.

The one time of the year when folks in my town had a little disposable cash was during the fall. Most of us picked cotton, and even though we only received three dollars per hundred pounds picked, by week's end, we had some money in our pockets. We were paid daily for our labor.

Each evening after working in the field, I counted my day's income and placed it inside a cigar box that I hid in my sock drawer. I knew it wasn't going to happen, but I sometimes wondered if I had saved enough money for a bus ticket to California.

There were two cotton gins in Marmaduke. During the fall, the smell of burning cotton hulls permeated the air. I often heard people say, "Smells like money to me." With money in hand on Saturday night, I, along with many other fellow cotton pickers, would go to an auction that was held downtown. I enjoyed watching people bidding and buying while I carefully kept my hand down. I was hoarding my cash for bigger purchases.

At the age of twelve, I bought a small horse. When I turned fourteen, I bought a small motorcycle. And at sixteen, I bought a 1952 Ford for three hundred dollars. Even though it wasn't a Cadillac, I felt rich having wheels of my own.

I'm glad that I grew up the way that I did, not judging folks according to their financial worth. Even though I thought those rich people in California were glamorous and interesting, I never entertained the thought that they were better. These days I'm comfortable enough, but I never did get rich, and I didn't move to California. However, I did own a poodle at one time. That's close enough.

Shopping in Memphis

While growing up in the Arkansas Delta, Memphis was our go-to metro area. Our television stations were broadcast from Memphis, and two newspapers, the *Memphis Commercial Appeal,* and the *Memphis Press-Scimitar,* were delivered to our home daily. If we needed to go to a specialist for medical care, we headed to Memphis. Besides going to the Overton Park Zoo in that city, what I remember most about Memphis was shopping downtown.

After crossing the Mississippi River Bridge and arriving in the city, my family would begin their shopping day at the large Sears store on Crossover Road. Sears was *the* place to shop. My younger sister and I liked going there because they had an escalator. While my parents shopped, my sister and I rode the escalator up and down and over and over again.

After we left Sears, we headed for the downtown area of Memphis. My father knew what he wanted to buy and went to two stores, the Thom McAn shoe store and Robert Hall men's store. He finished his shopping in less than an hour, and he spent the rest of the day sitting on a park bench and feeding pigeons in Court Square Park.

At noon, Daddy would join the family for lunch at the Piccadilly Cafeteria. Before entering the cafeteria, he would always advise, "Don't let your eyes be bigger than your stomach." The advice fell on deaf ears as my younger sister and I loaded up our trays. We were particularly fond of the shrimp cocktail that was served in a lovely glass with a tiny sterling silver cocktail fork. I enjoyed watching the young men employees who wore white jackets and white gloves. They balanced several trays of food that they carried to the tables. When very young, I thought, *That's what I want to do when I grow up, wear an elegant white jacket and white gloves, and juggle trays at the Piccadilly.* After we finished lunch, the serious shopping would begin.

My favorite time to shop in Memphis was during the Christmas season. Two major department stores, Goldsmith's and Lowenstein's, were decorated inside and out during the holidays.

Lowenstein's had a special Christmas spokesperson, Mr. Bingle, a snowman puppet who was featured in the store's window. He had his own television show that aired during the month before Christmas. I watched him on TV every day after school during December. I couldn't wait to get to Memphis and to see Mr. Bingle in person in the department store's window.

Christmas shopping in the city also included going to Goldsmith's for a visit with Santa. I would sit on Santa's lap and tell him what I wanted, things I had carefully selected from the Sears Christmas catalog.

When I got older, around twelve years of age, I was allowed to run around by myself to shop in downtown Memphis. One of my favorite stores was the young man's clothing store, The One-Two-Three Shop.

I had a "secret" favorite store, a small newsstand near Court Square. The newsstand sold adult magazines. By today's standards, the adult magazines were very tame. As a teen, I spent quite a bit of time at the newsstand during each trip. The owner didn't seem to mind that I looked through the adult publications.

Around the age of fifteen, I finally got the nerve to buy an adult magazine. I smuggled it home and hid it under my mattress. Then I volunteered to always change the sheets on my bed.

And I did.

You Say Potato, and So Do I

While I was growing up in the Arkansas Delta, the folks who lived there shared a common language that was slow, easy, and often colorful.

When I moved from that region, I had to learn different words and expressions in order to fit in, and for everyone to clearly understand just what I was trying to say.

There was a generational gap when it came to word usage. However, I had heard the "old-timey" words used by the older folks enough that I could interpret their meaning. When my grandmother said "vittles," I knew she meant food. She called pots and pans "vessels." What she called "ketchup" was a homemade tomato relish, something that I would never put on fries.

If she said to "sit pretty," I knew she meant for me to sit down and behave. When my grandmother was going to cook, or to do anything, we knew she was "fixin'" to do something. "Fixin'" is so embedded in my vocabulary that I still say that word without thinking.

If one was "fixin' to go to town," they were going shopping. "Town" for us was Paragould, Arkansas, ten miles away. On the way to town we would pass by several "mile crossings," places where a road crossed over the railroad track every mile.

While in town we went to Kroger's, the main grocery store. All paper sacks at my house were known as "Kroger sacks." If we bought a soda pop, it didn't matter if it was a Pepsi, an RC, or another flavor, we were getting a "coke." Manufactured clothes bought in town were "store-bought," not "homemade." Potatoes came in burlap bags that we called "tow sacks." We called French fries "fried potatoes." "Commodities" had nothing to do with the stock market. They were food rations that po' folk received in lieu of food stamps.

In the Delta, if folks said they were going to have dinner, then they were going to eat their noon meal. When my daddy worked at the bank, he put a sign on the door that said, "Gone to dinner, back in thirty minutes." Everyone in town knew he would be back early afternoon. The evening meal was called "supper." We did use the term "lunch" when referring to a lunch box, or the lunchroom at school. However, we put our dinner in the lunch box and ate dinner in the lunchroom. If we were going to eat supper out somewhere fancy, my daddy would say, "Wear your Sunday go-to-meeting clothes." That meant dress up. My grandparents and parents referred to the refrigerator as the "icebox," or the more modern term, "Frigidaire."

There are some words and expressions that I do miss hearing from the past such as "yes sir" and "yes ma'am," as well as several terms of endearment such as "darlin'," "honey pie," and "sugar."

When I'm back in the Delta, it takes no more than five minutes for me to slip back into a manner of speech that is as comfortable for me as an old pair of slippers.

Y'all know what I mean, you hear?

Dirty Hands, Happy Hearts

Nearly everyone grew a vegetable garden in Marmaduke in the 50s. There was an abundance of fresh food available for eating during the spring, summer, and fall, with plenty of produce left over to be canned and put up for the winter.

A one-eyed man, Bunk Tuberville, plowed up most of the town's gardens in the early spring with his two horses. One horse was red and named Lipstick, and the other was white and named Buttermilk. The soil in town that he turned was black and as rich as store-bought potting soil. It was fertile black Delta gumbo.

My grandmother Eva Belle Harvey gardened and canned everything from green beans to tomato juice. She also canned grape juice that on occasion fermented and turned to wine. I enjoyed the rich purple drink, and I never let her know that it sometimes made me tipsy.

My aunt Buena Ogles canned pickled peaches that were coveted by all who lived in town. Since we were relatives, we often got several jars of the prized canned fruit. My mother's pickles, stained a deep green from added food color, received rave reviews from all who bit into the sweet, crisp pickled cucumbers.

My father liked to garden, and he cultivated a large lot that he owned next to our house. He watered with gusto and left the hose running down the rows of vegetables until the dark dirt was soaked and gooey. The city water was not metered, and my father didn't have to worry about the cost.

The town sat atop the Memphis Sand Aquifer, one of the largest in the nation, and water was plentiful. Planting would start in late winter for some vegetables and harvest of produce would continue until late fall.

Winter onions could sometimes be harvested as early as February. The harvest of lettuce and greens soon followed. Potatoes were planted on March 17, Saint Patrick's Day. Between what my father grew, and the produce given to my mother by her beauty-shop customers, we ate well. Many of the fresh veggies were battered and fried. My mother fried green tomatoes, eggplant, okra, and yellow squash. No one seemed worried about their weight, and we weren't aware of such a thing as cholesterol.

While most everyone concentrated on raising vegetables, my grandmother, whom we all called Mom, also grew flowers. She would reserve a couple of rows in her garden for raising colorful flowers to cut for bouquets. She planted flowers here and there in her yard as well. Mom instilled in me the love of flowers. Each spring when planting flowers in my garden, I think of her. I loved my flowers, and I loved my grandma. I still do.

Bottoms Up

My father was the only person in my immediate family who drank. He liked Old Crow whiskey, and he had bottles of it stashed here, there, and everywhere. Every now and then, I would sneak a drink from one of his bottles. I didn't really like the taste, but I did it because I wasn't supposed to. My mother made me drink hot toddies as a cure for colds. Whiskey reminded me of medicine, but I drank my father's Old Crow anyway.

The first time I remember drinking in front of my parents was during a Christmas celebration. My parents had a very old bottle of champagne stuck away in a kitchen cabinet. The bubbly had been given to them as a wedding gift but had never been opened. There were several family members present that Christmas, and the amount of champagne given to each was not much more than a sip. Despite the small amount of champagne that I consumed that day as a fourteen-year-old, I felt that I had come of age because I drank alcohol in front of my parents.

I didn't turn twenty-one until halfway through my senior year of college. Until that time, I depended on older students or older-looking students with fake IDs to buy beer for me. Much to my dismay, I looked much younger than my actual age. I had zero chance of getting into a nightclub before I reached legal age. Having my ID checked went on for many years after I turned twenty-one. As much as I hated having to get out my driver's license, when the ID check stopped, I was rather sad.

When I could finally buy wine to drink at home, I bought Mogen David. The sweet, sticky wine was the only brand I knew. It's the wine I drank with my friends during my teen years when someone could manage to get their hands on a bottle. The deep purple wine came up as often as it stayed down.

After I moved to Memphis, I noticed that several of my fellow art student friends had empty Chianti bottles used as candle holders as part of their apartment's décor. Chianti became my wine of choice. Before long, I had the straw-covered bottle candle holders everywhere in my apartment as well.

As an adult, I felt comfortable drinking in front of my mother even though she did not drink. That changed for her late in life when radio talk show host Paul Harvey advised the elderly to drink a glass of wine to maintain a healthy heart. He endorsed Riunite Lambrusco as the best tonic to prevent heart disease. My mother considered Harvey to be the wisest of men, and she began drinking the recommended wine during her late seventies. Every few weeks I would visit her, and while there I would go to the liquor store to buy a couple of large jugs of Riunite Lambrusco. The jugs were almost too heavy for her to lift. During return visits I would find the last bottle close to being empty, and we would make another liquor store run.

Although not my favorite wine, I would join her in drinking an evening glass of the Riunite. She did have a bad heart, but she lived more than a decade after she started drinking the wine. Perhaps Paul Harvey was right.

After she passed away, we found a large number of the empty wine jugs in a shed behind her house. She was not one to throw away a good glass bottle. Following her funeral, my family gathered in her kitchen and opened her last jug of Riunite Lambrusco. She had it stored in the same cabinet where years earlier she had kept the bottle of wedding champagne. My family toasted my mother, and we emptied the last bottle.

That evening while I sat at her kitchen table drinking Riunite Lambrusco, I thought of a life well lived, and for the first time, the wine tasted delicious. Cheers.

Burn, Baby, Burn

There was a time when small Arkansas towns did not have trash pickup. My daddy piled noncombustible items in a shed behind our house. He didn't have to worry about adding glass jars or butter tubs to the pile. My mother never threw those items away. When enough disposables were accumulated, Daddy would load them into his vehicle for a trip to the dump. Because my grandmother didn't drive, my father would stop by her house to pick up her garbage too.

The dump was located west of town in the hills of Crowley's Ridge. The ridge was hilly with large gullies, and the trash, including large appliances, was tossed into the ravines. I don't know whether the land was sanctioned as an official disposal site or was privately owned and the landowner wanted to fill in the gulley. I enjoyed going to the dump with Daddy. He would let me toss items into the ravines. I liked to hear the crashing sounds that the junk made when hitting the ground.

Combustible items were burned in "burn barrels," metal containers that were found in most backyards in town. My mother kept burnable items in designated wastebaskets. There were a couple for the house and one for her beauty shop. When full, the baskets were emptied into the burn barrel and set on fire. When cut hair from my mother's beauty shop was set ablaze in the barrel, a putrid stench would fill the air.

My mother gave permanent waves to her clients. This required small chemical packets to be placed on hair that had been wound onto a metal rod. A hot metal clamp was then placed over the rod and the packet, burning a curl into the hair. I looked forward to days when the packets were to be thrown into the burn barrel. They would burn bright colors: yellow, red, green, blue, and purple. The fumes from the packets were ghastly, and if the wind blew my way, the acrid smoke stung my eyes.

Every once in a while, a grass fire would break out in town when some flaming paper escaped from an unattended burn barrel. This usually happened in the winter when the grass was dead, brown, and crispy. In early winter, my grandmother would do a controlled burn of the dried grass as an ounce of prevention. She would volunteer each year to do this for my mother. A few times the wind came up, and the fire got away from my grandmother while she was burning our yard.

Directly behind our house was a Baptist church that didn't have an inside bathroom. To accommodate the church members' needs, an outhouse was located near the alley that separated our two properties. Twice during my grandmother's burns the church's outhouse caught on fire.

One time it was just charred. Another time the outhouse burned to the ground. Some folks may have suspected that my grandmother did it on purpose because it was a Baptist outhouse, and she was a Methodist. My grandmother was too fine a person to do such a thing. The outhouse was just in the wrong place when my grandmother's "controlled" burn got out of control.

"They Say" and Other Beauty Shop Tidbits

My mother read the newspaper every day and listened to television news at 7 a.m., 6 p.m., and again at 10 p.m. She was as loyal to her favorite news programs as she was to her favorite show, *Wheel of Fortune*. I never called her between 5:30 p.m. and 7:00 p.m. I knew she would be watching *Wheel of Fortune* and the news.

Information received from customers in her beauty shop often took precedence over what she had learned from legitimate news sources. My mother and her customers often followed the advice of "they say," a source of unknown origin. "They say" informed my mother and her customers that to relieve the pain of arthritis they should spray their joints with WD-40. They did.

When "they say" warned my mother of a toilet paper shortage, she filled a closet with a year's supply of Charmin. When I asked my mother who "they" were, she would reply with something like, "I don't know but Lucille told me that they said it, and Lucille is pretty smart."

Another source of news in the beauty shop came from supermarket tabloids. My mother bought the *National Enquirer* and the *Star Reporter* papers each week for her customers to read. When she would tell me some bogus news that she had read in the tabloids, I would tell her that it could not possibly be true. My mother would shake her head in agreement and say to me, "Yes, you are probably right." I'm not sure she believed me because she continued to buy and read the papers.

When my mother and her customers started drinking copious amounts of apple cider vinegar to lose weight, I had no scientific evidence to prove them wrong. Mavis, a woman who worked for my mother, was the source of that diet tip. Mavis thought that she was an expert on dieting. She attended the weekly meeting of TOPS (Take Off Pounds Sensibly). However, Mavis never seemed to be able to shed those extra pesky five pounds. Maybe it was because the TOPS group went to Bonanza, a restaurant in Paragould, after each weekly meeting. Even though they drank gallons of apple cider vinegar, my mother and her customers did not lose weight.

My mother was a wonderful person. Even though she often believed everything "they" told her, right or wrong, when it came to living a good life, she rightfully believed, don't judge, don't discriminate, and love your fellow man. That's what she did, and that's the truth.

Break the Rules

When I was growing up in the Arkansas Delta, there were some things one did not do. Some were written into law, while other taboo activities were based on social customs and community mores.

Until the 70s it was against the law in Arkansas for a man to go to a beauty shop or for a woman to go to a barbershop. Even though my mother owned a beauty shop, my daddy went to the local barber. His reason for getting a weekly trim at Irby's Barber Shop had nothing to do with the law. He told my mother, "Since Irby's wife, Cricket, comes to you each week for a shampoo and set, it's only right that I go to Irby for my haircuts." I think he went for the gossip.

While my father went to the barber, some men would not. When Elvis Presley rose to fame, a few of the local fellows wanted to have their hair look like their idol's hair. Elvis had long, slicked-back hair—at least it was long for the time—and he had bushy sideburns. As good as Irby was as a barber, he was not capable of creating a longer style. The guards on his electric clippers wouldn't allow him to leave the hair longer than two inches.

In the dark of night, my mother would lower the shades in her beauty shop and allow select clientele to secretly enter. They were men. The guys trusted my mother to style their locks and leave them with a longer look. They left the beauty shop through the back door of our house while sporting an Elvis Presley–like hairstyle. One of the men went a step further and had my mother tint his hair Elvis black. She kept on hand a supply of Miss Clairol Black Velvet hair dye for that special customer. Although my mother was at risk of being fined or losing her beauty operator's license for styling men's hair, she thought the law was unreasonable and she willfully broke it. I also think she liked the thrill of being an outlaw of sorts.

Other Arkansas laws were just as silly. At one time it was against the law in Arkansas to walk a cow down the street on Sunday after 1 p.m. Some rather strange laws are still on the books. It is still against the law to keep an alligator in a bathtub.

Just as strange as the laws, and often as foolish, were rules and social mores that were prevalent in many towns in the South. A woman could smoke cigarettes, but societal rules prevented her from indulging while walking. To be a proper lady with a lit Salem in hand, she had to remain seated. Many of the rules regarding social conduct were more restrictive when it came to women.

At school, male teachers could wear comfortable slacks, while female teachers were required to wear dresses. Professional women, and that included teachers, did not wear form-revealing pants to work. Local social rules and mores kept provocative parts of a woman's body covered and protected from the lusty eyes of boys and men. It was thought that pants showed too much of a women's provocative shape.

Even during the heat of summer, men wore suits and neckties to church. Women were not thought to be properly dressed at church unless they had on a dress, gloves to cover their hands, and a nice hat on their head. My mother owned dozens of hats, and she had a large assortment of colored gloves. She had gloves to match every Sunday outfit.

My mother was a forward thinker who didn't take kindly to discriminatory rules and mores. When pants suits became fashionable, she was among the first in our town to attend the First United Methodist Church while wearing them, and she did it without a hat or gloves.

Breaking the "men's only rule," a bold young woman who was back in town during spring break defiantly marched through the door of my hometown's pool hall. She grabbed a pool cue, challenged a local shark to a game, and beat his butt. She proudly exited the building leaving many a drop-jawed man in shock. She was the talk of the town for several weeks.

In my life, I have defied social mores and rules, and admittedly, I may have broken a few laws, but please know that I have never kept an alligator in my bathtub. There are some things that one just does not do.

What's in a Name?

My great-aunt Precious Beulah didn't like her given name. I was around ten years old when I learned that what we called her was not her real name. We called her Boober. My grandmother Eva Belle Harvey, who was Boober's sister, didn't like that Precious Beulah refused to use her given name. My grandmother refused to call her Boober. The two women referred to each other as Sister.

My mother's name was Alice Allene. She was named after her grandmother, Alice Vashti Ogles. My mother disliked the name Alice, and she always went by Allene. My great-grandmother also must not have liked the name Alice. She was known as Vashti. My mother's sister was named Beulah Verlene. She was named after Precious Beulah, and she too disliked her first name. She went by Verlene.

My parents named my older sister Billie Cheryl. She was named after my mother's youngest sister, Billie Reba, who had drowned many years earlier at the young age of fourteen. My sister disliked her first name and went by Cheryl. She was upset when she started college and the professors called her Billie. My younger sister liked her name, Rhonda. She was named after my mother's favorite movie star, Rhonda Fleming.

My father's name was Zeek Wesley Taylor. His first name was the same as his grandfather's last name on his mother's side. They had come to America from the Netherlands. My father's middle name came from the founder of the Methodist Church, John Wesley. His father, Garland Cicero Taylor, had been a Methodist minister, and he thought it appropriate to name his only son after the founder of the church that he loved.

I was named after my father, Zeek. My mother wanted my middle name to be after her father, Arzo Estus Harvey. My father knew a guy named Harvey who he didn't like, and Harvey was out. That left either Arzo or Estus. They chose Estus. I wish it had been Arzo.

Because my father and I had the same first name, to avoid confusion I became "Zeekie Boy." That is the name that is on my report cards from elementary school. When I started seventh grade, Boy was dropped but Zeekie remained.

There have been times when I didn't like my name. Some folks considered it to be a hillbilly name, and more often than not it is misspelled. Over time I've learned to like it. It's been good for business because people tend to remember it.

A person's name is part of his or her identity. There have been several studies on how one's name affects them professionally and socially. On the other hand, it may be true that a rose by any other name is still a rose. Perhaps it would be good to let a person select their name when they reach a responsible age. If that option had been available, I probably would have chosen Zeek to honor my father. I'd still be the same rose.

Wash Days and Feeding the Monster

My mother worked six long days a week, and she often got behind doing the laundry. To help her keep up, my grandmother would walk the four blocks to our home and do the wash. There was an electric wringer washer on the back porch. In good weather, my grandmother would roll the washer outside onto a little wooden platform. She would then attach a hose from an outside faucet and fill the machine with water. She would add flake detergent before she put in the clothes. If the items were white, she would add bluing to the water. A lid was placed on the tub to prevent the water from splashing out. After going through a wash cycle and a rinse cycle, my grandmother would put the clothes through a wringer to remove excess water. After the wringing was finished, the clothes were hung on a nearby clothesline to dry.

When I was a child, my grandmother would let me put items into the constantly turning rubber rollers. I pretended that I was feeding a monster. When feeding the monster, I had to worry about a couple of things. If too much fabric was put into the wringer at once, it would hang up. Also, I had to be careful not to get my fingers caught between the rollers. I never experienced the monster pulling me in, but a cousin did have most of his forearm pulled through the wringer. He screamed like a banshee. He suffered a sore and bruised arm, but fortunately no broken bones.

My grandmother considered the electric wringer washer a modern, time-saving miracle machine. When she was a young mother of six children, she did laundry in two large iron kettles. The kettles were outside her home, and one was placed over a fire to warm the water. The heated kettle had soap in it. After the clothes were put in it, my grandmother scrubbed them on a washboard. The clothes were then rinsed in the second kettle that was filled with cool water. The rinsed clothes were wrung by hand to remove water and then hung on a clothesline.

During the 50s life became somewhat easier for my grandmother. She was able to do her laundry inside her kitchen in a big, galvanized washtub. She didn't have hot running water in her house, but she did have a hand pump at the kitchen sink. She heated water on her wood cookstove and put it in the galvanized tub. I remember seeing her stir the clothes with a large spoonlike paddle after the items were placed in the soapy water. Following the soapy wash, she rinsed the clothes with the hand-operated pump at her kitchen sink before taking the clothes outside to hang on the line.

Besides the once-a-week laundry that my grandmother would do for my family, my mother did small amounts of laundry almost every day in a room off the kitchen that we called the "washroom." The room held two galvanized tublike sinks that were on a stand, and each tub had a water spigot attached. In the tubs, my mother would hand-wash small loads of towels that she had used in her beauty shop.

Most of the time the clothesline in the backyard had dozens of shop towels hanging on it. I can still hear my mother yelling from her beauty shop that was attached to our house, "Go get the towels off the line. It's starting to rain." My sisters and I would run outside to retrieve the towels as quickly as we could. When my sisters and I weren't home, my mother would have to stop working and get the towels off the line.

During the wintertime, a sudden drop in temperature would freeze the towels solid. If the weather was too cold or too rainy, the towels were hung on a folding wooden rack that was placed inside the family bathtub.

Some laundered items were not hung on the clothesline. My sisters' sweaters were carefully laid to dry atop towels placed on flat surfaces. The method of flat drying prevented clothespin stretched puckers at the shoulders. My wet Levi's were put on metal stretchers. When dry, the jeans were wrinkle-free with beautiful crisp creases, the desired fashion look for the modern teen boy. During the winter, the Levi's on stretchers were placed atop the floor furnace. They stood there like little half men until the jeans were good and dry.

My father surprised my mother on her forty-seventh birthday with an automatic washer and an electric dryer. She said they were the best gifts she had ever received. I think she may have been right.

Even after getting the new appliances, my Levi's were still dried on the metal stretchers. As fine as the new electric dryer was, it could not put a nice, crisp crease in my jeans.

CHAPTER 4 — FAMILY ROOTS

Long Journey Home

My great-grandfather Julius Alonzo Ogles was born in Benton County, Tennessee, in 1871. In 1900 he left Tennessee in a covered wagon with my great-grandmother Vashti and their four children. The family crossed the Mississippi River on a ferry. They were traveling to Indian Territory, where they planned to claim available land and build a new life in the Great West. Indian Territory bordered the western boundary of Arkansas. The area became Oklahoma in 1907.

When they arrived at the territory, my great-grandfather was disappointed in the quality of the soil. The dirt where they had lived in Tennessee had been rich and black. Their oldest child, my grandmother, told me that the family was afraid of the Indians and that wolves would follow their wagon at night. They turned around, crossed the Arkansas border, and headed back toward Tennessee. During the return trip, my great-grandfather noticed that the soil in Northeast Arkansas was rich and black. Not wanting to cross the Mississippi River again, he decided they would settle there. He never left.

By the time I was born, Julius Alonzo Ogles was an elderly widower who lived on the edge of town with his daughter, my grandmother, Eva Belle Harvey. His many grandchildren and great-grandchildren called him Grandpa. My grandmother was called Mom.

Grandpa and Mom had electricity in their little house, but there was no indoor plumbing. The only heat source was a potbellied stove in the living room. Grandpa would get up at 4 a.m. and start a fire in the potbellied stove during the winter months. Early mornings all year long he would start a fire in the wood burning kitchen stove so it would be good and hot, and ready for Mom to bake biscuits for breakfast.

I enjoyed spending the night with them. I thought it was fun taking a bath in a galvanized tub in the kitchen in water that had been heated on the cookstove. When my younger sister and I stayed with them, an evening treat was popcorn popped atop the wood stove. There was no television in their house, and only one radio. While my sister, Mom, and I played cards, Grandpa sat in his rocker and listened to gospel shows on an old AM radio.

When I was eight years old, Grandpa and Mom moved to a house inside the city limits. For the first time in their lives, they were living in a house with indoor plumbing. During warm months, he spent most afternoons sitting on the front porch in a rocker, smoking his pipe and watching the world go by.

I was thirteen when my great-grandfather passed away. He died in the house after several bedridden days. The doctor dropped by each day to check on him, and he usually reported, "Nothing can be done. It's just a matter of time." On his last day, a low, almost growling sound came from his throat. The old-timers said it was the "death rattle" and that he would soon be gone. He died early that evening.

Dress Pants

My paternal grandfather, Garland Cicero Taylor, was a Methodist preacher, fairly liberal, fun, and jolly. He was born in Lawrence County, Arkansas, in 1886. He attended school in a log cabin and went to a church that dated back to 1815. He related that when he was young, "Men sat on one side of the church and women on the other. Nary an ankle could be seen." The church was served by circuit riders. The circuit riders were preachers who served several churches. They traveled on horseback. My grandfather was influenced by the traveling preachers, and he got "the calling." He gave up six hundred acres and his mules, and went into the ministry.

During my grandfather's career, he was assigned to several different parishes in eastern Arkansas. They were always within a couple of hours driving distance from my family's home. We would visit my grandparents every couple of months on a Sunday, arriving at their home, a parsonage, in time to attend church.

My grandmother, in her role as a pastor's wife, was more reserved. We referred to her as Grandmother Taylor. She came from a Dutch family, and she stuck to what was deemed proper. I was not allowed to wear blue jeans to my Grandmother Taylor's house. She thought that jeans were not proper attire for a young man to wear on the "Lord's day." While I hated wearing dress pants, my mother made me wear them when we went to see my grandparents. I was instructed to not get the trousers torn or stained, a difficult task for an active boy. I was to sit quietly and to not go in and out of the house too often for fear of letting in a fly.

When my grandfather retired, my grandparents moved to Osceola, Arkansas. He continued to preach as a guest pastor well into his nineties. His mind remained sharp. He once said, "While most old folk have trouble with their minds, my problem is on the other end. My feet hurt."

I can't remember when Rosie, a beautiful African American woman, joined the family as my grandparents' maid. My younger sister Rhonda and I were very energetic children. We found it very difficult to sit still and be proper during our visits to our grandparents' home. We often sought refuge in the kitchen where Rosie spent most of her time. Rosie pampered us and loved us. We loved her in return.

Soon after my grandmother's death, my Grandfather Taylor, at the age of seventy-six, announced that he would remarry. I crossed my fingers and hoped it would be to Rosie. Unfortunately, it was not. Drat.

Michigan Relatives

My great-aunt Precious Beulah didn't like her name. She preferred for us to call her Boober. She was my grandmother's sister and the youngest of her siblings. After World War II, Boober, along with her brother, two of my mother's brothers, and one of my mother's cousins, left the Arkansas Delta for Detroit. The men all moved to Michigan to work in the automobile plants. There were no jobs at that time in their home state. The women in the family were expected to stay home in Arkansas. Boober was rebellious by nature and insisted on moving north with the men. She was what my father called "a rounder."

Northern life suited her, and it let her be herself: a woman who smoked cigarettes, drank, and played honky-tonk piano. She even married twice, the first woman in the family to do so. She owned several poodles and she always had a parakeet or two. She crocheted like a fiend. She made us laugh and we loved her to pieces. She remained in Michigan until her death in 1979.

My mother's brothers who had migrated to Michigan, Vernon and Lowell, stayed there and married northern women. I remember visiting them when I was four years old. Uncle Lowell's family had a television, the first TV that I had seen. It was in a lounge area in their basement. I asked my mother if the room was a cave. My hometown of Marmaduke did not have houses with basements. In that room in Detroit, I watched Howdy Doody for the first time.

During our visit to Detroit when I was four years old, Uncle Lowell came home after work, took me by the hand, and walked me to the neighborhood tavern. He sat me on a tall red stool at the bar, and he ordered each of us a beer. He helped me lift the mug to my lips. I took a sip and made a face. I took another sip and told him that was all I wanted. He drank my beer and then he drank his. I think when he ordered me a beer, it was a way for him to circumvent my aunt's one-drink rule knowing that he would drink mine too.

I did eventually develop a taste for beer.

Marriage Is Not Always Forever

My great-uncle Floyd Ogles, unlike the vast majority of my family members, was married more than once. Members of my family in his generation did not divorce and rarely remarried following the death of a spouse. Uncle Floyd was married eight times. Despite his many marriages, he had only one child, a girl, and she was by his first wife.

He was a very successful businessman who went from one venture to another. He always managed to come out on top. He was also a gambler and a sporty dresser. At times he came across as a flimflammer. He had an enduring charm and was a family favorite. He wore lots of jewelry, including a diamond ring that he won in a poker game. He passed down that ring to my father, and my father passed it down to me. I consider it a good luck charm.

I only knew the last two of Uncle Floyd's wives, especially his next to last one, Luella. When I was a kid, my family and I would go visit Uncle Floyd and Aunt Luella. They lived in Dexter, Missouri, a town just north of the Missouri Bootheel. They owned a motel next to a drive-in movie theater. Guests could sit on the patio at the motel, watch a movie, and hear the film's sound through a speaker that Uncle Floyd had placed there.

My younger sister and I loved to go to Dexter because we could spend the afternoon at the drive-in movie's playground that was located in front of the movie screen. The playground had swings, seesaws, and a merry-go-round. During one visit, I discovered a ladder behind the movie screen that went straight up to the top. I had to climb it. After reaching the top of the screen, I waved down to my sister, who was sitting in one of the swings. I felt like I was on the top of the world.

My mama was helping Aunt Luella prepare lunch in my aunt and uncle's apartment at the motel. My mother looked out the kitchen window and saw me waving from the top of the screen. My parents ran from the motel, screaming at me to slowly come down. I carefully descended while everyone held their breath. My punishment was that I did not get a piece of Aunt Luella's lemon icebox pie. I never climbed the screen again.

Boxcar Johnnie

My great-uncle Johnnie Ogles and his wife, Grace, lived in a boxcar. He worked for the railroad, and when he was assigned to a new location, the railroad company would hitch his boxcar to a train and move it. The converted boxcar had all the comforts of a conventional home.

For several years, Uncle Johnnie and Aunt Grace had their boxcar parked in the town of Weiner, Arkansas. As a kid, I loved telling my friends that I had relatives living in Weiner. I liked saying the word *weiner*, thinking it was okay in this case to say a word that I thought was naughty. The town's name had nothing to do with hot dogs. It was known as "the Rice Capital of Arkansas."

When Uncle Johnnie died, his body was sent to his hometown of Marmaduke. The funeral service was scheduled to be held at the Methodist church with burial to follow in the family section in nearby Harvey's Chapel Cemetery. Uncle Johnnie's oldest sister, my grandmother Eva Belle Harvey, lived in Marmaduke. The wake was held in her home. His body was laid out in the same room where my great-grandfather's body had been. All the mirrors were again covered in black fabric. It was thought that if one saw themselves in a mirror with the corpse, they would be the next to die.

The wake went on for three days. The kitchen and dining room were filled with food that was brought to the house of bereavement by friends of the family. A wreath of white flowers with black ribbon adorned the door.

At the time of Uncle Johnny's passing, I was sixteen years old. The same wake and funeral rituals that occurred when my great-grandfather had passed away in 1959 were followed again. Funeral and burial customs were set in stone, and it was important that they were carried out properly.

On the first day of the wake, Aunt Grace confided in me something that I and the entire family already knew: she dipped snuff. In the early 60s it was no longer acceptable for a woman to dip, even though a good many of the older women I knew "dipped." Aunt Grace asked me if I would keep her secret. I assured her that I would. She then asked me to go next door to Mrs. Huckabee's and borrow some snuff for her.

For the next three days I was the secret snuff liaison. I would go to Miss Huckabee's house, and she would wrap a pinch of the smokeless tobacco in a small piece of tin foil. I would meet Aunt Grace on the back porch and place the little package in her hand. She would then retire to the bathroom for what she called her "alone time." I felt honored to be trusted to do this covert deed for Aunt Grace in her hour of need. We all want to be trusted, even if it is merely to secretly deliver snuff.

Strong and Gentle

My grandmother Eva Belle Harvey was born in 1893 in Big Sandy, Tennessee. To family members she was known as Mom. She left Tennessee at the age of seven with her family in a covered wagon on their way to settle in Indian Territory. She didn't like the new land; she was fearful of the Indians and the wolves that often followed the wagon. She was glad when they left the territory and resettled in the Arkansas Delta.

When I was young, my grandmother lived on the edge of town in a house without indoor plumbing. Her source of water was a hand pump in the kitchen. The only source of heat was a potbellied stove in the living room. When I spent the night at her house, I would sleep in an unheated room in a feather bed. The minute that I awoke, my feet would hit the bedroom's cold linoleum floor, and I'd make a beeline for the living room to get to the stove. Mom did have electricity in her home, but there was only one electrical outlet in each room. Bare lightbulbs hung from a cord in the center of each room. She washed clothes with an old-fashioned washboard, canned food, and preserved meat in a smokehouse. She cooked three meals a day on a wood cookstove.

Mom gave birth to eight children. The first two did not survive. She had an eighth-grade education, and she never worked outside the home except for picking cotton.

One fall I was home from college for Thanksgiving break, and Mom was sick. She had the flu. I insisted that she let me take her to the doctor, but she didn't want to go. I asked her why and she said, "I'm afraid that he will give me a shot. I've only had one shot in my life, and that was over forty years ago when your uncle Vernon was born." I took her to the doctor, he gave her an injection, and she felt better. I sadly thought of all the physical pain that she had endured in her life without the benefit of numbing shots. Besides the pain of childbirth, she had suffered major burns as a child that scarred a large area of her body. She had survived many hardships.

Mom was the strongest person I've ever known. She was also the kindest and most gentle person I've ever known. I think of her often, but I miss her the most during the holidays. When she got older, every Christmas she would say, "I may not be here next year," and we would all say, "Oh Mom, don't be silly." Then one Christmas she wasn't there.

In the Garden

My grandmother Eva Belle Harvey, or Mom, loved to garden. She raised vegetables to put food on the table, and she harvested enough bounty to fill the pantry with canned goods. She generously shared her harvest with family and neighbors. In the summer, her fingers were often stained different colors from handling the veggies. When she shelled bushels of purple hull peas, her fingers were a deep violet. She canned tomatoes, pickles, and spiced peaches, and she put up grape juice in fruit jars. In early spring and long before any fruit was ready to pick, she harvested some of the green unripe grapes and made a cobbler. The green grape cobbler had a nice sweet-and-sour flavor.

Even though she worked outdoors as much as she could, the only tan she had was on her hands and where the sun hit her legs below her hemline. She didn't believe in wearing pants; she always gardened in a dress. Her gardening outfit included a cobbler's apron and a head covering.

Mom could grow anything. Many times I saw her start a plant from a stem. She would spit on the stem's end, say something under her breath, and stick the stem into the ground. It grew into a thriving plant.

While vegetables fed her body, flowers nourished her soul. She had flowers all over her yard. She devoted two or three rows of her vegetable garden to growing flowers to be cut for indoor bouquets. She raised all her flowers from seed or from cuttings. She taught me to appreciate the beauty of flowers, and I enjoyed working alongside her.

One spring she set aside a small area of her garden just for me. We went to the store, and I picked out zinnia seeds to plant in my section. I chose zinnias because of the many bright colors displayed on the seed package. The very next morning after planting the seeds, I walked the few blocks to her house to see my plants. They weren't up yet. My grandmother explained that it took a while, and she told me to be patient. She said, "Good things are worth waiting for." The wait was worth it. When I showed excitement at the first zinnia blooms, I noticed that my grandma had tears in her eyes. She loved to see me happy.

One year she was given dozens of rose of Sharon shrub seedlings. I helped her plant them all in a row on two sides of my parents' large yard. She said, "I think next to the iris, rose of Sharon may be my favorite flower."

I replied, "Mine too, next to zinnias."

Many years later when I moved to Fayetteville, my parents came to visit very early one spring and brought my grandmother with them to see my newly purchased house.

While my parents toured the house, my grandmother immediately went outside to look at my yard. By then she was in her eighties and had very poor eyesight. Looking out my living room window, I watched her explore the garden. My mother said, "We better go get her, she can't see good enough to keep from stepping on the plants." I said, "No, let her go." Having a few plants trampled didn't bother me. She explored the flower beds and viewed the plants as best she could. She plucked a little marigold, smelled it, and held it close to her glasses. It was a joy for me to see her in my garden.

She died a couple of years later. Every time I paint an iris, I think of her. In the spring I delight in seeing a pink rose bloom in my backyard on a bush that was started from a cutting that came from one of her rose bushes. In my front yard, I have iris blooming from tubers that a friend gave to her in 1944. I only wish that I knew what she said when she spit on a stem before sticking it in the ground. She had magic. At her funeral, as she had requested, the choir sang the old hymn "In the Garden."

"I come to the garden alone, while the dew is still on the roses."

Fabric of Our Life

Everyone in our family and many of my friends called my grandmother Mom. Mom grew up very poor. I think growing up poor taught her not only to "make do" but also to "make." She could make a garden, make her clothes, and make canned goods. What I loved most, though, were her quilts.

Mom had a full-size quilting frame that hung from the ceiling that she used on occasion. Most of the time, she worked on a small frame that took up less space in the living room. She saved every scrap of material from numerous sewing projects, and family members and friends saved scraps for her too. She had dozens of patterns and enjoyed making quilts for gifts. She had a keen sense of color and design.

When I was a boy, Mom made a quilt for my bed. She let me pick out the pattern. I had recently bought a pet turtle from Woolworths, so I chose a turtle pattern. Most of the time Mom used unbleached muslin on the bottom side of a quilt. For my quilt, she splurged and bought special fabric for the flip side. The fabric was imprinted with red monkeys on a cream background. I felt "embraced" when sleeping under the turtle quilt.

Mom continued to give me quilts well into my adulthood. I ended up with more than a dozen. She gave the oldest that she had in her possession to me. She and her mother had made it in the 1920s. She also gave me the last quilt she made before her failing eyesight finally put a halt to her quilting.

The last one was a snake quilt. The pattern was not really snakes, but wavy lines of fabric weaving across the quilt top. On the backside she used a light blue fabric for the liner. She didn't have quite enough to finish the backside and had to use a little square of a darker shade of blue in one corner. She apologized for her mistake and fretted because her final quilt wasn't perfect.

I told her that it was perfect to me and that not everything has to be perfect to be beautiful. I loved it because she made it. It may be my favorite quilt in my collection.

Every quilt tells a story.

Sad Movies

When my grandmother, or Mom, was in her forties, she left Marmaduke, Arkansas, where she had spent most of her life. She and my grandpa Arzo Estus Harvey relocated to Walnut Ridge, Arkansas. My grandpa had secured a job as a clerk in a dry goods store. All of their children were grown and out of the house except for a fourteen-year-old daughter, Billie Reba.

One Sunday Billie Reba asked if she could go to the movies. Mom thought it was not right to go to a movie on the Sabbath. She told her no. Billie Reba instead went swimming in the Black River. Shortly after arriving at the river, she spotted a child drowning. Billie Reba was a strong swimmer. Without hesitation, she jumped into the river and pushed the child to safety. Then Billie Reba was pulled under by a whirlpool. She drowned.

Mom and my grandpa were devastated. Shortly thereafter, my grandpa, a man in his forties, died of heart failure. The family said, "He died of a broken heart." Mom moved back to Marmaduke where she lived the rest of her life as a widow and each day relived a what-if situation.

After the death of Billie Reba, Mom would not go into a theater to see a movie, not just on Sundays, but on any day of the week. She would go with us on family outings to the drive-in movies, but she would not set foot inside a theater building.

In 1956 the *Ten Commandments* movie was released. My mother, Mom's daughter, convinced her that it was just fine to see that movie because it was a religious film. Mom finally consented to go, and that seemed to be a turning point for her. I think she realized that she couldn't blame the movies, and more importantly, she should not blame herself for what had happened to Billie Reba.

While Mom lived in Walnut Ridge, a neighbor gave her some dwarf iris tubers. Although living there was a tragic period in her life, she loved flowers and could not leave that part of Walnut Ridge behind. When she returned to Marmaduke, she brought the iris tubers with her, and she planted them in her yard. She was very proud of them because no one in town had any like them.

In 1975 when I purchased my first home, she gave me some of the tubers. I've dug up and transplanted the tubers each time I've moved. In the spring when they bloom, I think of Billie Reba and Mom, and I know in my heart that no matter what, life goes on.

The Shawl

Of my grandmother's fifteen grandchildren, I am the only one she ever spanked. I deserved the spanking. I thought her coffee table would make a great dance platform, but it proved not to be sturdy enough for the weight of an eight-year-old boy. One of the legs broke off, and I tumbled to the floor. Before I could get up, my grandmother grabbed me by the arm and swatted my behind a few times. We were both shocked and remorseful for what we had done. Oddly enough, that event brought us closer, and we laughed about it often as she reminded me, "You were the only grandchild who I ever spanked."

We called my maternal grandmother Mom, and she lived a few blocks from my boyhood home. She came daily to our house to take care of me and my sisters while my parents were at work.

She had grown up poor and remained poor all her life. In 1946 her husband died from a bad heart while in his forties. Social security began in 1937, and my grandfather had paid little into the system. He had worked as a clerk in a dry goods store. Both of my grandparents had an eighth-grade education, and my grandfather felt fortunate to have landed an indoor job. My grandmother had never worked outside of the home except for fieldwork. Folks that chopped and picked cotton were paid in cash, and they did not pay into the social security system.

When my grandmother reached the age where she could draw on my grandfather's social security, she received the minimum payment of sixty-six dollars a month. She should have been eligible for the Commodity Supplemental Food Program, a government program that distributed food including dried beans, rice, peanut butter, and cheese. However, Mom had managed to save two thousand dollars that she held in a special account to pay for her burial. Because she had money in the bank, by law she could not receive welfare or commodities. My mother, Mom's daughter, offered to hide the money in her account, but Mom said that was not honest. She would rather have starved to death than to have told a lie. She was honest to a fault.

Mom never learned to drive an automobile. When my family went somewhere, Mom went with us. She loved to go, even if it was just a trip to the Kroger's in a nearby town. Mom's five living children made certain that she had everything she needed, including a place to live, food, and money. She loved and appreciated anything she received. She was overwhelmed by the amount of gifts she received from her family on her birthday and at Christmas.

When she was a child at Christmas, usually her only gift was an orange. That was the only time each year during her childhood when she got to eat an "exotic" fruit.

One Christmas I gave her a transistor radio. She thought that was a very lavish gift, a magic box that played music without electricity. She often played it while sitting on her porch or while working in her garden.

After I was grown and no matter how far away I lived, I always returned to my parents' home for the Christmas holidays. Along with many relatives, Mom was always there. One year for Christmas I gave her a very dressy lace shawl. She loved it, put it on immediately, and said, "I'll wear this all day today, but then I'll put it up for good." "Putting up for good" meant to save something for a special occasion.

Before I left that Christmas, I was alone in my mother's living room with Mom. She was sitting in a chair still wearing the shawl. I took her picture and gave her a kiss. I made it to the kitchen before I broke down. My mother came to see what was wrong, and I told her, "I'll never see Mom again."

I don't know how I knew, but I knew. She died three weeks later. When I went to the funeral home to view her body, I was touched and honored to see that she was wearing the shawl.

It had been "put up for good."

Held Up

My father, Z. W. Taylor, was born in Tyronza, Arkansas, in 1914. He had attended three years of college before being drafted during World War II. After a stint in the military, he got a job as a schoolteacher. Although he didn't have a degree, three years of college was enough to allow him to teach high school. He taught math and etiquette.

After several years as a teacher, my father got a job as the manager of our town's bank. It was a small-town branch and a one-man operation. He was also the teller and the janitor.

I often went to the bank at closing time to watch my father count the money. He did it with such speed that the cash looked like a green blur. My favorite part of closing time was watching him throw chemical floor sweep on the marble floor and then sweep it up with a large broom. Sometimes he would let me help. I had great fun throwing stuff onto the floor. I felt like I was getting away with something I shouldn't be doing.

While working in the bank, my father was robbed twice. During the early 50s, a lone gunman held up the bank and fled with $51,071 in cash. This was more than the usual amount kept in the bank. But the holdup happened during the cotton harvest season, and there had been a substantial amount of money deposited by cotton farmers the day before the robbery occurred.

My father said the bandit approached him at 8 a.m. while he was unlocking the bank door to get ready for the day's business. "What time do you open up?" the man asked. Daddy told him that the bank opened at 8:30.

My father later told the FBI, "As I was opening the door, the man pulled an automatic from under the cotton-pick sack he was carrying and poked the gun in my back. Then the robber said, 'I'm fixing to take the money. Don't try any funny stuff. Open up and go to the vault.'"

They walked into the bank while the robber held the gun to my father's back. They both went to the vault door. The man then said, "All right, open that thing up." My father was nervous and had trouble with the combination. The impatient bandit said to my father, "Hurry up and get it open." He finally did.

Once inside the vault, my father had to open a safe that contained the money. He told the robber, "I don't know if it will open," and the robber said, "By God, it better."

The inner safe was opened and the man stuffed the currency into his sack, forced my father to get down on his knees in the back of the vault, and warned against "any funny stuff." He then left, slamming the vault door that locked behind him. My father pounded on the vault door until he attracted the attention of two men in the drugstore next door. He shouted the combination to them, and they managed to free him after about twenty minutes.

My father described the robber as about thirty years old, nearly six feet tall, and about 170 pounds. He was dressed in brown coveralls, a dark felt hat, and sunglasses. Despite a fairly accurate description, the crook was never caught.

Following the first robbery, a button was installed underneath a drawer handle in the bank that, when pressed, alerted the druggist next door that a robbery was in progress.

During the second robbery, four armed men came in, demanding cash. My father pushed the button before telling the four robbers that he would go into the safe and get the money. After he entered the safe, he closed the door behind him. The robbers panicked and fled. The druggist had called the police, who quickly apprehended the four men before they got very far down the road.

My mother was relieved when my father finally left the job at the bank and took a job as the town's postmaster. Stamps were cheap at the time, so there was little cash in the post office till and little danger of it being robbed. While I was glad that he was out of harm's way, I was sad that there would be no more exciting stories to tell my friends at school about my father's fearless encounters with mean and dangerous outlaws. Also, I sure did miss throwing stuff on the floor. Nothing exciting ever happened at the post office.

Big Daddy

My father was a very large man. My sisters and I called my father Daddy until the day he died. I think that term is more commonly used in Southern states, especially when used by grown children. My cousins from up north called their paternal parent Dad or Pop. My father was Daddy and still is when I speak or think of him.

My daddy's father was a Methodist preacher. In his case, the apple *did* fall far from the tree when it came to religion. My daddy resisted going to church and did so only for funerals, weddings, when his parents came to visit, or when we visited them. However, his raising did affect him in some ways. Although he was good at cursing and cussing, he never used the Lord's name in vain. That was an ingrained no-no. He was a good person, just not a churchgoer.

Because his father's profession required frequent moves, Daddy lived in several towns in the Delta. In high school, he landed in Marmaduke, Arkansas, met and married my mother, and remained there for the rest of his life. Following high school graduation, he did attend Arkansas State in Jonesboro, where he studied math and played football.

My father was reputed to be a very good football player. While in college, he and several of his friends went to a nearby carnival. One of the attractions at the carnival was a wrestling match that pitted a man against a very large live bear. After failed attempts by several of Daddy's friends to wrestle the animal, my father stepped into the ring and successfully won the match. His prize was a hundred dollars, a large sum of money at the time.

Daddy had one year of college remaining when he was drafted into military service. After serving in the military, he taught school, and then managed a branch bank. In 1962 he was appointed to be the postmaster of our town, thanks in part to political pull and his friendship with Senator J. William Fulbright. Daddy's appointment certificate was hand signed by President John F. Kennedy. While serving as postmaster, he also served a couple of terms as the town's mayor.

Of all his achievements, I think the greatest one was his role as a loving, supportive, encouraging, and understanding father. If asked when I was a kid, I think I would have said, "Wrestling a bear."

Keep On Dancing

One of the first dances I learned to do was the Charleston. My mother, Allene Taylor, was born in 1913. She lived during the Roaring Twenties, the era when the Charleston was popular, and she is the one who taught me the dance. She grew up in a progressive family, and that was unusual considering that they lived in the Northeast Arkansas Delta. Her father, Arzo Harvey, wanted his family to live a "modern" lifestyle.

Even though he had only an eighth-grade education, my grandfather kept up with popular culture by reading magazines. One evening after he got home from his job at a dry goods store, he told his wife and daughters that he was going to cut their hair. He had seen a magazine that day featuring the latest flapper haircuts. The haircuts were very short, and at the time were considered to be shocking and too manly for women to wear. He cut off his daughters' hair and my grandmother's hair. They were the talk of the town for weeks.

Besides wanting his family to look fashionable, Arzo wanted them to take advantage of modern fads, including the most popular dances. The Charleston was the dance of the day, and he learned to do it. He taught it to my mother, and many years later, she taught it to me.

My mother, like her father, wanted her children to be modern and know the latest dances. My father said that my sisters and I would be socially handicapped when we started college if we didn't know how to dance. My parents enrolled my two sisters and me in ballroom dance classes at the Westbrook School of Dance in nearby Paragould. When I turned ten and for the next several years, my parents took us to weekly classes.

I loved to dance, and in addition to ballroom I learned other dances like the new dance craze, the bop. I taught my mother to bop, and she taught the dance to my father. Once a month on a Saturday night, my parents dressed up and went to the Kingsway Supper Club to dine and dance. The night they returned home after going to the supper club and dancing the bop, she could barely contain her excitement when she told me about "taking the floor" while dancing to "Rock Around the Clock."

I was never much of an athlete, and I was relieved that I was able to take dance courses to fulfill my physical education requirements at Arkansas State University. I made an A in choreography and an A in ballroom dance. I was thrilled that I had made such good grades in both PE classes. Physical education had never been an area where I had excelled.

There were three young ladies and two other guys in my college ballroom dance class. During the semester, the class was asked to provide the halftime entertainment at one of the university's basketball games. My instructor said that to receive credit in the class we must do the performance. We were to perform a waltz to "The Blue Danube" by the

Austrian composer Johann Strauss II. I was nervous before I entered the shiny basketball court while wearing a blousy shirt and white stirrup dance pants. I didn't know how we would be received, and I was afraid we would be jeered. The crowd loved us. I thought it ironic that my daddy would be proud that I was "cheered on a college basketball court," although not quite the way that he had wanted it to happen.

Years later while attending the Memphis College of Art, I received a full scholarship to study and perform with Ballet South. I had art classes during the day and dance classes at night. I studied with George Latimer, who had been a principal dancer with the San Francisco Ballet, and Daniel Buraczeski of the Royal Winnipeg Ballet.

Many years earlier I had learned the Charleston in my mother's beauty shop on an old linoleum rug. In Memphis, I danced on a stage where Rudolf Nureyev and Margot Fonteyn had performed.

Every time I dance, I think of my mother.

Waste Not, Want Not

My mother, Allene Taylor, was born in 1913, to Eva Belle and Arzo Harvey. Her family lived in the Arkansas Delta town of Marmaduke. They lived in poverty, but they were industrious and "made do." My mother was the oldest child. She had two brothers and two sisters. Her father worked as a clerk in a dry goods store, her mother worked at home, and they all worked in the cotton fields.

As an adult my mother hesitated to throw anything away that she thought could possibly be of use. I attribute that to the fact she grew up poor and lived through the Great Depression.

In the room that housed her washer and dryer, there were hundreds of plastic bags. Most came from Walmart, Kroger's, or the dollar store. Next to the stash of plastic bags were dozens of yellow margarine tubs with lids. In a shed behind the house, there were countless glass jars and cardboard boxes. In an adjacent shed there were dozens of small defunct appliances that included can openers, electric skillets, and coffee makers. When questioned as to why she was saving them, she replied, "In case I ever decide to get them fixed."

My mother was one of the sweetest people on Earth. This one little quirk, her need to save, did not bother me. It didn't border on real hoarding. It was just an effort on her part to not be wasteful. She did occasionally use some of the jars, plastic bags, and margarine tubs.

The saving did bother my younger sister, and when she visited my mother, she would sneak some of the stash into the garbage. She thought our mother wouldn't miss "the junk." My sister was wrong. My mother would call to let me know that my sister had thrown away some of her "stuff." Then she would go through the garbage and retrieve the discarded items.

One thing that did bother me about my mother's saving of items was when she put things up for good. "Putting things up for good" is a practice of saving items for special occasions. For my mother, those items were brand-new and never-used towels, washcloths, nightgowns, and bathrobes. When I would visit, she put out new, pristine towels for my use. However, in her towel cabinet were some of the most threadbare, raggedy towels imaginable. She saved the perfect towels for use by company while she kept the raggedy ones for her own use.

I objected most to her saving nightclothes. My mother had a large old cedar chest at the foot of her bed. Inside were many brand-new nightgowns and bathrobes. Most had been gifts to her. When I asked her why she didn't wear them, she answered, "I'm saving them in case I have to go to the hospital and then I'll have nice things to wear when visitors show up."

I laughed while assuring her that if that situation occurred, I'd see to it that she was properly attired. "In the meantime," I told her, "wear those nightgowns and enjoy."

She, too, laughed at herself and said that she would, and she did. One Christmas I gave her a big, fluffy bathrobe. When I gave it to her, I said, "You can't have this if you're putting it up for good." We laughed again.

My mother was such a good person. She deserved only the best. I tried to see that she had the best, even if it was just a bathrobe. Her idea to "waste not, want not" is not a bad rule to live by. And I confess, I do have some things that I've put up for good.

Tradition

Because my birthday was on or near Thanksgiving Day, my mother would bake a cake for me as part of our holiday dinner. Well into my fifties and as long as my mother was alive, I went home for that holiday. The family would gather for the Thanksgiving meal around the same dining table that was in the house when I was a child. The table would be surrounded by various family members, and regardless of the number attending, my mother had more than enough food to feed an army.

Another family tradition was to begin shopping for Christmas gifts the day after Thanksgiving. My father on that day headed for the duck blind while the rest of us piled into the family car and journeyed to Memphis to shop. We began our shopping spree at Sears before going downtown to Goldsmith's and Lowenstein's, both landmark department stores in the city.

Our holiday shopping spree took place long before the term "Black Friday" was coined. We would shop for hours, have a very late supper at Shoney's before leaving Memphis, and head back home in the dark.

For many years, I spent the Saturday that followed Thanksgiving Day putting up my mother's Christmas tree. Because the tree would remain up for a month, there was a danger of fire if the tree dried out. My mother often forgot to water it. I convinced her that it would be easier and safer to buy an artificial tree. We bought a fake tree at an after-Christmas sale. The purchase took care of my concerns. It was 75 percent off, and my mother got to brag about getting it at "such a price." She loved a bargain.

Mama had collected countless ornaments over the years. Many were handmade and were gifts from her beauty clients. When decorated, it didn't matter whether the tree was artificial or alive. There was not a lot of green showing by the time I finished putting everything on it. The tree was in my mother's beauty shop, a large room that adjoined the rest of our house. Her customers spent lots of time looking at each and every ornament.

Every year my mother would tell me, "Everyone says it's the prettiest tree they've ever seen." She would tell them, "It should be. My son decorated it, and he's an artist." It was far from the truth that it was the prettiest tree ever. However, because it made my mother happy and proud, I, too, thought the tree was pretty.

I saw it through her eyes. She was looking at it with love.

Steel Magnolias in Marmaduke

My mother was a hairdresser. Her parents, both with eighth-grade educations, wanted my mother, their oldest child, to attend college. However, realizing that she had a passion for hairdressing, they agreed to send her to beauty school. The nearest beauty school was in Memphis. My mother's parents didn't think it proper for a young lady to live in a city unsupervised. They sent her to a cosmetology school in Birmingham, Alabama. She had two aunts and an uncle there who watched out for her. After completing the course, she opened Allene's Beauty Shop in Marmaduke, Arkansas, on Groundhog Day in 1935.

My mother secured a commercial space in the downtown area for her business. She paid forty dollars a month in rent. She and my father lived in the back area of the building behind a partition in what was essentially one room with a bed, a kitchenette, and a small bathroom. When my older sister was born in 1942, my parents decided they should buy a house and move the business to their residence. They purchased a home that was a couple of blocks from downtown. It was a large house built in 1900 with double parlors. They had managed to save the entire purchase price of six hundred dollars, and they bought the home outright. They had a little extra money left above the purchase price, and they used it to install plumbing and an indoor bathroom.

My mother used the front parlor as her beauty shop. She had built up a loyal and large clientele. Her customers in the little Delta town of 650 people included several personal close friends. During the early 70s some of her closest friends, Jean, Nettie, and Anna Faye, all decided they would each make their weekly standing appointments on Friday afternoons. My mother had one employee, Mavis, who was also a close friend. My mother would not take additional appointments on Friday afternoons. She reserved the time for only Mavis, and her other three friends.

The three ladies would arrive at 1 p.m. even though some of their scheduled appointments didn't start until much later. One or more of the women would bring refreshments, and often the food they brought to share was the result of a newly found recipe. They were all ardent collectors of recipes.

My mother would have her twenty-cup percolator hot and filled with brewed coffee. She used the large coffee maker only on Friday afternoons. If the ladies wanted to sweeten the coffee, they did it with saccharin. Even though the snacks they brought contained lots of sugar, they all claimed to be dieting and thought using saccharin would lead to weight loss. The group remained in the beauty shop all afternoon, sharing laughter, gossip, snacks, coffee, and most importantly, friendship and support. It was close to 5 p.m. when the last lady had her coif firmly in place and coated with Aquanet hair spray.

During the 70s my older sister was suffering from Crohn's disease. She spent many days in hospitals, and my mother would go with her during those stays. My mother's Friday afternoon friends always pitched in when she needed to be away. They cleaned her house and beauty shop and made certain my father had supper. Mavis worked extra hours in the beauty shop.

In 1978 my sister passed away at the age of thirty-five. She died in one of my mother's bedrooms while my mother was working. The Friday afternoon beauty shop friends kept my mother propped up and smothered her with love, helping her make it through those darkest of times. Their love and support ran deep.

As time went by, Anna Faye and Nettie passed away. Mavis retired in the early 90s. Jean was the last one still going to Allene's Beauty Shop on Friday afternoons in 2002. That year my mother, at the age of eighty-eight, was still working behind the chair. One cold morning, just a couple of weeks before Groundhog Day, my mother's heart gave out while she was dressing for work. Her first scheduled appointment that day was a permanent wave. My mother passed away still doing what she loved. She lived her passion, and she left the world with countless fond memories of Friday afternoons spent with friends.

Looking Good All the Way to the End

In the Upper Arkansas Delta, funerals are important events. Particularly among the older generation, there are time-honored funeral traditions with set guidelines and little room for variation.

The traditions include visitation with the family at the funeral home, usually with an open casket so the body can be viewed one last time. Prior to the funeral and during the wake, there is much socializing, and the bereaved family is gifted with enough home-cooked food to feed the entire county.

The funeral service takes place the day after the visitation in either a funeral home or a church. After the indoor service, a slow-moving procession of mourners in cars with headlights beaming follows the hearse to a cemetery for the graveside service.

When I was a kid, there was a woman who lived in town and enjoyed going to funerals. If there was not a funeral to attend for someone she knew, she would go to services for strangers. She would listen to the obituaries on the radio every morning. She attended any funeral that was within driving distance of her home. On average, she went to two or three funerals a week.

Women in my mother's beauty shop critiqued funerals, with particular attention paid to how the body looked. The appearance of the body was important to them. They discussed whether or not the deceased looked "natural," and they talked about the dead person's clothing. Did they have on their jewelry? How did their hair look? Were there many flowers?

My mother worked as a hairdresser for sixty-seven years. During that time many of her customers passed away. At the request of the bereaved family, my mother would go to the funeral home and do the hair of the departed prior to their viewing. It was upsetting for my mother to style the hair of a dead person. However, she considered it an obligation to her customers. She wanted to make them look good one last time. Perhaps to lighten the situation a little, she would jokingly say, "At least I don't have to worry about how the back of their hair looks."

My mother knew exactly how she wanted her funeral. She planned every detail years before it took place. She wrote down the songs she wanted to be played. She made a list of the names of pallbearers along with an alternate list in case one or more of the preferred had preceded her in death. She chose the color for the spray of flowers that would be on top of the casket. She prepaid for everything including the casket that she herself had selected. The only thing she did not pick out was what she would be wearing. She said to the family, "I might buy something prettier to wear between now and then, and y'all can choose."

The call came early one January morning in 2002. My mother at the age of eighty-eight had died while getting dressed for work. I immediately packed and rushed across the state. I needed to be home. The family gathered the next morning at the funeral home to make arrangements. There was not much to do since my mother had taken care of everything. We did take a recently purchased outfit for her to wear. While making the arrangements, the undertaker asked, "And who do you want to do her hair?"

I found myself saying, "I will do it." I had been styling her hair for years, and I couldn't bear for anyone else to do it. I wanted her hair to look just right, and I knew that my mother would want it to be perfect. It was one of the hardest things I've ever done, but it was very important for me to do. I knew that it was the last thing that I could do for my mother.

She looked good.

You Can Go Home Again

My parents bought their first and only house in the early 40s. The house in the Arkansas Delta town of Marmaduke sat on three big lots. It was one block from downtown in the little town of 650 people. The house had been built in 1900.

They paid six hundred dollars cash for the property. It took them a while to save that amount of money on my father's meager schoolteacher salary and my mother's earnings as a hairdresser. At the time she was doing shampoo and sets for twenty-five cents. It was a struggle for them to save a few hundred dollars.

Prior to purchasing the house, my parents had rented a commercial space downtown where my mother had her beauty shop. They had living quarters in the rear of the building behind a partition. Their downtown space was small, and they had acquired very little furniture. When they moved into their newly purchased seven-room house, it took them a while to furnish it. In addition to the price of the home, they had managed to save enough to install indoor plumbing in their new house. That allowed them to install an indoor bathroom, water in the kitchen, and a shampoo bowl in the front parlor, where my mother had her beauty shop.

The house, like most in the Delta, sat on concrete piers rather than a slab or actual footings. During the summer months, the house was kept cool, or at least bearable, by a whole-house attic fan. The thirteen-foot ceilings helped keep hot air aloft. Heat in the winter came from a floor furnace and strategically placed Warm Morning freestanding stoves.

By the time I was born, my parents were well settled in their home. The house was in the middle of Marmaduke. It was an easy walk for me to go downtown and to school. It was also a good location for my childhood friends to gather. At night, the beauty shop became a teen hangout.

My parents always welcomed all who entered our home. My mother kept plenty of food and drink available to serve. My friends and I often messed up her kitchen when we cooked French fries or baked Chef Boyardee pizzas. My mother never complained about the mess or my frequent company. She knew that if we were at home with friends, my sisters and I were safe. We were happy and content to be there.

I had my own bedroom at the rear of the house. I decorated it to my taste and changed the wall color every couple of years. After I left home and went to college, I knew that my room was still there. No matter my age, when I went back home, my room was a familiar refuge. While there, I was comfortably engulfed in a tender space where nothing changed. The same pictures hung on the walls, and the same knickknacks sat on the dresser.

My mother lived in the house for sixty years. After she passed away, the property was bought by the Methodist church. They needed additional parking for the parishioners.

I vividly remember the last night I slept there. I took pictures of every detail in the room with my mind, and I touched every knickknack. I kept the items that were most important to me, including a picture from a calendar that my mother had framed for me when I was five years old. It now hangs in my current bedroom.

The church tore down the house. I've not been back to see the vacant lot where the house once stood. I do not plan to go back. However, I do not believe that "you can't go home again." I do. With fond memories I often visit the home that is forever in my heart.

Sign of the Dove

I remember my great-grandfather, but I did not know my great-grandmother Vashti Ogles. She was born in 1871 in Tennessee and died shortly after I was born.

She was named after Queen Vashti in the Bible, who defied her husband's request to appear nude before male guests at a banquet. Because Queen Vashti defied the orders, her husband, King Ahasuerus, banished her and chose another queen. Vashti's refusal to obey the orders of her husband has been admired as heroic in many feminist interpretations. From stories that I heard about my great-grandmother, she lived up to the reputation of being a strong woman just like Queen Vashti had been.

My great-grandfather Julius Alonzo Ogles talked fondly about his wife. Other family members also had nice memories of Vashti, but they rarely mentioned her without recalling her frequent trips to the liquor store where she purchased alcohol for "medicinal purposes." She liked whiskey. My great-grandfather was a teetotaler, but he knew better than to forbid his wife from purchasing her "medicine."

Their daughter, Eva Belle Ogles Harvey, took care of both of her parents, my great-grandparents, during their later years. They lived with her on the edge of town in a small two-bedroom house.

When it became evident that Vashti was dying, my grandmother stayed by her bedside. Vashti lay in a coma with her eyes closed, and she did not speak a word for several days.

My grandmother told me that late one evening, Great-Grandmother Vashti Ogles opened her eyes and said to my grandmother, "Eva Belle, do you see the white dove? He is flying toward me." She extended her arms upward while holding her hands close together. She closed her palms as if the dove had flown into her waiting hands, drew her closed hands to her chest, and died.

When I was a child, I was fascinated by the tale of my great-grandmother's experience on her deathbed. My grandmother told me that a white dove was a good sign, and a sign of peace. Vashti had found peace.

Years later when my mother had passed away, I went to my childhood home, where my family had gathered to mourn. Although it was January, the weather was warm, and I would often go outside into the backyard. I wanted to spend time outside where I had played as a kid many years earlier. One morning I looked up and saw three white doves flying overhead. Other family members also saw the white birds several times during the days between my mother's death and her burial.

My family felt that the three white doves that flew over my mother's house represented the three generations of women who had gone before us: my grandmother, my older sister, and my mother. I thought, *They are together, and they are at peace.*

There are signs if we allow ourselves to see them.

Groundhog Day, New Beginning

After attending beauty school in Birmingham, Alabama, my mother, Allene Taylor, opened a beauty shop in Marmaduke, Arkansas, the second of February, 1935. It was Groundhog Day, a new beginning for her, and a calendar date easy to remember.

The beauty shop was attached to the home where I grew up, and my two sisters and I spent a lot of time there. We enjoyed the attention of my mother's clients. Each of us had favorite customers who considered us to be their "pets." Most of the women who came to the shop had standing weekly appointments for shampoo and sets. I quickly learned the shop schedule and knew the times that my favorites would be sitting under the hairdryers. I enjoyed showing off for them, singing songs, dancing, and drawing pictures for the ladies. They were a captive audience.

Sometimes my sisters and I went a little too far, and we embarrassed my mother. One of the beauty shop customers wore big bows in her hair. My older sister informed her, "My mother said old ladies shouldn't put ribbons in their hair."

My mother turned red and quickly said, "Uh, bows are not ribbons. Bows look nice." My sister looked puzzled, but she knew to keep her mouth shut and say no more.

One day in the shop, I asked my mother what a brassiere was, and Ruth, one of my mother's weekly shampoo and set appointments, raised her top to show me her bra. I appreciated the information and visual demonstration. That evening my mother explained to me that there are some things one shouldn't ask in public. Questions about undergarments were included in the no-no list.

Different Drums

My father was the middle child and only son of Blanche and Garland Taylor. When my father started high school, his father, the Reverend Taylor, was assigned to be the pastor of the First Methodist Church in Marmaduke, Arkansas. That is where my father met my mother.

Following high school graduation, he attended three years of college at Arkansas State before being drafted during World War II. Shortly before he left for boot camp, my parents decided to get married. With little time to plan a wedding, the nuptials took place in the living room of the Methodist parsonage, and my preacher grandfather officiated. After my father returned from military service, my parents settled in Marmaduke where they lived the remainder of their lives.

My father and I shared the same first name. We shared little else. He was interested in sports, woodworking, fishing, and duck hunting. Those things did not interest me. I was interested in reading, entertainment, and the arts. I liked the movies. The last movie my father saw was *Gone with the Wind* in 1939, and only because my mother made him go with her. He read several newspapers each day, but he never read books. Not once in his life did he go to an art museum, a concert, or the ballet.

I went hunting with him only once. I didn't like it. I couldn't sit still long enough to fish. When the family went out in a boat with fishing poles, I was left on the bank to play. While my father was watching boxing on television or listening to the St. Louis Cardinals baseball game on the radio, I was reading a book.

My father was a good carpenter, but I couldn't drive a nail without it bending. He built the cabinets that were in the family kitchen and the cabinets in our bathroom. He built a wooden corral and a stable for a small horse I purchased, and he built a large carport for the family's cars. When I started painting, he made frames for my art.

While we didn't share common interests, my father and I were appreciative of each other's talents. He did not try to mold me into someone who he may have preferred to be his son. He supported and encouraged me in everything I did. Despite our differences, my father was proud of me, and I was proud of him. That is love.

Strong Woman

My mother, Allene Harvey Taylor, was ahead of her time in many ways. Born in 1913, my mother was the oldest child in her family. She had two brothers and three sisters. She told me that her father, Arzo Harvey, encouraged his daughters to be strong individuals.

My mother was the first woman in her family to drive a car. Not long after she purchased it, she rolled it over a couple of times, and the car landed upside down in a ditch. When my mother's younger sister heard about the accident and saw the wrecked car, she refused to ever drive again. Not my mother. She immediately replaced the car, and she continued to drive well into her late eighties.

My mother's parents each had an eighth-grade education. My mother was the first in her family to graduate from high school. Even though she wanted to become a hairdresser, she did agree to give college a try out of respect for her father, who encouraged his children to get as much schooling as possible. After she had attended one semester at Arkansas

State College, her father could tell that she wasn't happy. He told her that she should live *her* dream, not his. She dropped out of college and enrolled in beauty school in Birmingham, Alabama.

After she completed cosmetology school, she returned to Arkansas and opened her own business. She then married my father, who had been her high school sweetheart. Though most of her peers were married and having children, my mother told my father that they should wait until they were well established and financially comfortable before starting a family. They did. My mother was thirty-one before having my older sister, thirty-four when she had me, and thirty-six when she gave birth to my younger sister. All the time she kept working. She was able to juggle raising children and having a career.

Most of my mother's female friends did not work outside the home. Typical of the time, their husbands were the breadwinners. Because my mother had her own business, she had her own money, and she spent it as she pleased. She didn't ask my father if she could, or how she should, spend her money. He never said anything about her purchases. He knew better.

In the early 40s, my mother and several of her lady friends thought their small town was not being properly governed. They decided to run for office, and they formed an all-female slate of candidates. One lady ran for mayor, and my mother and the other women ran for city council seats. While standing in front of the city hall with brooms in their hands, the group had their photo made, and it was on the front page of the *Paragould Soliphone*. They wanted to "sweep the city clean." Unfortunately, they all lost their races to the men. When my mother would mention the unsuccessful takeover, she would say, "At least we made a statement." Just like her mother, Allene Taylor was living proof that one could be kind and gentle but still be strong.

Calls and Whistles

My father had many talents, and that included running up and down the sidelines of a basketball court for two hours and blowing a whistle. My father was a referee. During my childhood, he was the manager of a branch bank, and later he was the postmaster in our little town. Both were stationary jobs. However, during basketball season, which began in early fall and ended in late spring, he got plenty of exercise. He officiated at both junior high and high school basketball games.

Twice a week my father and his referee partner, Neilis, would put on black-and-white striped shirts and travel to nearby schools to referee two games each night. They wore black pants and black-and-white high-top tennis shoes. Whistles hung on chains around their necks. The two men ran up and down the sidelines on opposite sides of the basketball court. While running, they kept the whistles in their mouths, and they would blow them loudly when an infraction occurred.

I got to watch my father referee when he officiated in my hometown gymnasium. I watched proudly thinking that my daddy had a certain amount of power. I knew that he would use that power fairly. Never once did I hear anyone boo him because they thought he had made a bad call. I was amazed at his ability to run fast and hard, watch the game, and still have enough breath to loudly blow the whistle.

Daddy kept his whistle in a box in my parents' bedroom. Occasionally while he was at work and my mother was in her beauty shop at the front of the house, I would slip the whistle into the backyard and pretend that I was a referee. I would blow so hard that my face would turn red, but I never could blow as loudly as my father could.

I was slightly more successful when it came to blowing on one of my father's duck calls. My father was an avid duck hunter. To be a successful hunter one had to be able to talk to the ducks by blowing into a wooden duck call. My father had three different handmade wooden calls that were five or six inches in length and finely crafted.

He would place one of the short flute-like instruments into his mouth, blow through the opening, and manipulate the outgoing air with various finger movements. The way his fingers moved created an array of sounds that attracted different types of ducks in various situations.

I enjoyed hearing the quacking sounds, and I asked my father to teach me to work the call. I learned to do a few calls on the smallest instrument, one that had a beautiful ebony finish. I did not become a duck hunter; I went on only one hunt, and I never shot a duck. I did like knowing that if ever needed, I knew how to talk to a duck. So far that hasn't happened.

Saving Allene

My mother, Allene Taylor, was an avid shopper and a collector of coupons. My father subscribed to four daily newspapers, and he read each one. When he finished the papers, they ended up on the kitchen table in the hands of my mother. She carefully searched the pages for coupons, and she cut out each one. After my father passed away, my mother continued to subscribe to the papers to get the coupons.

She spent a great deal of time cutting out coupons not only from the papers but also from many magazines. She bought magazines for her beauty shop patrons to read while they sat under hairdryers. She cut out and saved every coupon that she saw, even if she had no intention of using it.

Long after my father had passed away, I asked about the men's grooming coupons that she had saved. She told me, "Someone may want them." One time I found Barbasol shaving cream in her bathroom. I kidded her, asking if she had a secret boyfriend who needed shaving cream. She laughed and said, "No, but I had a coupon for it." Every so often I would go through her huge stash of coupons, and she reluctantly would let me throw away the ones that had expired.

My mother also liked freebies that came with the purchase of some of the items that she used in her beauty shop. A very good-looking salesman from the Memphis-based Kar-Hill Beauty Supply called on my mother's shop each week. During one promotion, he didn't have to use his good looks and charm to convince my mother to purchase more perms than she needed to get free place settings of Noritake china. She wanted to buy enough to get twelve place settings of the dishes to give to me. She bought way more perms than she needed, but she got the twelve place settings along with matching serving pieces. I still have the Noritake Blue Orchard china dinnerware, and I have plenty of it.

My mother collected S&H Green Stamps and Kroger's Top Value Stamps. The number of trading stamps given by a store to a shopper would depend on the purchase amount. The stamps were placed in little books, and when filled they were traded for merchandise at a stamp store. My mother especially liked shopping on double stamp day, and lucky for her, the local Kroger's double stamp day was on Wednesdays. My mother took off Wednesday afternoons from work. She also made an effort to buy the advertised products that offered double stamps. When I moved into my first unfurnished apartment in Memphis, I was able to get a bookshelf, TV stand, and serving cart at the local S&H Green Stamp store with stamps my mother had collected. After reaping the benefits of her trading stamps, I, too, started collecting stamps from the nearby Piggly Wiggly grocery store.

My mother studied the grocery ads in the newspapers to see which stores had the best prices. When I visited her and we went grocery shopping, we would go to two or three stores in nearby Paragould. If we were in Kroger and she picked up a can of kidney beans, she could tell me how much it was selling for in the other stores. She bought where it was the cheapest. Gas was inexpensive at the time or she would have burned up her savings while she drove all over town to get a bargain.

I don't fault my mother for being thrifty. She grew up poor and had suffered through the Great Depression. I also think her savings activities were somewhat of a hobby. She enjoyed the hunt for bargains. A penny saved is a penny earned, but that may not hold true when that penny is saved while purchasing unneeded items.

Mother's Day

My grandmother helped raise me. My mother worked long hours in her beauty shop, so my grandmother, whom we called Mom, walked the few blocks to our house to take care of me and my younger sister while my mother was in the shop. We really didn't need taking care of, but it was a way for my mother to give my grandmother money for babysitting. My grandmother would not have accepted unearned money. No matter how hard the struggle, she wanted to make her own way. When my mother told her that she needed her to watch us kids, my grandmother felt wanted and needed. And she was.

My mother's sister and her husband, my aunt Betty and uncle Leroy, bought a house in Marmaduke for Mom to live in. They told her that they needed her to take care of the house they probably would move into after Uncle Leroy retired. My aunt and uncle never intended to retire in Marmaduke, but they wanted Mom to have a comfortable home with gas heat and indoor plumbing, unlike the house where she had been living. One Christmas, my grandmother's children chipped in and bought her a television. She spent many hours sitting and watching the "magic box" with her dog, Bullet, by her side in her nice home.

I loved my grandmother, and I noticed and appreciated the love and respect that my mother and her siblings gave to her. On Mother's Day before going to church, we pinned a red rose to our lapels in honor of our mother. My sisters and I wore red roses that had been cut from a bush in my mother's yard. Mom wore a white rose plucked from a bush that she had planted. When I asked her why her rose wasn't red, she said, "When your mother has passed on, you wear a white rose in her honor."

The first time that I saw my mother pin a white rose to her lapel on Mother's Day, I cried a little. At the same time, I was happy in my heart knowing that my grandmother had been loved. I learned to love my mother by watching her love her mother.

The Innocent Years

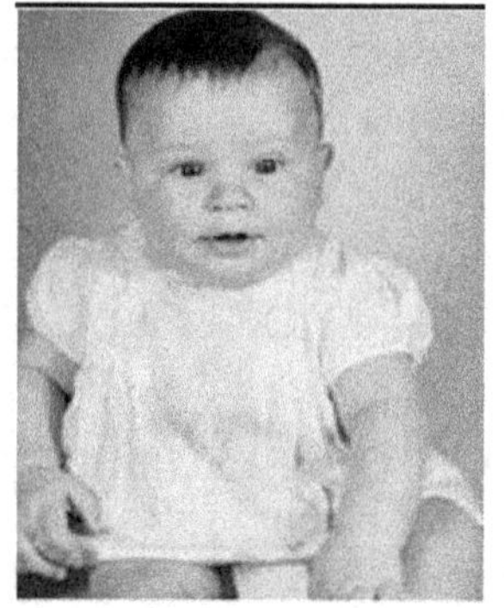

Fat baby Zeek

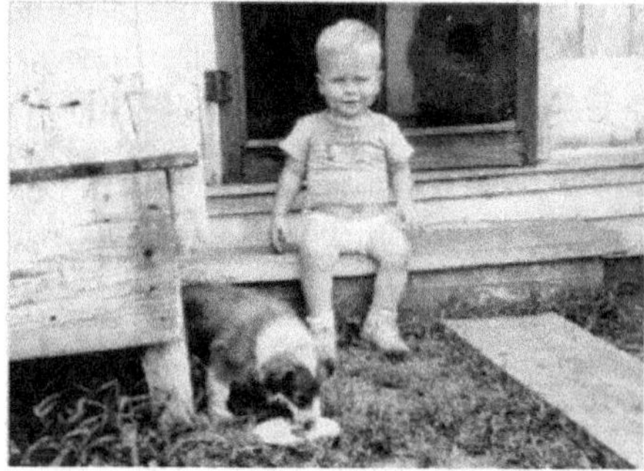

Feeding the dogs

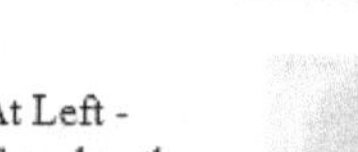

At Left - Grandmother & sisters in our Sunday finest.

At Right - A boy's best friend, Jiggs

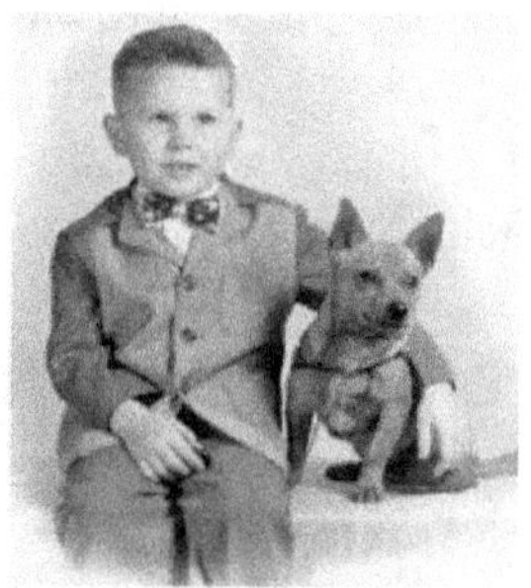

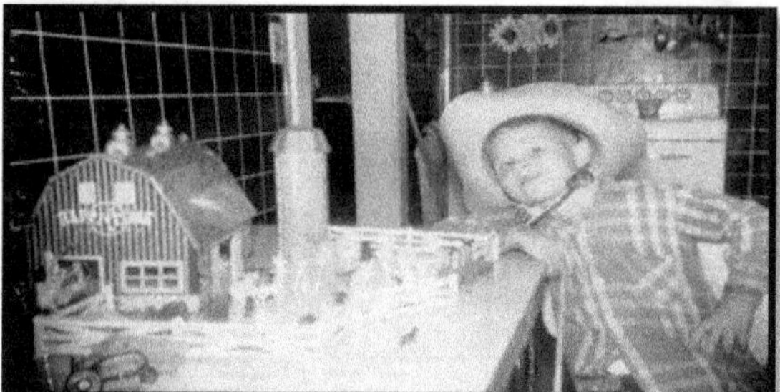

Santa Delivers

Temptation and Spirituality

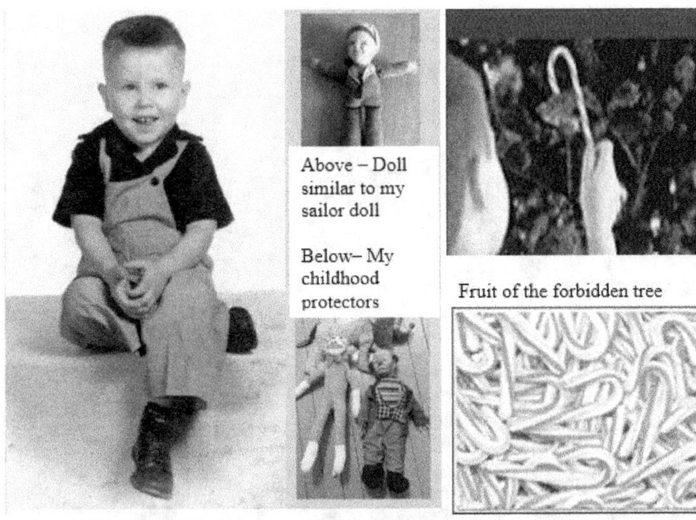

Above – Doll similar to my sailor doll

Below– My childhood protectors

Fruit of the forbidden tree

Four-year-old Zeek

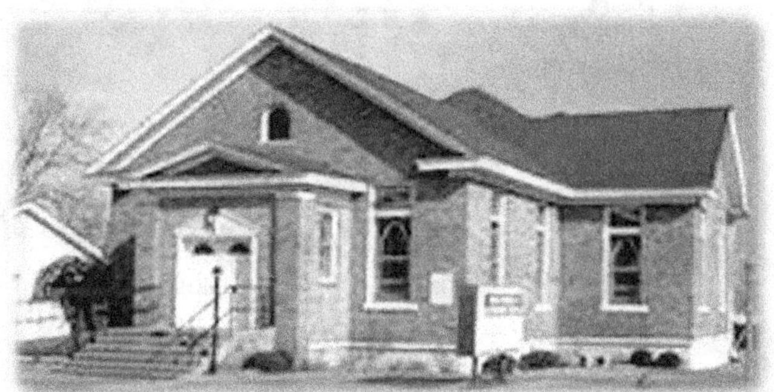

The Marmaduke Methodist Church

In the Delta Cotton is King

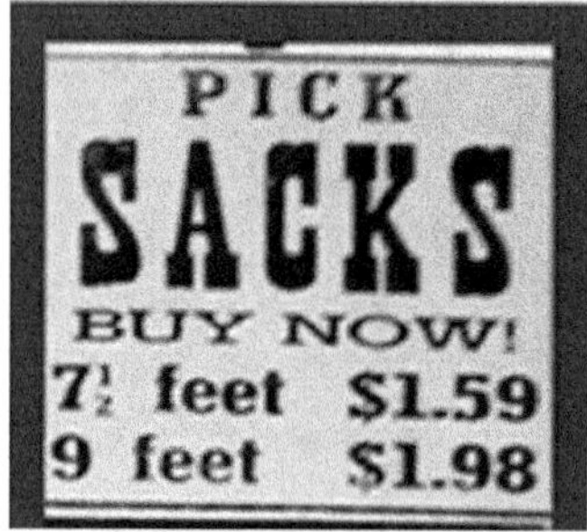

Into the fields at age five

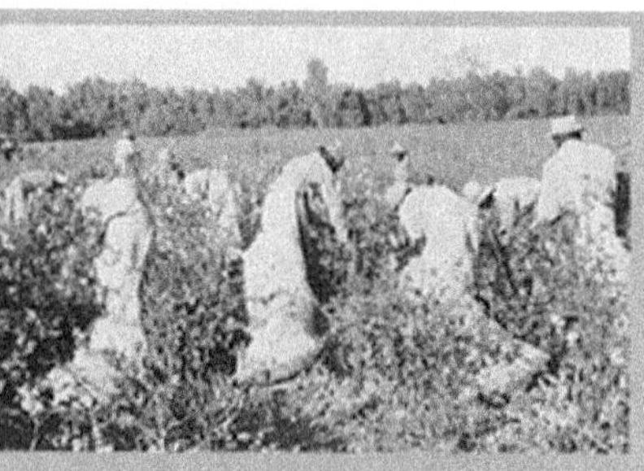

Working beside my beloved grandmother

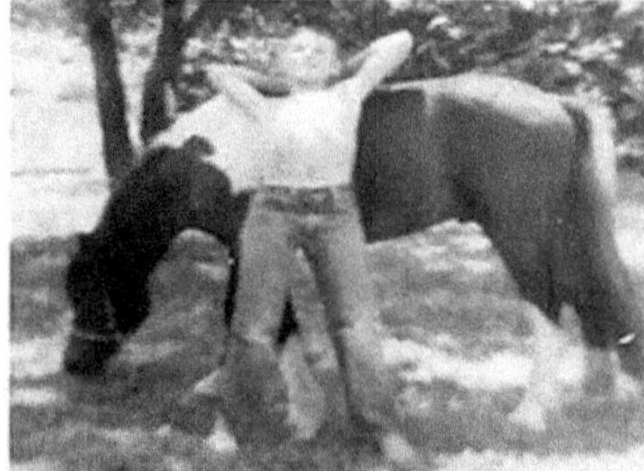

One small horse = 4,200 lbs. of cotton

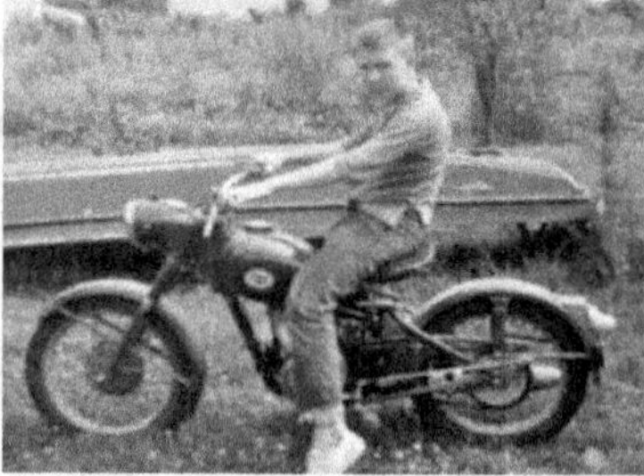

Hard work brings rewards and freedom

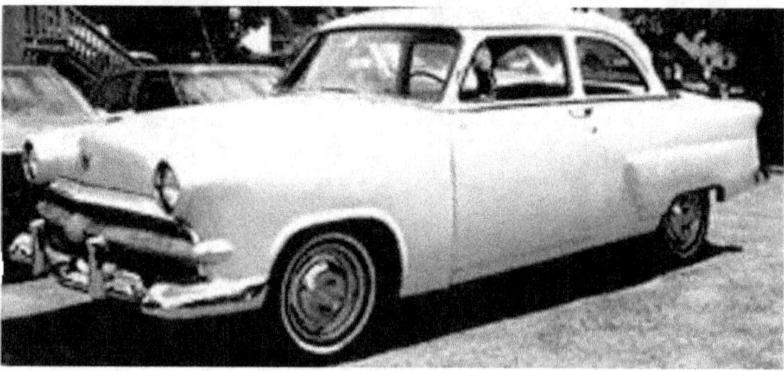

There's nothing more beautiful than your first car, particularly if you paid for it yourself

Family is Everything

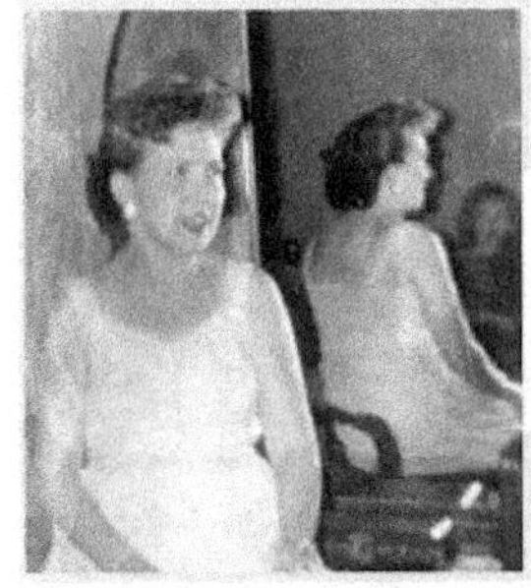

Mother at play and at work

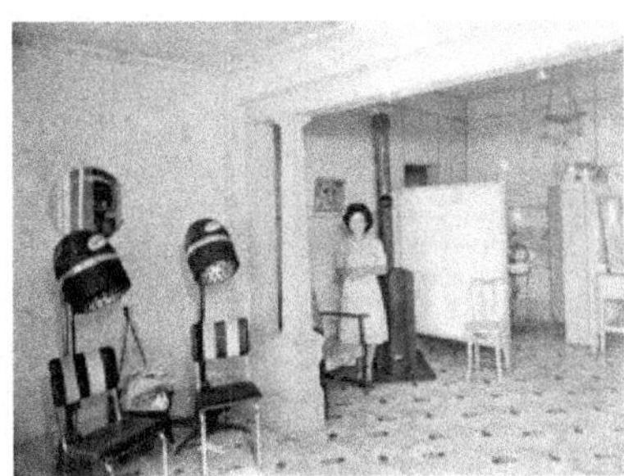

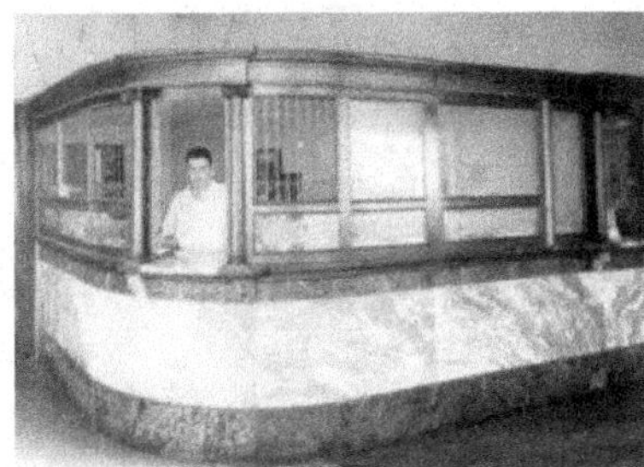

Dad at work and at play

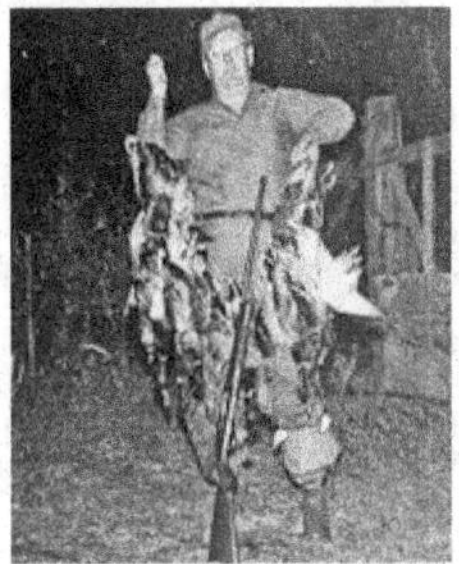

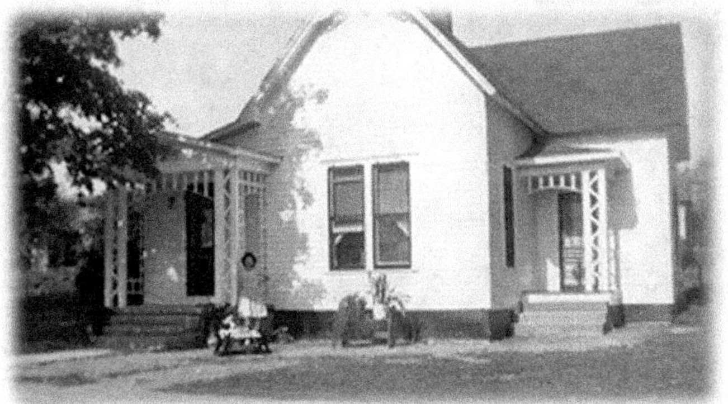

Our family home in Marmaduke, Arkansas

The Family Unit

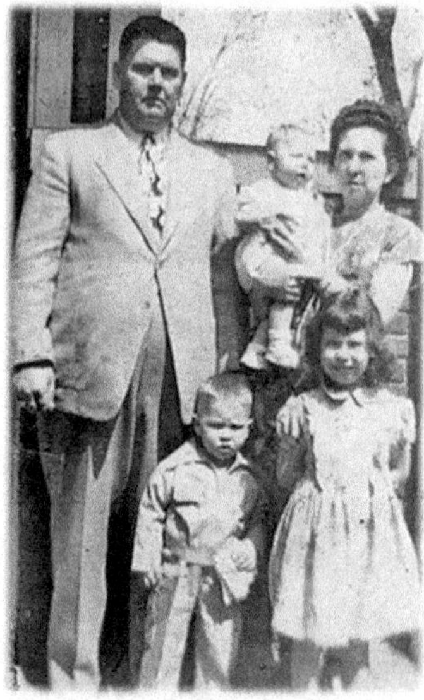

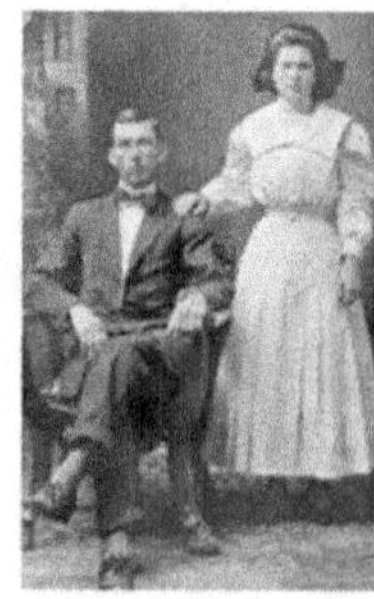

At Left – The Taylor family in Happy Days

At Top Right – My maternal grandparents Arzo Estus Harvey and Eva Belle Harvey

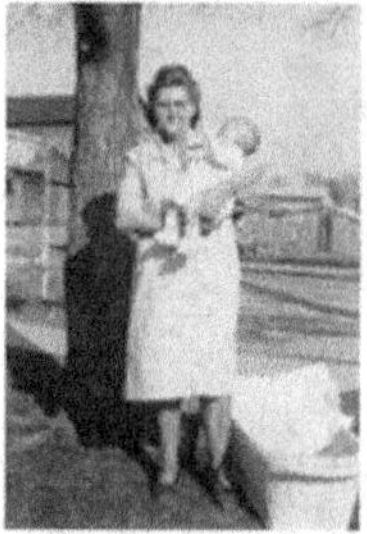

At Right – My maternal grandmother, "Mom" Harvey

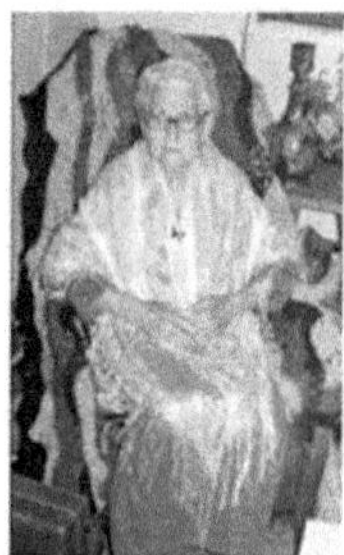

At Right – My Grandfather Garland Cicero Taylor

At Left – Mom in her shawl Christmas 1978

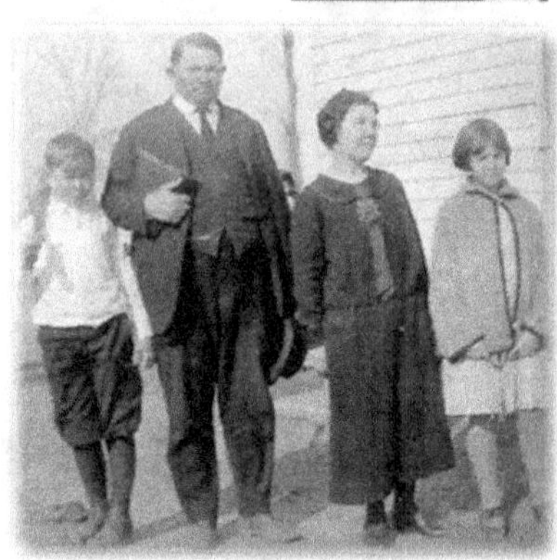

Family Ties

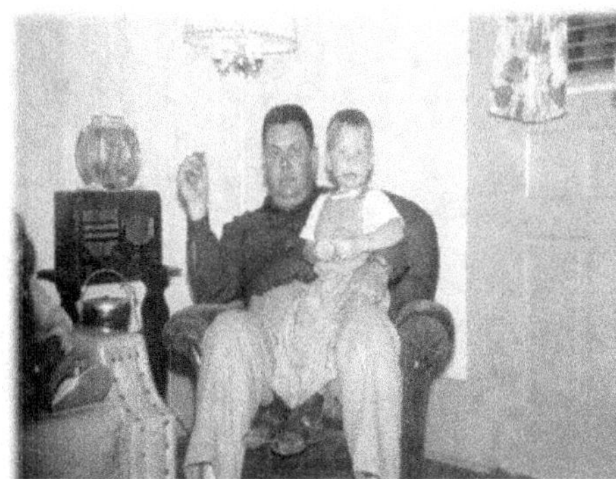

Listening to the radio with my Dad

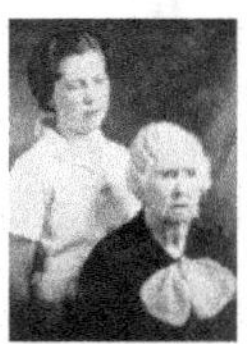

Mother started dressing hair in 1935. Here she is giving a 90-year-old woman her first permanent wave.

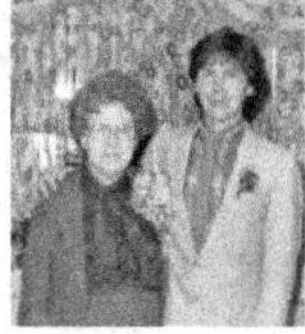

With my Mother in 1985 at her celebration of 50 years as a hairdresser

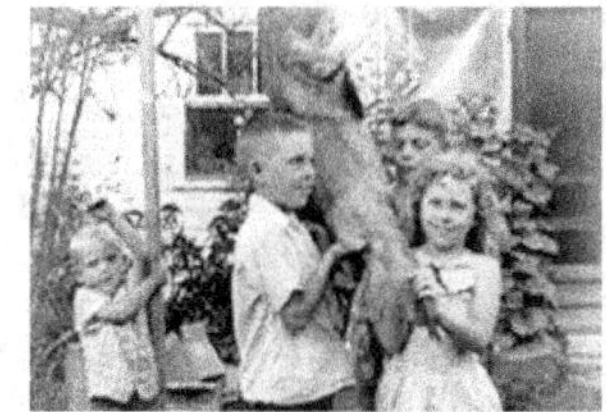

Me, my sisters, my cousins, and a giant catfish

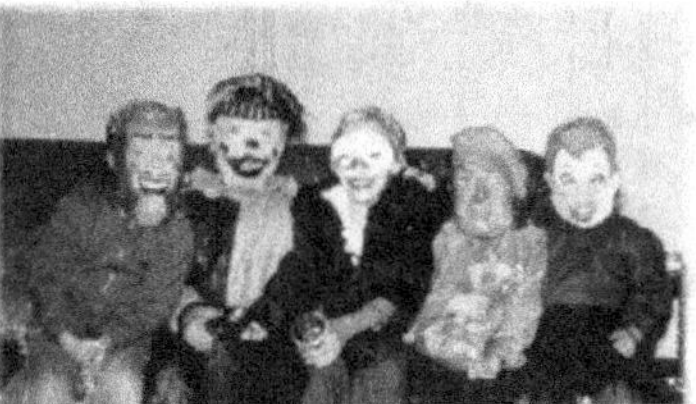

Just another typical Halloween in Marmaduke

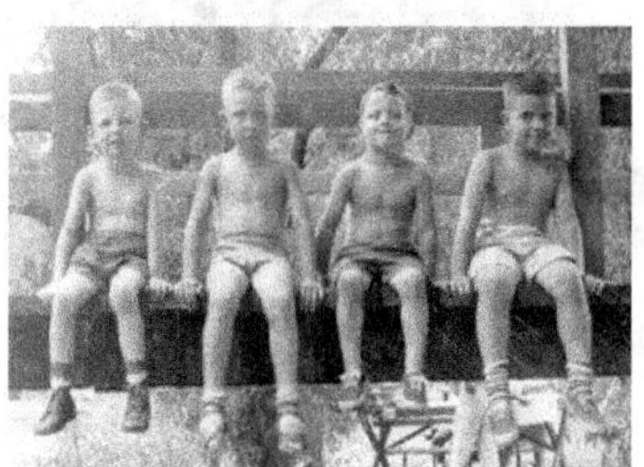

Me and my cousins at a family reunion in Paragould

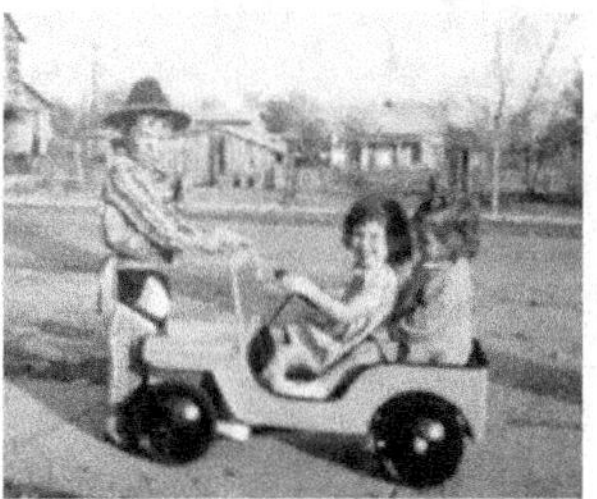

Pulling my sister Cheryl and cousin LeJean

Waxing Nostalgic

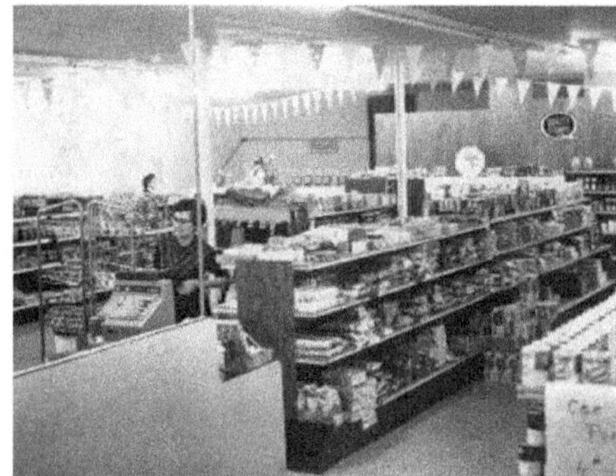

This was our "super" store

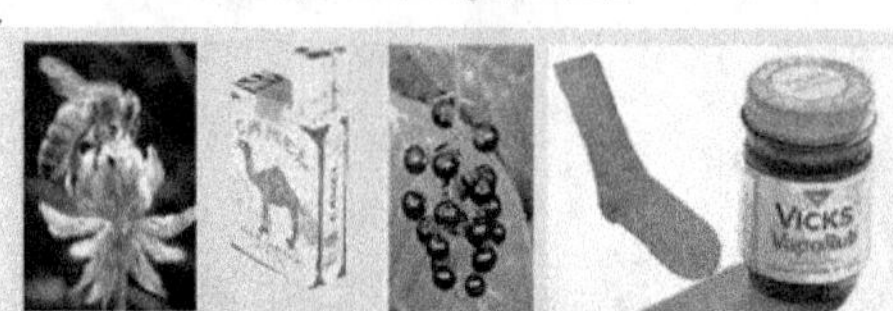

Home remedies for bees sting, arthritis and colds or flu – just add hot toddy

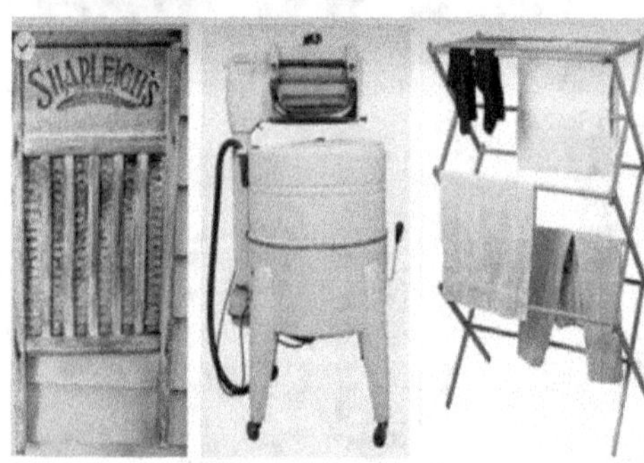

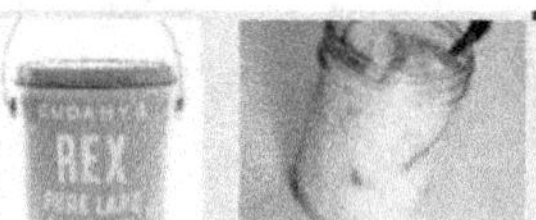

Coke, coke, coke, coke & coke

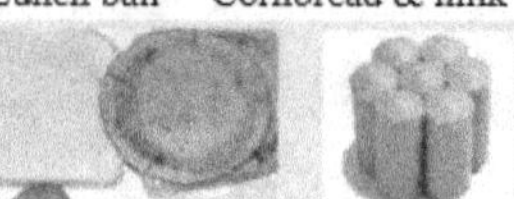

Lunch pail   Cornbread & milk

Fried bologna   Vienna sausage

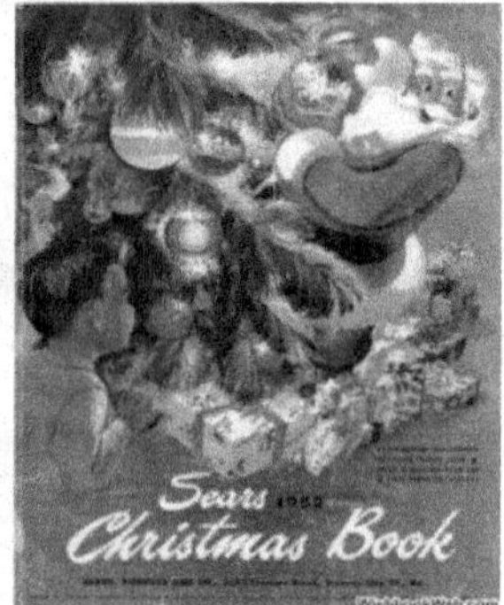

Above - The "Wish Book"

At Left – Modern conveniences
to make clothes washing easier

More Nostalgia

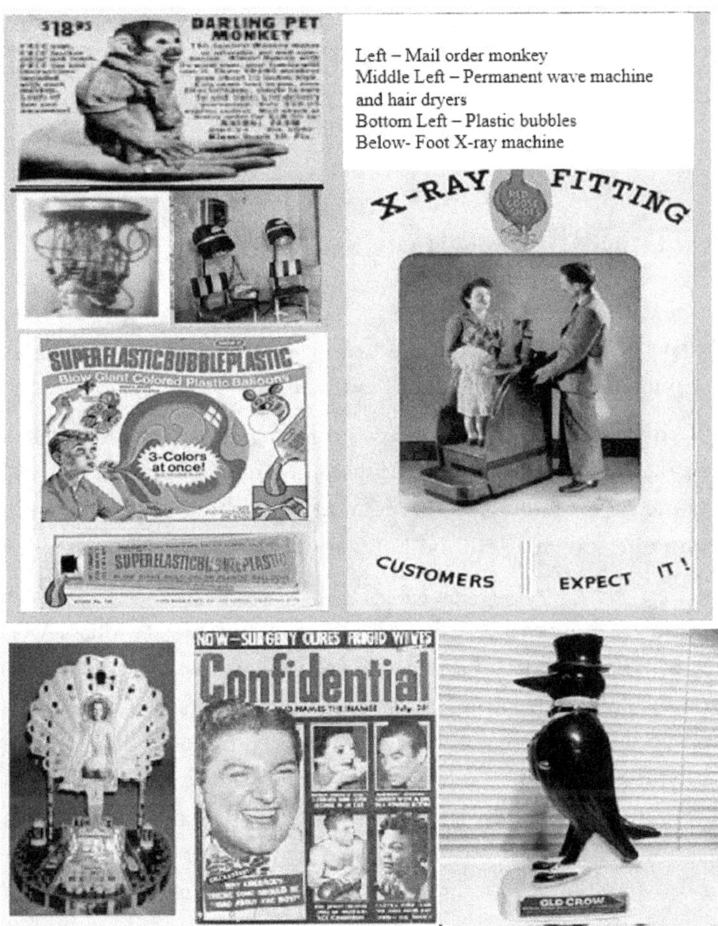

The King Lives   Before There Was an Enquirer   Always Had An Affinity For Crows

CHAPTER 5 — THE STUDENT BECOMES THE TEACHER

Cain't Talk Rite, Lik It or Not

In the fall of 1964, at the age of seventeen, I enrolled in college at Arkansas State University. When selecting a major, I decided to combine my interest in art and journalism.

My dream job at the time was to be a graphic artist for a television station. I didn't realize that while studying broadcast journalism, I would be doing some on-air radio announcing. During my junior year of studies, I was required to do an afternoon radio show each week that was one hour in length.

The news show was broadcast on the college radio station, KASU. My parents, who lived thirty miles from the school, were excited about hearing their son on the radio, so they purchased a new FM radio. The radio had a long telescoping antenna, and it had an honored place on the kitchen table for the next forty years. At the time, there were very few FM stations available compared to the large number of AM stations. Although my parents thought their son was a radio star, I soon realized that I was not cut out for broadcasting. I found doing the show unnerving.

Reading the obituaries on air was particularly troubling. I was worried about mispronouncing names during a time of the deceased's family's grief. However, I doubt that many of the bereaved had FM radios. It was difficult for me to "talk right." For on-air announcers "talking right" meant speaking as if one hailed from the Midwest. The region of the Arkansas Delta where I grew up was influenced culturally by its proximity to Memphis. That influence included the way we spoke. When outside the Delta, I avoided saying words such as *bike, like, tire*— any word I could not pronounce properly. Despite my pronunciation shortcomings, I did make a B in the broadcasting course.

Since then, I have done more than twenty-one radio and television interviews. I also read stories for two *Tales from the South* shows that were heard by 130 million radio listeners worldwide, and I was featured on a StoryCorps segment on the *Morning Edition* public radio show that was heard by 50 million listeners nationwide.

I've learned to appreciate regional dialects, and I'm glad that we don't all sound alike. I have embraced my culture, and I have learned to accept the way that I talk. I now own my Southern voice.

I rather like my accent . . . y'all.

Not a Very Good Soldier

When I attended Arkansas State University, all male students were required to take two years of Reserve Officers' Training Corps (ROTC). The four semesters of classes during the freshman and sophomore years counted as physical education hours.

Even though I had no intention of becoming an officer in the military, I had no choice but to sit through the classes and learn about modern warfare techniques. I was issued a military uniform complete with hat and black patent leather shoes. I was issued a rifle and assigned to F Company. My company was jokingly referred to as "F Troop," a bungling military unit featured in a popular television show of the same name. The name was appropriate. We were the worst marching company on the field.

It was required that I keep my uniform and rifle in tip-top shape and ready for inspection. I cleaned the gun and shined brass buttons and shoes each week before drill class. Although I thought I had fairly good coordination, I often dropped my rifle during the drills. F Company not only marched together, we sat together in the classroom. We were a unit, and we were all given the same grade. One semester we all received a D–, and it was the only D– I ever made. In actuality, I probably deserved an F.

During the spring semester, all ROTC students were required to participate in a General Inspection, a dreaded affair when the Pentagon sent the big brass to ASU to inspect the troops. I was terrified about the inspection. The first year I didn't go. My sophomore year, an order was issued, "Attend the General Inspection or receive a failing grade." The only accepted reason to not attend was to have a written doctor's excuse.

The week before the big inspection, after having a few beers, I decided to go skinny dipping with friends in nearby Craighead Lake. Shortly after entering the water, I stepped on a broken bottle and ended up getting fourteen stitches in my foot. I was on crutches and had a wrapped foot, and I had a written doctor's excuse. Therefore, I did not have to go through the General Inspection. During the drill, I sat in the bleachers in my civilian clothes and watched the inspection. I was relieved that I was not on the field marching with my bungling company.

After two years of military studies, I had fulfilled my ROTC obligations. To earn PE credits in the following semesters, I took tennis, bowling, ballroom, and choreography. I was a much better dancer than I was a soldier.

White Skin and Fangs

When spring arrived at Arkansas State University in the late 60s, I was ready to put down the books, get outside, bask in the sun, and turn my pasty-white skin to a beautiful bronze.

In early April of my junior year, my roommate and I ventured to nearby Craighead Lake to soak up some rays. After we finished our morning classes, we loaded the car with a beer-filled cooler, a picnic lunch, a transistor radio, suntan lotion, and our tie-dyed hippie beach towels.

When we arrived at the lake, we found the beach area was crowded with sun lovers. We spread our towels in the grassy field near the water, opened a couple of beers, and plopped down to work on our tans. A short time later we heard screams. When we looked up, we were surprised to see many of our fellow sun worshippers running away from the lake and toward us. Then we saw them. There were dozens and dozens of cottonmouth snakes heading our way.

A large nest of snakes had broken up near the shoreline. Snakes often huddle together in a den to stay warm during the winter months while they conserve their energy until food becomes more abundant in the spring. The sight of the snake stampede was like viewing a scene from a horror movie.

My roommate and I left everything on the ground. We got on top of my car, which was parked nearby. The two guys next to us did not move quickly enough and one was bitten. The young man who had not suffered a bite asked us if we would watch their cooler and other belongings while he took his friend to the hospital. We said yes. They sped off leaving towels, cooler, and other belongings on the ground.

We sat on the hood of my car while we watched the snakes pass by us. The cooler with its contents of beer was not in reach. We sat there on the hood of my 1959 Chevy, thirsty but too terrified to risk getting down from the car to grab a couple of cold ones. We stayed put long after the snakes had moved on. A couple of hours later, the unbitten student returned and reported that his friend had received anti-venom medication but was still in the hospital for observation. Still fearful, we got off the car, loaded up, and made a hasty retreat.

I never again went to Craighead Lake.

Hiding from the Wind

Tornadoes appear quite often in the Arkansas Delta. The violent storms seem to thrive on the warm, moist air and easily sweep across the flat landscape. My hometown of Marmaduke, Arkansas, has been hit several times. I was in my high school gym when the town's warning siren went off to alert everyone that a tornado was heading our way. Rather than seek shelter, I climbed to the top of the bleachers and watched the funnel cloud go by a few blocks away.

That tornado hit a nearby house trailer. A young woman who had been a classmate and had quit school to marry was inside the trailer baking a chocolate cake when it hit. She was almost nine months pregnant at the time. The mobile home rolled several times before exploding. Debris from the trailer was scattered over an area of one square mile. Miraculously, the young woman was barely injured. She was taken to the emergency room and had a nail removed from her leg, and she carried her baby another couple of weeks before she delivered a healthy child.

Marmaduke did suffer severe damage in 2006 when two to three hundred homes were destroyed by a massive tornado. That was a large portion of homes in the small town. There were more than forty injuries but fortunately no fatalities.

My closest encounter with a tornado was in Jonesboro, Arkansas, in the spring of 1968, my senior year in college. An F-4 tornado ravaged much of the town, killing thirty-four and injuring more than three hundred. The twister hit less than one mile from my apartment. During the storm it was pitch black, wind howling, rain falling, sirens going off, and no electricity. I heard sirens wailing all through the night.

The next day a friend of mine called and asked if I would accompany him to the hardest hit area. My friend was a reporter for the local TV station. I would occasionally accompany him while he reported. I went with him to help carry his equipment. He didn't really need me to help, but we were friends, and we enjoyed each other's company. Going with him on assignment allowed me to get into places that only the press could go. This time I wish that I had said no. At the site, I saw things that I never wanted to see, and I have tried to erase the images from my mind. From then on, I only went with my friend to report on happy events.

The next assignment I helped him cover was a backstage interview with pop star Dionne Warwick. Images from the Warwick interview are the ones I try to hold in my mind from the spring of 1968. However, some things are hard to unsee.

Delta Politics

Early on I learned how politics works. When I was thirteen years old, I was standing with my father at the Marmaduke Fourth of July picnic when he took a one-hundred-dollar bill out of his pocket and handed it to Governor Orval Faubus. My daddy said, "Sure wish that road between here and Lafe was paved." A half dozen other men standing in the circle followed suit and each handed the governor a one-hundred-dollar bill. Faubus placed the "campaign contributions" into his pocket. Later that fall, the road was paved.

My father was a Democrat of the yellow dog variety as was everyone else in our town with the exception of one woman, Miss Lucy. When anyone mentioned her name they often followed it with "that Republican woman." Miss Lucy was attractive and somewhat flamboyant. I personally thought she was quite glamorous. I was in her home several times and was very impressed with her decorating skills. Her bedroom walls were covered with yellow wallpaper that was splattered with big, bold, multicolored flowers. Her bedspread and curtains had the exact same design. She had a bedroom like no other in town. She liked being different. I think that's why she was a Republican.

I turned twenty-one during my last year in college. I could legally drink and vote. The next spring, I volunteered to be a poll worker during a primary election. Miss Lucy was the only person who came to vote and requested a Republican ballot. In those days, ballots were tallied by hand after the polls closed. The poll workers spent a lengthy time tallying the Democratic ballots. It took us a few seconds to tally Miss Lucy's Republican ballot. It was the only one.

My father was such a loyal Democrat that he could never under any circumstance vote for a Republican. In 1966 Winthrop Rockefeller ran for governor against Democrat Justice Jim Johnson, a devout racist much like George Wallace. My father would not vote for a Republican, but he could not vote for a racist. Disgusted, he stayed home on voting day that year. It was the only time I remember him not voting. In 1966, only 11 percent of Arkansans considered themselves to be Republicans, but Arkansans were also tired of being labeled racist. Rockefeller won the election, the first Republican elected since the Reconstruction period following the Civil War.

My mother, out of respect for my father, also didn't cast a vote for governor in 1966. Shortly after the election she did tell me a secret. She said, "I have to confess that one time I voted for a Republican, but your daddy can never know that I did." She continued, "I voted for Eisenhower."

I was shocked by her confession. I kept her secret. My father went to his grave never knowing that my mother had voted for a member of the GOP.

Some things are best left unknown, especially when it comes to politics.

Learning While Teaching

After graduating from Arkansas State University, I pursued a teaching job in order to get an occupational deferment from the military draft. I was hired as a junior high art teacher in the Mountain Grove School District in Missouri, a town located in the state's south-central Ozark Mountain region.

I decided that if I was going to teach, I would go where the money was, and at that time, Missouri seemed to be the place. In 1968, the starting salary for teachers in Arkansas was $4,600. In Mountain Grove I was under contract to receive a yearly salary of $5,100. That amount seemed sufficient to warrant the purchase of a brand-new 1969 Chevrolet Camaro SS. I wanted something cool to drive to work. The cost of the car was $3,600.

After taxes and teacher retirement were withdrawn from my check, I received $430 each month. For the first couple of weeks of each pay period, I felt rich. That was followed by two weeks of feeling poor. It took me a while to learn to manage my money. However, living was cheap in Mountain Grove. I had a roommate, and we shared a furnished garage apartment, utilities paid. The monthly rent was $25 each.

There were not many places to spend money in town. There was one movie theater, but it did not have heat and air. Moviegoers fanned in the summer and bundled up in the winter. I never went to the movies while living there. There was a liquor store, and I spent part of my salary on beer. Most weekends were spent playing poker with fellow teachers.

During the time I taught there, the county where Mountain Grove was located was one of the five poorest counties per capita in the USA. The school district was huge, and some of the students spent a couple of hours a day on a school bus. Some of the kids lived in homes with dirt floors. I had a friend who taught Head Start. She told me there had been times when she had to teach children how to use silverware. Not every student in the district was poor, but there was a disproportionate number who did live in poverty.

Due to the poverty in the district, the school received a large amount of supplemental government funding. I had art supplies in abundance.

I really did like the people of Mountain Grove. The students were very supportive of each other, and socioeconomic status seemed to make no difference to them when it came to clubs, cheer teams, and social groups.

It was a rewarding experience for me to be with them, and to experience their excitement for living and learning. I, too, learned a lot that year. One thing that stuck with me is that zest for living and learning is more important than money and possessions.

However, I do wish I still had that 1969 Camaro.

Hard-Hitting Teacher

I was twenty-one when I got my first teaching job. I was fresh out of college, green behind the ears, and not prepared to teach. I think that may be true for many teachers when they enter their first classroom. College-level education courses do have some value, but a rookie teacher really learns how to teach through on-the-job training.

I was hired to be the junior high school art teacher in Mountain Grove, Missouri. The school was fairly small, and the seventh through twelfth grades met in the same building. I was terrified on the opening day of school while I waited in my assigned classroom for the first-period class to enter. Even though I was standing by my desk and wearing the required coat and tie when the first group of young students came in, they weren't convinced I was their teacher. I was twenty-one years old, but I looked like a scrawny sixteen-year-old. I had to convince the students: "Yes, I'm Mr. Taylor, and I'm your teacher."

I was not accustomed to wearing a necktie, and I was not used to being addressed formally. It took a couple of weeks before I realized someone was talking to me when they said, "Mr. Taylor." I made it through the first four classes on opening day. I became less nervous as the morning passed, but I was glad to have a break when the lunch bell rang.

After lunch, my nerves flared again when I entered a stand-alone building where I was assigned to be in charge of a study hall. The building at one time had been the school lunchroom. The study hall room was huge and had dozens of desks that were soon filled with kids.

My job as the study hall teacher was to watch more than eighty students, making sure they studied and, most importantly, keeping them quiet. The students ranged in age from twelve to nineteen. From day one it was a nightmare task.

I was fortunate that the class period following the study hall was my teacher's preparation hour. I did not prep but spent the hour unwinding in the teachers' break room. I shared the room with the language arts and Spanish teacher, Miss Octavia Hale. We were the only teachers on break that period. Miss Hale was elderly and had been teaching most of her life. I learned a lot from her. She was a great mentor who taught me to chill, and she assured me that everything was going to be just fine. For the rest of the year, we enjoyed spending the prep hour with each other. We became good friends while sitting in the break room, gossiping, drinking Coca-Cola, and chain-smoking cigarettes.

The hour that I spent in the break room was a much-needed time to unwind following the study hall assignment that was a constant headache for me. I did not have enough eyes to watch eighty students and make them all behave. I knew that the kids liked me, but they were kids, and they could not sit still and be quiet for an entire hour.

One of the eighth-grade students who was in the study hall gave me the gift of a very large paddle. It was a fine piece of woodwork that he had crafted during shop class. He gave it to me only if I promised to never use it on him. It was easy for me to agree to his request. It was not in my nature to harm another person. That is until one day when I felt I had no choice but to use the paddle.

The building where the study hall was held was not air-conditioned, and the windows were left open to take advantage of breezes when the weather permitted. One spring afternoon I had just finished helping a young study hall student with an assignment when I looked up and saw three senior boys jump through an open window. They hightailed it across the lawn. There was little I could do about it at the moment. I was very fond of the three students, but I also knew that as their teacher I had to get the upper hand and punish them.

The next morning, I talked with the principal, explained what had happened, and told him I would like to paddle the three boys. He agreed that was a fitting punishment. I agonized the next day about my decision during the periods before the study hall.

I wasn't certain I could go through with the paddling. I didn't want to physically hurt the young men, but I did think it was the only way to show them that I was in charge. When the three arrived for the study hall, I had them wait by my desk in front of the room. Soon the principal arrived. State law dictated that when teachers paddled a student, another adult had to be present as a witness. The principal was there to serve as the witness.

I had the first boy bend over and put his hands on the desk. I gave him three good whacks with the paddle. He grinned, nodded, and took his seat. The second boy smiled at me and put his hands on the desk, and he took his three whacks. He gave me a tough guy smile, a shrug, and he took his seat.

The third young man gave me a "don't do it" look but bent over the desk when I told him to bend over. I gave him his three whacks. He gave out a big "whoop," grabbed his butt, and started laughing. The entire class laughed, and I could barely keep from laughing. I thanked the principal before he left the room. The three students came to my desk, shook my hand, and asked to sign the paddle. From then on, I didn't have a bit of trouble from the rowdy three. At the end of the school year, I asked them to forgive me. They laughed and said, "We deserved that whooping."

I retired the paddle after using it that day. I've never hit another person since, and I still can't believe I hit those three young men. I admit that I still laugh a little when I think of the last guy grabbing his butt and giving out a loud "whoop."

I hope the three young men have had a good life.

Poor in the Pocket, Rich in Experiences

I was looking forward to Christmas break at the end of my first semester of teaching in Mountain Grove, Missouri. However, due to the poverty in the area, I worried that some of the students wouldn't have much of a holiday.

Two weeks before the break, I decided to bring a little Christmas to the classroom. It was a fitting time to do 3-D origami construction and have my eighth-grade art class students make Christmas ornaments. One of the students volunteered to bring a cedar tree from his property and said that his daddy would deliver it in their truck. I bought a stand that night, and the tree was delivered to the school the next day. It was perfect for displaying our handmade paper sculpture ornaments.

I had an abundance of white-as-snow, velvet-like paper in my art supply closet. The paper was the perfect material for the ornaments. The students worked from two different patterns: a rose and a dove. The class had fun working with the paper while listening to Christmas music.

They enjoyed the easing of classroom rules while working on the project. I brought candy canes to hang on the tree. Not many made it to the tree. We ate them. While we worked on the project, we had a good time. I quit worrying that we were making excessive noise that may have disturbed the nearby classrooms. I made the decision that laughter was not noise, and that learning should be fun. No one complained. When the tree was finished, many teachers stopped by to admire the students' work.

On the last day of class before Christmas break, I let the students take home the ornaments. Many had penciled their initials on the white paper and knew exactly where on the tree they had placed their handmade decorations. They were proud of their work, and I was proud of them.

I hope that some of my former students still have their ornaments and that somewhere a white rose or a white dove is hanging on one of their Christmas trees during the holidays. Most of all, I hope the former students have fond memories of a time when "We need a little Christmas, right this very minute" came to their classroom, and all seemed right with the world.

I Don't Like Math, but I Love Figures

When I walked into my first figure-drawing class as a young art student, I was very uncomfortable. When the unclothed model took her first pose, I was flush and red in the face. It didn't take long before I got over being uncomfortable. I enjoyed the challenge of drawing the human body, and I soon realized the benefit of practicing figure drawing.

Each model presented a new challenge, and my ability to draw improved. During countless sessions, I drew and painted all body types: female, male, tall, short, thin, heavy, black, white, duos, dancers, construction workers, and even a couple of very pregnant models. I thought each and every one was beautiful in their own way. That is until I encountered Breda. She was old.

My second teaching job was in St. Louis. While living there, I took painting courses at Washington University. In one class, our subject matter was the human body. Breda was the instructor's favorite model. The first time she showed up to model, I thought, *Yuck, I don't want to see this old woman naked.* Breda was seventy-something years old. As a twenty-two-year-old, I thought there was no way that anyone that old could look good and be worthy of me spending time drawing them. When Breda removed her robe, she revealed a potbelly, saggy flesh, and veins showing through her thin skin. I thought, *Okay, get over it and draw.*

By the end of that first session, Breda had become my favorite model. Her body revealed great character, and I could sense the history of a lifetime of living. What I noticed more than anything is that Breda's gentle, beautiful spirit shone through even though she was not saying anything, and she was sitting perfectly still. Her beauty radiated.

I was particularly drawn to her hands. They were somewhat gnarled with knotty joints, veins showing through, and age spots. I loved her hands. Many people think the eyes tell a story, I thought and still think that the hands tell a story and are a true reflection of a life lived. The older the hands, the more chapters that are revealed.

For the next two semesters, Breda was our only model. Most of the time she was nude, but at times she would add accent accessories such as a large hat or feather boa. During breaks, Breda and I chatted and soon became good friends. Many times she would bring me homemade goodies. She was an excellent cookie baker.

I appreciate the time I spent with Breda. I learned a great deal. Not only did my drawing and painting skills improve, but I learned that age has nothing to do with beauty. Beauty truly does come from the inside.

I Didn't Move to California

From the time I reached puberty and until I graduated from high school, I would not say the word *homosexual.* I was afraid that if I said the word aloud, someone might think that I was "one of those." During my high school years, I had no one to talk with about my sexual orientation. I didn't know how friends and family would react if they knew, and I was afraid of being ostracized, made fun of, or disliked.

I knew there were guys out there like me, even though there were none where I lived, at least no one I knew. I thought they probably lived in New York City or in Hollywood. I bought every possible issue of *Confidential* that I could find. The magazine was a gossip rag that hinted about the homosexuality of several male movie stars including Rock Hudson, Tab Hunter, James Dean, and Liberace. I wanted to move to California where gay men lived, and I decided that after college, I would.

After graduating from high school, I attended Arkansas State University. I was seventeen when I moved into a dorm and met my roommate. I didn't know the guy; we were randomly assigned to share a room. He was straight, but my two suitemates were obviously not straight. They were flamboyant, listened to opera, and wore fancy silk robes while in the dorm. The suitemates shared a room separated from mine by a large bathroom. Most of my encounters with them were in the mornings while we were getting ready in the shared bathroom. I was in awe of them, but at the same time, they scared me. I didn't know how to converse with them. I was afraid I would come off as the inexperienced yokel that I was.

I graduated from college at the age of twenty-one, and I took a job as an art teacher in Mountain Grove, Missouri. The Vietnam War was waging, and as long as I was teaching, I was not subject to the draft. I had an occupational deferment as an educator. Moving to California was not an option. I felt that I needed to stay in the closet in the small rural community where I was teaching, or I may have lost my job.

During the summer following my first year of teaching, I returned to Arkansas State for summer classes, and it was there where I met a drama professor who swept me off my feet. I experienced romance for the first time. Soon after we had met, the professor asked if I would like to go to a gay bar in nearby Memphis. I said, "Oh yeah, let's go to the bar."

I wanted to look good for my first venture into a gay bar. Before leaving for Memphis, I spent a great deal of time selecting an outfit to wear. I decided to wear some tight wheat-colored Levi jeans that were in style at the time. The pants were too tight for me to put my wallet into the back pocket. I decided I would carry it in my hand.

When we arrived at the bar, I took a deep breath before walking through the door. I was green behind the ears when it came to the bar scene, and especially a gay bar. Once inside, I immediately relaxed. For the first time in my life, I was in a room filled with men who were just like me.

I had a great time in the bar. When it came time to leave, I stood up and looked at everything and everyone in sight. I wanted to imprint a vivid mental image to keep forever of my first gay bar visit. The image didn't include my wallet, which was lying on our table. We left. The wallet stayed.

I realized my wallet was missing a couple of hours after we had left Memphis. I didn't have much money in it and no credit cards, but I did worry about losing my driver's license. A couple of days later, my wallet arrived in the mail. A guy sitting at our table noticed it, picked it up, and took the time to mail it to me. It made me think, *Wow, gay guys are really, really, cool, and they are honest.* After that mishap, I bought my first "man purse." It had a strap on it that went across my shoulder. I kept my wallet in the purse, and I never again lost my wallet.

During my first visit to that gay bar in Memphis, I thought, *Finally I'm here, and I'm where I belong,* and I wasn't even in California.

Papers on the Lawn

My father was a news junkie. When I was a kid, one of my jobs was to retrieve the daily papers that were thrown into the yard by the carriers. Every morning I would pick up three papers: the *Arkansas Gazette,* the *Memphis Commercial Appeal,* and the *Paragould Daily Press.* By the time I got home from school, the afternoon edition of the *Memphis Press-Scimitar* would be lying on the sidewalk. Once a week, the *Clay County Democrat* would arrive in the mail.

I began reading the papers at an early age. I rarely had time to read all the papers, but I would scan the major news articles. I would look at all the comics, and I would read "Dear Abby." I particularly enjoyed reading the feature stories. My favorite columnist was Eldon Roark, who wrote for the *Memphis Press-Scimitar*. He wrote human interest stories in his column "Strolling." The stories were about Southern culture.

Often Mr. Roark would include in his column the writings of Mattie Dear. Mattie Dear was an African American folklorist who had been born on a Mississippi plantation in 1884. Her columns were often humorous, but at times they were touching. The photo that accompanied the column showed her to be a beautiful, skinny, elderly woman with her head wrapped in a bandanna. In the picture, she was smoking a pipe. At the end of each story, she signed off with "Be of good cheer, Mattie Dear." That became one of my favorite quotes, and I said it often. Her work exposed me to good storytelling and inspired me to write my own stories.

My small high school did not have journalism classes, and the students did not publish a school newspaper. Despite not having received training in journalism, I was offered the opportunity to write a school news column that appeared weekly in the *Paragould Daily Press*. I titled my column "Dukes Den." The writing bug bit me, and I liked it when my friends would say to me, "Neat column this week. Could you mention me next time?"

While in college, I pursued two fields of study: art and journalism with an emphasis on television and radio. I hoped to combine the two fields and get a job doing graphic design for a television station. I also liked writing scripts for television commercials. After graduating from college, instead, I took a job as a public-school art teacher, and I put writing and journalism on the back burner.

It was forty years following college graduation before I had the opportunity to use my journalism training. I took the position of editor of *iOnArt* magazine, a Northwest Arkansas regional art publication. I signed my "Letter from the Editor" that appeared in the magazine with "Yours in Art." "Be of Good Cheer" had already been taken. Inspiration has no expiration date.

Thank you, Mattie Dear.

From Paul and Paula to Paul McCartney

From the time I bought my first stereo at the age of twelve, music became an important part of my life. The first album I purchased was by Connie Francis, and the first 45 record I bought was "To Know Him Is to Love Him" by the Teddy Bears. I looked forward to Sunday nights when *The Ed Sullivan Show* aired on television. Each week the variety show would introduce the newest popular singer or band, who would then perform live during the broadcast.

When I was old enough to get my driver's license, I drove to concert events to see live music performances. The first concerts I went to were at the *Hornersville Watermelon Festival* in the Missouri Bootheel. The shows took place in the local high school gymnasium, where I saw Paul and Paula, Bobby Vinton, Chuck Berry, and Brian Hyland of "Itsy Bitsy Teenie Weenie Yellow Polka Dot Bikini" fame.

Many concerts followed that featured artists from different musical genres. I saw everyone from Tammy Wynette to Bette Midler to the Who. The best concert that I attended was the Beatles.

In early 1964 the Beatles became international stars. I was a senior in high school that year, contemplating my future and wondering, *Who am I?* The Beatles showed me that it was all right to be different, and to not conform to rigid societal expectations. The band members had long hair; at least, it was considered long at the time. They defied convention through their gender-bending dress and progressive philosophies. The group was influential in advancing the hippie movement of the 60s. I admired the Beatles' "I don't give a damn; I am who I am" attitude.

Before the British invasion, rebellious young men had a hood-like, motorcycle-riding, slicked-back hair persona. Their look was completed with a cigarette dangling from their mouths. They hung out in pool halls, and they were tough guys. That wasn't me. I also didn't fit the flattop, white shirt, squeaky-clean, good boy persona that was prevalent in the 60s.

In the fall of 1964, I started college at Arkansas State University. Occasionally I would spot a Beatlesque-looking guy who had long hair, wore mod clothes, and had on love beads. The hip guys did get stares of disgust from some, but they received stares of admiration from me. I wanted to be like them, and I wanted to be more like the funky, fun British rock stars who were defying mainstream straitlaced ideas.

During my freshman and sophomore years in college at ASU, I begrudgingly took the mandatory Reserve Officers' Training Corps classes. I was far from being the military type, but I had no choice. I certainly didn't want to be a soldier; I wanted to be a counterculturist. I did let my hair grow into a Beatles-style haircut. I mastered the art of tucking my hair up under my uniform hat when I attended the required ROTC military drills. It took some practice and lots of hair spray, but I pulled it off. Underneath my military garb, I was a British rocker hippie at heart.

I bought every Beatles record the minute it was released. I attended concerts in Memphis that featured British rock bands including the Dave Clark Five, Gerry and the Pacemakers, Chad and Jeremy, and Herman's Hermits. I thought seeing British bands would be as close to seeing a Beatle as I would ever get.

In 1966 during the Beatles' final tour, it was announced that they were coming to Memphis. I ordered tickets the first day they were on sale. I was shocked at the price. They were $5.50 each. I had been paying $3.00 to see big-name groups like the Beach Boys. The higher ticket cost didn't deter me. I paid. I wanted to see the Beatles.

The Beatles' final tour was mired in controversy arising from John Lennon's comments that the Beatles were "more popular than Jesus." The band tried to downplay the statement in press conferences and interviews, but there was a lot of opposition to the Fab Four because of the comment. There were staged record-burnings of Beatles' albums, radio boycotts of their songs, and protests outside their concert venues. That made my planned attendance at the concert even more exciting and rebellious.

On August 19, 1966, I stood in line outside the Memphis Coliseum while I waited to get inside and take my seat. The line was long, the wait even longer, but no one cared. I entered and took my seat. I was directly behind the stage on the first mezzanine that faced the back of the stage. It was a great seat because the Beatles turned around and faced those who were sitting there almost as often as they faced the other direction.

I'm not sure if I heard much of the music over the screams of the thousands of fans. I didn't care. I was in the same room with the Beatles. Hundreds of flashbulbs exploded each minute and created an unreal light show. I thought, *It doesn't get any better than this.*

There are places I remember . . .

— From *Rubber Soul* by the Beatles

Don't Look and Watch Your Mouth

By the time I reached college age, I had an extensive bad-word vocabulary. I used it only in certain situations, and just around the guys. Bad language was not used in polite society. It was rarely used in the movies, and actors were never allowed to curse on television shows.

Well into the 80s there was rigid censorship of both television and movies. The Federal Communications Commission was established in 1934, and it became the body that decided what should and should not be seen and heard by television viewing audiences. Insinuating that sex did or could occur was forbidden on television shows, even between married couples. A husband and wife could not be shown lying in the same bed. Ricky Ricardo and Lucille Ball, who were actual husband and wife in real life, could not be shown in bed together on the popular *I Love Lucy* show. The bedroom set in the sitcom contained twin beds.

NBC Today Show anchor Barbara Walters was one of the first TV personalities to say the word *pregnant* while on air. She said the word while showing the latest in maternity wear during the show's fashion spotlight. During the show, Ms. Walters lifted the top of a miniature maternity dress that was on a foot-high mannequin. She wanted to show the maternity skirt underneath and how it fit across the belly of an expectant mom. My father watched the *Today Show* each morning before going to work. I was with him in the living room the morning of the maternity dress reveal. When the segment began, he had me run to the kitchen to get my mother. He didn't want her to miss the shocking segment.

In 1966 the movie *Who's Afraid of Virginia Woolf?* was released. The movie was controversial, and many theaters refused to show it. It was deemed unfit to view because of vulgar words said by the actors. Most theaters near my hometown banned it. My mother and four of her good friends were determined to see it. The ladies piled into my mother's station wagon, and they drove thirty miles to the nearest town where a brave drive-in movie owner dared to screen the movie.

They watched the film while anxiously waiting and hoping to be shocked. Finally, there it was, the line that was the reason for the movie being banned in most cities. Elizabeth Taylor turned to Richard Burton and said, "Goddamn you." In the original stage version, she said "Screw you," but censors nixed that phrase even though *screw, monkey nipples, hump the hostess*, and other off-color phrases were said in the film.

The ladies were mildly shocked, but even more, they were confused by the abstract and wordy script written by playwright Edward Albee. They didn't understand what they saw, but they still had a giggly time. Thereafter when they talked about the movie, one of the ladies would laugh and say, "I think we got screwed."

As Mark Twain once said, "Under certain circumstances, profanity provides a relief denied even to prayer."

Hippie Dreams

Before I started college at Arkansas State University in the fall of 1964, I had not met a real hippie. It was early in the movement, and there was no one in my hometown that came close to being one. I was hoping that perhaps my dorm roommate would be a hippie, gay, or both. He was none of those. He was a straitlaced baseball player. While I was happy to finally meet a couple of gay guys, my dormitory suitemates, they were not hippies.

During the first semester at school, I took a theater course. The class was held in the Fine Arts Building. It was there where I met a woman who I considered to be countercultural, and she was a Beatles fan. That was a big plus in my book. She told me that her name was Mary Full-of-Love, and she invited me to her apartment for a beer. Finally, I had met a hippie.

When I arrived for the visit, I found Mary dressed in her usual black attire. The apartment was dimly lit by a few candles. In one corner of the room, there was a Christmas tree. It was obvious that it had been there for several months. All the needles had fallen off the tree onto a black satin tree skirt. Mary had decorated the tree with photos of fallen soldiers that she had clipped from newspapers. She told me that the decorations were to honor the dead and to protest the Vietnam War.

Mary's darkness frightened me. I thought, "Maybe she's not a hippie. She might be a witch or something." She started coming on to me. That scared me even more. I drank my beer, left, and I never went back.

Eventually, I did meet several self-described hippies who were the opposite of Mary Full-of-Love. They wore colorful clothes, they were joyous, and their main purpose in life was to spread love and peace. Because I had conservative instructors in my journalism classes, and I had to take ROTC, I could not always dress in hippie attire. Regardless of what I had on, I was a colorful, free spirit in my thoughts and attitude.

Many years later, I am still a hippie at heart. I still love the Beatles, I like long hair and bellbottom pants, and I still wear tie-dye. I still have hope, and I still believe, "Love will win."

Big Time in the Big City

I enjoyed the year I spent teaching junior high art in Mountain Grove, Missouri. I made many good friends while living and working there. Although my experiences were good ones, I decided to seek employment elsewhere. One of the main reasons I decided to leave Mountain Grove was my desire to live in a city. I grew up in a town with a population of 650, and I attended college in a town of 30,000. I thought if I lived in an urban environment, I would have more opportunities to advance my art career beyond teaching.

I had friends who were teaching in the House Springs school district on the outskirts of St. Louis. They notified me of an art teaching job that came open at one of the junior high schools in the district. I interviewed and got the job. It was hard saying goodbye to my friends in Mountain Grove, but I was excited to have a new adventure awaiting me in the city.

Before moving to the St. Louis area, I spent the summer of 1969 taking additional courses in art education at Arkansas State. My salary at the new teaching job was going to be $6,600 a year. That was a substantial increase from my yearly salary at Mountain Grove where I earned $5,100 annually. I soon learned that the increase didn't matter that much.

The cost of living in the St. Louis metro area was far higher than what I had previously experienced. While living in Mountain Grove, I had a roommate, and we shared a two-bedroom furnished apartment. We split the monthly rent of $50. In St. Louis, I rented a small studio apartment, and I paid $125 each month. The cost of groceries, eating out, and utilities was also more expensive.

The students at the new junior high were different from the kids I had taught in southern Missouri. Many of the students at my new school had street-smart city ways. Because I grew up in a small town, I better understood the kids in Mountain Grove. It took this Southern boy a while to understand the ways of the folks I considered to be Northerners, but I did eventually get there.

I did take advantage of city living. I enjoyed shopping in urban malls and finding merchandise not available in smaller towns. I discovered ethnic restaurants, and I tried dishes that I didn't know existed. I attended the St. Louis Symphony concerts, and I spent many hours in the city art museum. I attended art gallery openings.

I took night classes in painting at Washington University, one of the nation's best colleges. Attending the classes increased my desire to become a professional fine art painter. I decided to no longer teach and to go back to school. I sent an enrollment application to the Memphis College of Art, and I was accepted. I declared painting as my major.

I am glad that I had the experience of teaching. When I taught, I was asked questions that I hadn't thought to ask myself, and I had to come up with the answers. When I returned to school, I realized that being a teacher had made me a better student, and being a better student made me a better artist.

CHAPTER 6 — MEMPHIS BLUES

Living Large While Living Poor

In 1970 I gave up a teaching position and left St. Louis. I had decided to return to school to further my studies in art and was excited to be accepted at the Memphis College of Art, where I enrolled as a painting major. I wanted to get better with a brush. However, my choice to go back to school left me without steady income.

While attending the art school, I survived on very little money. The tuition at the school was $700 a semester, which was a lot of money at the time. When I had attended Arkansas State University a few years earlier, the cost of a semester was only $140.

My parents helped with the expenses by paying my $60 monthly apartment rent and the utility bills. The apartment was unfurnished. I did have a bedroom suite that my mother had bought for me when I was a child, and I had a black-and-white portable television. I had nothing else to put in my new digs.

My mother gave me several books of S&H Green Stamps, enough to secure a metal bookcase and a rolling baker's cart for the kitchen. I had $100 in cash to furnish the rest of the apartment.

I went to the Royal Discount Furniture Store in downtown Memphis. I thought it would be a good place to shop not only because the prices were good, but because it was there that Elvis had bought the living room suite for his Jungle Room at Graceland. I purchased a $30 plastic studio couch and a $30 dinette set.

After leaving the Royal Discount Furniture Store, I went to Barzizza Brothers, an import store. I bought a director's chair, some decorative dried grass fronds, and a large vase. I then bought curtains at Kent's Dollar Store and returned to my apartment with $2 in my pocket.

My mother faithfully sent me $10 through the mail each week to spend on groceries. I could take that $10 to the Piggly Wiggly grocery store and buy a week's worth of groceries and still have a couple of dollars left to buy a beer or two during a weekend visit to a bar.

I ate lots of beans and rice. I was a vegetarian and often the beans were soy. They provided an excellent source of protein. I would cook a week's worth at a time. I blew the top off my pressure cooker a couple of times. After spending hours cleaning beans off the kitchen ceiling and cabinets, I finally did get the hang of using the cooker.

I had lived in Memphis for more than a year when I met Dick, a man who would become my life partner. He was a working man, and he enjoyed sharing part of his weekly salary with me.

He earned $136.50 a week working as a bookkeeper in an auto parts store. That was a good wage back then. Soon after our initial meeting, he started lavishing me with gifts, including a potted philodendron and a collection of Edgar Cayce books. I felt rather spoiled. Except for weekend visits to a local bar, we spent little money on entertainment. We passed free time hanging with friends, sitting on the Mississippi River levee watching the barges go by, sunning in Overton Park, and exploring the city. We were easily entertained, but we were never bored.

One place in the city that we enjoyed visiting was Beale Street in downtown Memphis. In the early 70s the street was somewhat seedy, and numerous pawnshops were located in the area. We went to the area only during daylight.

There was one major retail establishment on Beale Street, A. Schwab Dry Goods Store, established in 1876. The store's motto was "If you can't find it at A. Schwab, you're probably better off without it!"

The store owners' never removed any of the merchandise from the shelves even if the products were from decades earlier. There were shelves stacked with handwritten sales receipts that had been in the store for decades.

I was intrigued by the store's voodoo items that included magical love potions, powders, and several kinds of blessing candles.

However, I was not convinced that spending my money to buy the "money blessing" candle would increase my income.

During one visit to Beale Street, I spotted a ring that I liked. It was in a pawnshop window. It didn't matter to me that it had a plastic stone and was made from pot metal. I thought it was pretty.

Dick insisted on buying it for me and happily paid the $5, a sum equal to one-half my weekly allowance for food.

I still have the ring. The stone long ago clouded. It probably is now worth less than $5. However, to me it is priceless. It was purchased with love.

In the Arms of the Ghetto

When I enrolled at the Memphis College of Art, the small college did not have on-campus housing. Before the semester began, I drove around Midtown Memphis and searched for apartments. I found a not-so-fancy, affordable-looking apartment complex that was within walking distance to the school. The sign in front of the office stated that a one-bedroom was available for sixty dollars a month. I rang the office doorbell and was promptly greeted by Ms. Butler, the apartment complex manager. The office was not an actual office but Ms. Butler's apartment. It was heavily decorated in a Chinese theme. The room had several ceramic lamps in it that featured Chinese figures posing under red lampshades shaped like pagodas. The landlady's Pekingese dog plopped down next to me on the couch while I signed the rental agreement. If ever a person and pet looked alike, it was Ms. Butler and her dog Chan. I immediately liked my soon-to-be landlady.

After moving in, it wasn't long before I had met several of my neighbors. About half the residents were students at the art school, and like me, they were living on a budget. If any of the student residents were low on funds, we fed each other. We had potlucks; anyone who could contribute a dish did so. The potlucks seemed like royal feasts because we had such a wide variety of foods from which to choose.

Several of the tenants who were fellow art students became my close friends. We hung out with each other, ate, drank, and smoked together. It was the 70s. We encouraged each other in our desire to make art.

I could walk to school in less than ten minutes via a large concrete drainage ditch that ran underneath busy Poplar Avenue. The deep ditch was about ten feet wide and lined with huge trees covered in ancient wisteria vines. When the vines were in bloom, the air was filled with a heavy sweet scent. My walk ended in Overton Park. The school, Brooks Museum of Art, the city zoo, and acres of old-growth forest were located within the 342-acre park. At night, raccoons from the park would use the drainage ditch as a pathway to our apartments, and they would raid the garbage cans that were by our rear door stoops. From my apartment, I could hear the screams of peacocks and the occasional roar of lions coming from the zoo.

Our back door stoops were located in the alley between the buildings. They were popular places to sit, drink beer, and gossip. There was always something to discuss, and we spent a lot of time guessing who was sleeping with whom and how many weeks the tryst would last. A young good-looking musician named Dewie and his girlfriend lived across the alley from me. I could watch them coming and going from my kitchen window. They wore glam rock attire, and they made a striking presence as a couple.

That is until the day they had a big brouhaha and I heard them yelling. Dewie's girlfriend was sprawled out in the alley, mascara-stained tears running down her cheeks while Dewie threw her belongings from their stoop. Feather boas and sequined dresses littered the pavement. Dewie threw his girlfriend's shoes at her one at a time while she lay there. She had a lot of shoes. My neighbors and I spent several days speculating about what could have caused the breakup. No one was brave enough to ask Dewie. There may still have been some shoes left for him to throw.

One evening I heard the sound of gunshots from a nearby apartment. Soon the police showed up, and rotating blue lights illuminated the complex. During the domestic squabble, the woman who had fired the gun had missed her mark, her live-in boyfriend. The bullet had pierced a plaster wall and gone into the adjacent apartment. No charges were filed, but Ms. Butler did request that the couple vacate the premises.

Across the street from the apartments, there was a complex that at one time had been the Jewish Community Center. Even though a new center had opened in East Memphis, the large swimming pool at the abandoned center was still filled with water and in operation. After a few beers, a few of my guy friends and I would scale the chain-link fence and go for a nighttime skinny dip. The water was nice and cool, and it was a refreshing way to cool off during hot summer nights in steamy Memphis.

I had some of the best times of my life while living in the Ghetto Arms even though financially it was one of the leanest of times. My life was rich with experiences and, more importantly, rich with friendships.

It truly was the best of times.

Picnicking and Riding a Wooden Zebra

One of the highlights of summertime during my childhood was day trips with my family to the zoo in Memphis. Because my mother worked six days a week in her beauty shop, our zoo excursions were always on a Sunday. The night before the trip, my mother would prepare a picnic lunch to take with us. We would leave for Memphis early the next morning with the family sedan filled to capacity with my parents, two sisters, my grandmother, and me. The trunk was filled with ice chests, paper plates, and food. My grandmother, whom we called Mom, would bring a bag of fried peach pies. She kept them with her in the back seat in case the grandkids needed a snack during the drive.

Once we arrived at Overton Park, the location of the zoo, we would find a picnic table, and my mother and grandmother would begin putting the food out. Taking food from home for a picnic was an inexpensive way for my parents to feed us. It was also fun. My family didn't grill outdoors at home, and it was a rare treat for us to eat outside. While the table was being set, my younger sister and I would swing at a nearby playground. We would race back to the picnic table when my father yelled, "Come and get it." As much as I enjoyed eating in the park, I wanted everyone to eat fast. While gobbling down my food, I could hear the sounds coming from the zoo. I was anxious to visit with the animals.

I became excited when we approached the entrance to the zoo. Each side of the entry gate was flanked with ornate concrete lion statues. Once inside, we followed our usual path to the right and viewed the polar, grizzly, and black bears. I kept a map of the zoo layout with me, and I played tour guide to make certain we didn't miss a thing. I wanted to see every animal, but I was partial to the primates. I would reluctantly leave the primate house when the rest of the family was ready to move on. My favorite exhibition was "Monkey Island," a large manmade hill surrounded by a moat. Dozens of monkeys roamed freely on the island, playing and interacting with each other. Monkey Island was a good spot for the family to take a break, eat a pineapple whip ice cream cone, drink a coke, and sit a spell while watching the monkeys.

Before leaving the zoo, my parents would let my sisters and me enjoy the kiddie rides. I especially liked riding the miniature train and the carousel. I would hurry onto the carrousel and hop astride the wooden zebra, my favorite animal on the ride. If I wasn't the first to get to the zebra, the wooden lion was my second choice.

Before leaving the zoo, we would go through the gift shop. My sisters and I were each allowed to pick out one souvenir. During one trip, I chose a small plastic crocodile that was a pencil holder. The pencil that slid into the croc had a man's head on it that stuck out of the critter's mouth. I never used the pencil. I didn't want to sharpen it and whittle it away. It was a treasured souvenir.

Years later I enrolled in the Memphis College of Art. The college was in Overton Park adjacent to the zoo. Because the college and the zoo were both city-owned, students had free access to the zoo. I went often. It was an ideal place to sketch. Fellow students and I would take our lunch to the zoo and eat while watching the animals, and I got to know many of them as individual beings. I fell in love with a newborn orangutan, and I enjoyed watching him grow into a feisty young adult. In cold weather, I would spend time in the building that housed a large aviary. I'd sit on a bench and draw the birds while enjoying warm, tropical-like temperatures.

During the time I lived in Memphis, my family would still come to the city to visit the zoo, and I would serve as the host for the outing. The last summer that I lived in Memphis was the last time my grandmother was able to go to the zoo. She was feeble at the time and slow to move. I was surprised but pleased when she consented to being pushed around in a rented wheelchair. She would never have asked for help, but I think she was relieved when help was offered. She knew if I pushed her, she wouldn't slow everyone down.

That trip to the zoo, her last, and my last while living in Memphis, may have been the best zoo visit I had experienced. While pushing my grandmother around in the wheelchair, I enjoyed viewing the animals and sharing memories with her of past zoo trips. We looked at everything together, two generations apart, and we shared our love for all creatures while sharing our love for each other.

Odd Couple

After I enrolled at the Memphis College of Art to further my studies as a fine art painter, I felt that I no longer had to hide who I was. I no longer had to worry about students, their parents, school administrators, or anyone else knowing that I was gay. Art students were expected to be free spirits. I grew my hair long, pierced my ear, and wore paint-splattered jeans and T-shirts. The only time I spiffed up was to go dancing at one of the city's gay bars.

I had been living in Memphis for a year when I met Dick. A mutual friend suggested that he go to the bar where I hung out Saturday nights to check me out. Our mutual friend thought that I would be Dick's type. I was. There was one problem. He was not my type.

Dick was too corporate in appearance for my taste. He was a short-haired, squeaky-clean looking guy, and he was a bookkeeper for an auto parts store. My disinterest in him did not stop his pursuit of me. He wined and dined me and gave me gifts. After I mentioned that I was interested in the American clairvoyant Edgar Casey, Dick showed up at my door with a stack of books that Casey had written. When he learned that I liked plants, he brought me a philodendron. When I complained about being cold, he repaired the faulty wall heater in my apartment.

I began to fall for him, but there was still hesitation on my part. I had been warned about his reputation of "love 'em and leave 'em." I wasn't going to let that happen. I wanted to be sure of his intentions before I committed to entering into a relationship with him.

As best he could, Dick tried to conform to my way of life. He decided to let his hair grow and to grow a mustache. Before long, the white-walls over his ears began to disappear and dark fuzz appeared above his upper lip. I complimented him on his new look.

When his hair touched his ears, he was called into the office where he worked. He was advised to get a haircut. The parts store's policy handbook stated that hair touching the ears was against company policy. He was told that if he didn't get a haircut, he should look elsewhere for work. Dick said, "No, I'm not getting a haircut. You will just have to fire me." They did. Dick had the store manager write on the termination slip that the reason for letting him go was because his hair was too long.

Dick applied for and was approved to receive unemployment compensation. At the time, his former company would cash checks for anyone who walked into the business. When Dick's unemployment checks arrived in the mail, he would take them to his former place of employment, walk up to the counter with his ever-growing hair, and cash the checks.

When the unemployment checks stopped, Dick was hired to work in maintenance at Memphis State University. At the new job, he was not restricted when it came to dress styles or length of his hair. He felt free.

I decided that anyone who would lose their job to please me had good and honorable intentions. I committed to sharing my life with him. Dick continued to go out of his way to please me. He took Transcendental Meditation and Silva courses with me. When I declared that I would no longer eat meat, he too became a vegetarian.

In many respects, we are still an "odd couple." We do not always think alike. While he is very pragmatic and practical, I am often spontaneous and impractical. We complete each other. We talk to each other, and more importantly, we listen to each other. We have learned that the key to being together and staying together for the long run is to let each be their own person. For several decades that has worked for us.

Water and oil do not mix, but oil and vinegar do. It's an unlikely mixture, but it makes a tasty dressing. It's all about balance.

Standing Proud

I was a sensitive child, and I admit that I was a mama's boy. My mother loved and protected me. She loved me unconditionally, encouraged me to be myself, and did not try to change me.

When my sister received an early Christmas present of tiny twin baby dolls from our fraternal grandmother, I was sad because I wanted the same dolls. The present I received from my grandmother was a picture book about Christ's twelve apostles. Out of politeness, I had to thank her and to pretend I liked the book. My mother could see that I was disappointed, and she saw nothing wrong with a boy receiving a doll as a gift. A week later on Christmas morning, my mother saw to it that Santa had left twin baby dolls under the tree for me.

My father didn't say much one way or the other. He never pushed me to hunt, play sports, or participate in activities expected of the male gender. Both parents encouraged me to pursue activities that made me happy, and that included my interests in the visual arts and dancing. My parents did expect me to attend college. My choice of a major was never discussed or challenged. I was encouraged to choose my own path.

In the small Arkansas Delta town where I grew up, and like many towns throughout the South, some differences were tolerated if not celebrated, and that included being gay. It has been said that Southerners are proud of eccentric local characters and colorful relatives. Instead of hiding them away, they proudly sit them on their front porches for all to see. In our town, there were a few grown men who had never married. They were "bachelor men," and that description probably meant they were gay. One of the town's bachelor men was a friend of my parents, and he was the first one called on if they needed an odd job done around the house.

After I had left home, I would return for weekend visits, and I often had my boyfriend of the moment with me. The young men were always welcomed by my parents. If the boyfriend relationship lasted a while, then the young man became "Zeek's friend," and that's how he was introduced.

After I met Dick, I began taking him home with me. He soon became a part of my family. He was the only partner of mine that my nieces and nephews knew, and he became another uncle to them. If I planned to visit my parents, they expected Dick to be with me. He spent most holidays with my family, and my father was crazy about him. They spent many an afternoon together sitting in the backyard under a shade tree.

My parents loved me and taught me to love myself. They were proud of me, and they gave me the gift of "pride."

Dancing in the Dark

It was socially acceptable in the 70s for two women to dance together. They danced together in nightclubs, at street fairs, and even on telecasts of the popular *American Bandstand* show.

The same was not true for two men. It was so taboo that when I lived in Memphis in the 70s, it was actually illegal for two men to dance together. I don't know if it was a city law or a state law, but it was one that was enforced in Memphis. Arrests did take place. Four male couples were arrested for dancing together at a bar called the Closet. The arrests were reported in the *Memphis Commercial Appeal.*

My partner Dick and I enjoyed dancing. On weekends we went to a bar called the Psych-Out on North Cleveland in Memphis. The bar closed at midnight on Saturday. However, no one left the bar at closing time. The tables were cleared from the center of the floor, doors were locked, and we would have a "private dance party." The cops were aware of what was happening inside the bar and would periodically show up.

The bar owner kept a lookout on duty, and if the cops pulled into the bar's parking lot, lights inside the bar would flicker on and off. Everyone would quit dancing. By the time the cops were let in, we were all seated. After the cops left, everyone once again danced.

The popular 70s song "American Pie" was a favorite of the bar patrons. When that song played, everyone would stand together, place arms over shoulders, and form a huge circle. The circle, with up to forty guys in the formation, would then go round and round in the bar. We whirled around the room for the entire length of the eight-minute song, locked together and having a great time. We were young and reckless, and enjoying an activity that was perhaps made more exciting because it was illegal. We were brothers, arm in arm, sharing a secret that involved more than dancing.

We danced all night long. At dawn we left the bar, and several of us would go to the Ohman Inn, a diner on Union Ave, where we ate breakfast and made plans to do it all again the following weekend.

While the sergeants played a marching tune

We all got up to dance

— "American Pie" by Don McLean

Wet and Wild

In the early 70s while a student at the Memphis College of Art, I attended a lecture by Jimmy Driftwood. He was a famed folk singer and folk historian who had written thousands of folk songs. He was most famous for his songs "The Battle of New Orleans" and "Tennessee Stud." He lived in Timbo, Arkansas, near Mountain View. Mountain View hosted a yearly folk festival each April. During his lectures, Mr. Driftwood invited college students to attend the festival.

Dick, two fellow art students—Linda and David—and I thought it would be fun to attend the folk festival. We decided the most cost-effective way to make the trip was to camp out. Dick had an army surplus canvas tent that was large enough to accommodate the four of us. Linda and David had never camped, and they were excited about experiencing a new adventure. I planned to take my toy poodle, Chelsea, with us.

We prepared picnic food to avoid the expense of eating out. Dick owned a Coleman camping stove that we would use for cooking. The night before our trip, we loaded everything except the food into the pink 1959 Chevy Impala. The car was loaned to me by my father, and it was the same car in which I had learned to drive many years earlier.

The next morning when we were to leave Memphis, I could not find the car keys. Alas, the trip was off. Disappointed, I started unpacking. I had boiled a dozen eggs that I had wrapped in tin foil. When I unwrapped them, my keys were with the eggs. The trip was on once again.

Three hours later we were in the Ozark town of Mountain View. It was like stepping back in time. On the quaint square, there was music everywhere. There were fiddlers, banjo players, singers, and cloggers. Authentic hill music filled the air.

Along with hundreds of folk devotees, we spent a wonderful afternoon and evening enjoying the festival. Earlier that day, we had pitched our tent in a camping area at Sylamore Creek, five miles from town. We were joined by dozens of other campers. During the night while we were sleeping, the skies opened and heavy rains came. The small meandering creek in the park became a roaring river. The campground quickly flooded. Cars and tents were washed down the swollen creek. Fortunately, no lives were lost.

We had pitched our tent a little ways from the creek. Although we were spared the worst effects of the flood, we did get some water in our tent. The weather front that brought in the massive rains that April night also ushered in unseasonably cold temperatures. The temps fell into the upper 30s. A brisk breeze created an even lower wind chill temperature. We abandoned the tent and took refuge in the car. After the rain stopped and daylight came, we loaded up our soggy belongings and moved into town.

We found a spot in downtown Mountain View behind a Laundromat filled with folks washing their wet, muddy clothes. The dryers were constantly in motion. We pitched our tent near the dryer vents at the rear of the building. Hot air blew in through the tent's front door. We were toasty warm. We celebrated our survival with a breakfast of hot oatmeal. Every now and then, we ventured into the Laundromat to watch naked people barely covered by towels wash and dry their clothes.

Through it all, the music never stopped.

Performance Anxiety

When I was in high school, I had roles in both the junior and senior class plays. The plays were comedies that had been written for high school productions and typical of school plays produced during the 60s. They were not performed beyond that venue. The small-town school that I attended did not have a drama or a music department. The teacher who was that year's class sponsor was the director of each class's annual theatrical production. My role as Luigi Lanconi during my senior year allowed me to ham it up while using a far from perfect Italian accent. I enjoyed the applause, and I was bitten by the acting bug.

During my first semester in college at Arkansas State University, I took an acting course. My drama teacher, an imposing and handsome man, scared me. I was intimidated by his gaze and his booming voice. His diction was flawless. He was nothing like the soft-spoken class sponsor who had directed me in the high school plays. I didn't dare try out for the productions that he was directing, and I couldn't wait for the semester to end. I thought, *I don't think I'm meant to be on stage.* I took no more drama courses after that first semester.

A few years later I did work in the theater, but it was a paid backstage job. I was hired to run props one summer for the Memphis Summer Opera Lyric Theater. The theater produced two musicals that summer: *The Desert Song* and *Fiddler on the Roof.* The director of *The Desert Song* was a nice, gentle person. The director of *Fiddler* was stern. He yelled at the actors, and he made some of them cry. I tiptoed around him. The experience made me glad once again that I had not pursued acting.

I did get back on stage again but not as an actor. While attending the Memphis College of Art, I received a full scholarship to study with the Ballet South dance school, and I was asked to join the school's company. The ballet company was semi-professional. I occasionally received a small salary, but it was not enough to live on. After I finished my studies at the art school, I had to give up dancing with the company and concentrate on making a living.

I did have another dancing gig while living in Memphis. For a short time, I worked as a go-go boy at a bar in a seedy section of Memphis. The applause was good, and the tips were even better. I made more money performing in that bar than at any other time I had been on stage.

Applause is the sound of appreciation from a collective body for a job well done. Whether performing in a bar or on a stage, I did like hearing it.

Oh, Where Did That Twenty-Eight-Inch Waist Go?

While in art school in Memphis, I danced with Ballet South. George Latimer had come from the San Francisco Ballet to work with the Memphis Civic Ballet in the mid-60s. He was disappointed when he arrived to find that the company was segregated. George left the Civic Company and formed Ballet South and became its artistic director. He recruited African Americans to be in the company. R&B singer Isaac Hayes was on the company's board of directors. The dance company was the first to be integrated in Memphis. I was proud to be a member of Ballet South.

Dance required a great deal of time. I had classes four nights a week, company class on Saturday, and rehearsals on Sunday. It was very rewarding and downright fun. Unlike the city's more traditional Civic Ballet company, we did traditional ballets *and* contemporary pieces. We would dance to Memphis music that included songs by Isaac Hayes and Elvis.

Ballet South was a semi-pro company. I would receive an occasional check, but the pay was not steady. I realized that I couldn't depend on dance for my livelihood. Several of the folks I danced with did go on to larger professional companies such as the Atlanta Ballet and the Dance Theater of Harlem. That wasn't in the cards for me. My professional path led me elsewhere.

I am thankful that I had the experience, and I loved every minute of it, with the exception of having to occasionally wear white tights. Physically, I was in my prime. I still enjoy dancing. As an older person, my plié is still spot on, but my relevé is not so good. What goes up must come down, but what goes down isn't always easy to get up.

Summer Jobs

After completing my first year of art school in Memphis, I found summer employment as a flower vendor working for a very laid-back hippie company. I sold carnations on a street corner in Midtown. Each morning I went to the city's market warehouse district where I boarded a VW bus along with the other flower vendors. We were dropped off with buckets filled with carnations in various locations around town.

I had a great spot on the corner of Parkway across from Overton Park. For each bucket full of carnations that I sold, I received seven dollars. There were about thirty flowers in each bucket, and they sold for a buck each. I stood on the same corner every day for eight hours, and I was picked up at the end of the day by the VW bus. There was a gas station on my corner, and the attendants were kind enough to let me use the restroom. However, each time I needed to go, I had to haul all of the heavy, water-filled buckets into the restroom with me. I couldn't leave them on the corner unattended.

My second summer in Memphis, I worked as a prop person for the Memphis Summer Opera Lyric Theater at Memphis State. One of the shows that ran that summer was *The Desert Song*, a fun and campy musical that was set in the Sahara Desert.

The director decided that he wanted to have a live donkey in the show. The prop crew went to a farm in nearby Covington, Tennessee, to secure a donkey. Ironically, the guy that owned the donkey farm was named Mr. Burros. We loaded the donkey into our trailer to take him to Memphis State for his stage debut. When we arrived, it was decided that I should ride the donkey into the building. All went fine until I rode the beast into the elevator, where he started bucking for all that he was worth. I hung on for dear life, two floors up and two floors down. We promptly reloaded him into the trailer and took him back to Mr. Burros. The donkey was not in the show. There were no pictures of the incident, but there was a story about it in the *Memphis Commercial Appeal*.

In *Desert Song*, the leading man played a Frenchman who also had a secret identity as an Arab sheik, the Red Shadow. Not only was I the prop guy, I was also the dresser for the lead. He had many fast costume changes from Frenchman to sheik. I had a hell of a time getting his very tight knee-high boots off him during the changes. I cussed a blue streak while trying to remove them. During the closing night cast party, I learned that the leading man in real life was a Church of Christ preacher. I think that because he valued my assistance, he never said a word about my cussing. However, I'm sure that I was the subject of many of his prayers.

Pierced

I was back home at my parent's house for spring break from the Memphis College of Art when I noticed the strange looking gold hoops lying on the sink in the bathroom. They were perfectly round, about the size of a nickel, with an opening that had a gold ball on one end and a very sharp point on the other. Next to the hoops was an instruction pamphlet that read, "Place the earrings on the lobe, leave in place, and the earrings will self-pierce in a matter of weeks." I realized they belonged to my mother, who was going to use the devices to get something she had wanted for a long time—pierced ears.

I laid the hoops back down on the sink, walked into the kitchen, poured myself a cup of coffee, and laced it with a shot of my daddy's Old Crow whiskey. My parents were away for the day visiting my aunt Verlene. Because I had the house to myself, I thought it would be safe to have a little morning cocktail. I figured that my daddy wouldn't miss one shot of whiskey from the bottle that he kept hidden under the sink.

He had bottles hidden here and there—in his sock drawer, in the shed out back, under the seat of his old truck, and several other places. He hid the bottles thinking my mother wouldn't know just how much he drank. She knew. If I was careful to get a little bit of whiskey from different bottles, he would never know that I had borrowed from his stash.

As I sat there drinking the mixture of coffee and Old Crow, I thought about how happy I was to be enrolled in art school, a world so vastly different from the little Delta town in Northeast Arkansas where I had grown up, and where I had picked cotton each fall. Even though I felt at home in the little town of 650 people, I had never felt more comfortable than I did when I was with my fellow art students, a bohemian bunch who seemed to have a view of the world so unlike the Delta folks with whom I had grown up. I had found my tribe.

There were a couple of guys at school, sophisticated boys from up north, who had pierced ears. I admired their roguish fashion statement, but I did wonder whether they were ever harassed—called sissy boys, or worse—when they were off-campus. It was a time long before it was socially acceptable for a man to wear an earring.

I sat there at the kitchen table, my fingers tracing the outline of the flowers on the plastic tablecloth and wondered how I would look with a pierced ear. Would I be brave like those boys from up north and wear an earring in public?

I went to my daddy's sock drawer, found another bottle, and added a little more Old Crow to my coffee before returning to the bathroom. I placed one of the sharp-pointed earrings on my left lobe and lightly pressed. It hurt a little but not enough to make me want to remove it. Even in the dimly lit bathroom illuminated by a single light bulb hanging about halfway down from the thirteen-foot ceiling, I could see that my earlobe was turning red. However, as I peered into the medicine cabinet mirror, I thought I looked dashing and debonair, like a forward thinker and one not restricted by the norms of society. I looked cool.

My ear was smarting, but I saw no blood. I thought, *Oh, what the hell, it couldn't hurt much more than it does right now.* I reached up with my right hand and pushed the pointed end of the earring on through my lobe and out the other side. I cussed and fell to my knees in pain. Back on my feet again and peering into the mirror, I said out loud, "Well, I did it and I'm glad as hell." I was thinking, *Wowee, I can't wait to get back to school to show off this shiny gold hoop to my friends.* There was just one problem. In a few hours, my parents would return home, and I was worried about how they would react to my pierced ear. My earlobe had swollen to twice its normal size. I needed more whiskey.

Seventeen years earlier, I had made the decision to become an artist. My parents were accepting of whatever I did—not always understanding but accepting—and that included my desire to have a career in the arts. They at times would ask, "Now how do you make money doing that?"

Besides my career choice, they accepted without question or criticism other things that I'd done during my first year while in art school, like letting my hair grow down past my shoulders, wearing raggedy bell-bottoms, wearing strange sandals imported from India, and refusing to eat meat. Neither did they understand my practice of Transcendental Meditation. After all, they were Methodists.

While I sat at the kitchen table on that day during my spring break, I kept thinking that I may have gone a little too far with the ear piercing. Having a son wear an earring might be too much for them.

I spent a long afternoon drinking more spiked coffee, being careful to not take too much whiskey from any one bottle. I thought the whiskey would calm my nerves while the coffee would keep me somewhat sober.

Every so often I went into the bathroom to look at myself in the mirror and admire my new look. At the same time, I was regretting my action. I doused my earlobe with rubbing alcohol, cussed some more at the stinging it caused, and waited nervously for my parents to return. Time seemed to crawl, and I got more anxious. My ear continued to throb.

It was going on 4 p.m. when I heard a car drive up. There was no mistaking the smooth purr from the V8 motor of my mother's Chrysler station wagon. My parents were home. When they got out of the car, I peeked at them through the gingham curtains hanging above the kitchen sink. They were smiling and they looked happy. That seemed like a good sign.

With my courage bolstered by the Old Crow, I bravely awaited my fate as they came into the house. However, when the doorknob turned, I didn't feel so brave. I made small talk and asked about their visit while keeping my head turned at just the right angle so there would be no glint of gold. While my mother was setting her purse down on the table, she saw it. She tilted her head slightly to the side and gave it a little shake like people do when they see something not quite right. She straightened her head and then, to my surprise, all she said was, "How come you only pierced one ear?"

My father didn't say a word. His silence continued for the next few days. On the last day of my spring break, my father and I were sitting in lawn chairs in the backyard under a mimosa tree. It was not that hot, but I could feel sweat running down my spine from the nape of my neck all the way down to my waistband and dampening my bell-bottoms. I looked over at my father, who was as cool as a cucumber.

He was wearing a very dressy yellow straw hat with a green hatband. When not in the house he always had on a hat. He was also wearing an orange-flowered Hawaiian shirt. My father was a very large man, and he seemed even larger when wearing wildly colored shirts, but then, that was the only thing I can remember him ever doing that was outside of what I considered to be his safe zone. That day, he looked bigger than ever.

I sat there in that green metal chair, getting hotter and more nervous by the minute. I was going back to Memphis that afternoon, and I could not leave without knowing what my father was thinking and feeling. Was he disappointed in me? Was he ashamed of me? He shifted a little in his chair, retrieved a bottle from his back pocket, and took a swig of Old Crow.

I couldn't stand it any longer. "Daddy, did you notice that I pierced my ear?"

He looked me straight in the eye, and said, "Yes, I saw the earring. It's your damn ear. You can do with it whatever you want to do." He continued, "There is a big world out there that I don't understand. You do. You need to do and should do whatever it takes to make you happy."

I knew then that everything was going to be all right.

Walking in Memphis, but Not Alone

The Memphis College of Art was in a part of the city known as Midtown. I rented an apartment near Overton Park where the school was located, and I was within walking distance to the campus. A few blocks to the south and also within walking distance was Overton Square, an entertainment district with trendy restaurants, bars, and galleries. I could walk to the grocery store and the Laundromat as well.

Midtown was in an older part of the city and only minutes away from downtown and the Mississippi River. The area was frequented by tourists who could be seen strolling the streets at all times of the day and night. Directly across the street from my apartment there was a dairy distribution center and the abandoned Jewish Community Center. A few blocks to the west was a neighborhood filled with shotgun-style homes. The small houses were occupied by the disadvantaged poor. In contrast, just a few blocks to the north were well-maintained, older, large mansions that sat on beautifully landscaped lawns.

I loved my neighborhood. Most of the time I was able to leave my 1959 Chevy Impala parked behind my apartment and go places on foot. I could walk to the 7-Eleven, Purdy's Drug Store, and Burkle's Bakery. I often walked home late at night after working on projects at school, and many times I did the walk while alone. All that changed when several young men reported being raped while walking at night in Midtown. Local newspapers dubbed the rapist "The Midtown Molester."

I was afraid. I thought, *This must be how women feel with the constant threat of being assaulted.* It made me sad that anyone, man or woman, should have to walk in fear. My male friends and I became very cautious and only ventured out in pairs or groups while the Midtown Molester was on the prowl.

All this happened around the time I met Dick. He was very protective of me, and he worried about my safety. He made an effort to spend more time with me. One evening, several weeks after the first reported attack by the rapist, Dick and I were in my apartment watching the movie *Patton* on my television when we heard the loud whirling blades of a helicopter. It was flying low and close to the top of the apartment building. Searchlights flooded the living room windows. The invasive noise and the flashing lights continued for several minutes.

Earlier that evening the molester had attacked a young man in the park, blindfolded and bound him, put him in the trunk of his car, and drove him to an apartment where he was raped. The young man was a sailor from the nearby Millington Naval Base located north of the city. Despite the terrifying situation, the victim kept his wits, and he was able to count and estimate the distance the vehicle traveled between the site of the abduction and the molester's apartment. The young sailor also memorized the direction the car had turned at each intersection.

Following the assault, the rapist put the victim back into his car trunk, took him somewhere, and dumped him. The sailor contacted the police, and they returned to the site of the abduction with him. By counting and remembering each turn the rapist had made while the sailor was in the trunk, he retraced the drive and led the authorities to the abductor's apartment. The helicopter that had flown over my apartment complex was a lookout in case the rapist tried to escape on foot.

Later that night and after the helicopter had stopped circling, it was reported on the news that the authorities had arrested the Midtown Molester. He had been living in a nearby garage apartment, and he, too, had been watching *Patton* when the police entered his apartment. He was identified as a teacher at a local boys' school. The Midtown Molester was tried and sentenced to prison.

Following the arrest, all the guys in my apartment complex breathed a sigh of relief. We felt safer—not safe, but safer. I don't live in fear, but since that time, I have been cautious. I often look over my shoulder, especially when I'm walking in the dark.

Where's the Beef

While attending the Memphis College of Art in the early 70s, I was eager to explore alternative religions, philosophies, and lifestyles. I had been raised Methodist in a small town with a population of 650 people. Besides the Methodist church, the town was home to four Baptist churches and one Church of Christ. In that setting, I think that Methodism may well have been considered an alternative religion. While the other churches practiced immersion, we were the only congregation in town that considered sprinkling to be an acceptable form of baptism.

While at art school, I became interested in Eastern Philosophy. Some of my "with it" student friends recommended that I read the *Autobiography of a Yogi*. After reading and re-reading the book written by Paramahansa Yogananda, I was eager to give meditation a try.

Two friends of mine were certified instructors in Transcendental Meditation, a movement started by India native Maharishi Mahesh Yogi. Members of the musical group the Beatles were practicing TM. I was a huge Beatles fan, and that was all the endorsement I needed.

I had not known Dick for very long, but because I was eager to give TM a try, he decided to do the same. We were each given a mantra and began practicing meditation. As part of my spiritual journey, I decided to stop eating meat, and Dick went along with that decision. I wondered how my family would react to my new diet.

My mother was a great cook. Cooking was her way of creating and serving others. When I told her I was a vegetarian, she eagerly began collecting veggie recipes, and she created meatless dishes to serve to me. She seemed to enjoy the challenge. My father never understood but never criticized. I'm not sure that my younger sister ever got it. Shortly after Dick and I stopped eating meat, we were at her house for lunch. She served pork and beans. We said, "We can't eat that." She looked puzzled and asked, "Can't you just eat around the pork?"

Eating out became a challenge. At times, we ordered cheeseburgers and told the server to "hold the beef." I was often asked, "What do you eat?" and I would reply, "Everything that you eat except for meat." Unless I was eating a meal with someone, I didn't let anyone know that I was a vegetarian. It was easier than explaining the "why" and the "what," being judged, and many times being considered weird.

It was easier to eat at home. I cooked lots of rice and beans and kept a copy of the book *Diet for a Small Planet* on a counter in the kitchen. I followed the book's nutritional plan that showed which foods to combine to create complete proteins.

One day Dick came home very excited and said, "I want to take you out to eat at this new place. You will not believe it."

The place was the newly opened Ranch House Café on Highland Avenue near Memphis State University. Upon entering, I couldn't believe what I was seeing: yards and yards of vegetables arranged for self-serve. It was the first salad bar in the Mid-South.

Many years later, I'm still a vegetarian, and I still get excited when I see a good salad bar.

A Chance to Be Saved

In the early 70s I taught junior high art in St. Louis. The people I worked with became my running buddies. One of my friends, Evelyn, was a music teacher. Due to her position, she scored two free season tickets to the St. Louis Symphony. I often went with her. I was appreciative of her generosity because as a poorly paid teacher, I could never have afforded to attend the symphony. However, there was a torturous trade-off. Evelyn had become involved in a charismatic Catholic-based faith healing movement. I had to feign interest and attend the healing sessions with her. I was not going to give up a free seat at the symphony, even if I had to pretend to be interested in a religious activity that was somewhat strange to me.

The healing sessions would begin with the testimonies of believers who had been healed. There were always many nuns in attendance. I was a skeptic who was raised a Methodist. The teachings of the church of my childhood didn't include the belief in contemporary faith healing. We were prepared to "take what is" and limp all the way to the grave.

Despite being somewhat bored during the testimonies, I was fully awake when the star of the show took over. He was a priest, Father McNut, and the leader of the local movement. He was tall, dark, and handsome. He resembled a young Charlton Heston, and he was very charismatic. I think the combination of looks and charm gave him the edge to be persuasive. It didn't work on me. However, I kept going in order to keep in Evelyn's good graces. I wanted to keep my seat at the symphony.

When I quit my job and moved to Tennessee, I enrolled in the Memphis College of Art and immediately took up a hippie persona, vowing to never again wear a necktie. I let my hair grow long. I wore love beads and ragged bell-bottoms. I was free.

I had been living in Memphis for about a year when I received a call from Evelyn. She asked me to accompany her to a Kathryn Kuhlman event that was to take place in Memphis. Miss Kuhlman was a flamboyant and prominent faith healer with a huge following. Evelyn, Father McNut, and his followers had become groupies of the popular evangelist. I said, "Oh, what the heck, sure I'll go." Then I forgot all about it.

A couple of months later, Evelyn called early one Sunday morning to tell me that the day had arrived. She had saved me a seat to see Miss Kuhlman at the Assembly of God Church. It was a very large church, the one that Elvis attended when he was in town. When the phone rang that morning, I had just walked in the door from being out all night dancing, and I have to admit, I was still tripping on LSD. No excuse—except that it was the 70s.

I was wearing a black see-through shirt, black-and-white striped bell-bottoms, and platform shoes with stars painted on them ala Joe Cocker. I looked down at my clothes and thought, "Hey, these are good enough."

I jumped into my car and drove to the church. Evelyn had ridden to Memphis from St. Louis with a busload of faithful followers of the St. Louis charismatic Catholic movement. The group included a large number of nuns. I found my seat in the church and sat with Evelyn and the sisters.

Fortunately, the row in front of me was also occupied by nuns. If I had sat behind one of the many women that were there with high hair, my view of the stage would have been blocked.

We were there early that morning in order to get a seat. We had to sit through the entire morning service while we waited for Miss Kuhlman's afternoon performance. For lunch, we shared peanut butter and jelly sandwiches that Evelyn and the nuns had brought with them on the bus. By this time, I was really starting to suffer and was wondering if Miss Kuhlman might be able to heal a drug crash.

At 1 p.m., Kathryn Kuhlman took to the stage wearing a very gauzy white dress and gold lamé high heels. She was slender with bright red hair, and she was very theatrical. Shortly after she took the stage, folks lined up one by one to be healed.

Miss Kuhlman would describe the person's ailments to the audience and touch the afflicted on both sides of the neck. They would immediately fall backward into the hands of her attendants. If the attendants missed, the person would fall to the floor. They arose healed, or so it appeared. Folks were falling all over the place on stage, including some of the nuns from the bus. They fell to the floor like shot penguins.

As bad as I felt, I did find the healing service interesting and entertaining. However, if I had been a praying man, I would have prayed for the service to end. Two hours in, Miss Kuhlman called for all folks who needed to be saved to come down to the altar. I thought, *I have found my avenue of escape!* I got up from my seat and brushed past the many kind churchgoers and the nuns. They were patting me on the back and congratulating me. They thought I was about to be saved. When I got to the end of the aisle, I made a beeline for the door, jumped in my car, and went home. I was far from healed.

I never heard from Evelyn again.

Oceans Away

My family rarely traveled. While I was still living at home, we did venture from Arkansas to Detroit a couple of times to visit relatives. Other than the trips to Michigan, we did not travel any farther than four hours from home. The other family vacations that I remember were to Hot Springs, Arkansas; Mountain View, Arkansas; and Lakeland, Tennessee.

While I enjoyed visiting those places, I really wanted to see the ocean. My parents and my grandparents had never been to the ocean. Finally, around the age of sixteen, I traveled with my aunt, uncle, and cousins to Virginia Beach and checked "seeing the ocean" off my list of things to do.

It was ten years later before I had an opportunity to go to the beach again. I was living in Memphis and had already met Dick. We planned a trip to Florida for our first real vacation together. We decided that it would be fun to camp on the beach.

Dick had an old pickup truck. He rented a camper shell to place on the vehicle's bed to serve as our sleeping quarters. We loaded the truck and headed south to the Gulf. After several hours of driving, we arrived at our destination, Fort Pickens campground on Santa Rosa Island near Pensacola, Florida. We got there just in time to set up camp before dark. We built a fire on the beach and relaxed in folding lawn chairs. It was then that Dick told me a story that put the fear of God in me.

A few weeks earlier, he had read the book *Jaws*, and he proceeded to tell me the entire story. I kept glancing at the moonlit ocean and experienced fright akin to the fear that I had experienced as a Boy Scout while sitting around a campfire and listening to ghost stories.

The next morning after assurance from Dick that it was only a story, I put fear aside and waded into the Gulf. After swimming for a while, we blew up our two-man inflatable boat and ventured far out into the water.

Dick manned the oars while I relaxed and looked down into the crystal-clear water. I was fascinated by the sea life, especially the jellyfish that were swimming below us. Out of the corner of one eye, I saw large fins. I screamed. I panicked. I stood up in the small boat, demanding that Dick head for shore. We almost capsized when I tried to grab the oars.

All the while, Dick was laughing. He finally calmed me down enough to tell me that the large gray leaping creatures with the fins were dolphins. I relaxed, but only slightly. I could still see them, and I insisted that we go ashore.

Even though I was traumatized by the experience, I still enjoy going to the beach. However, when I'm there, I'm always very cautious. I know somewhere out there is a shark waiting to eat me. Fear runs deep.

The written word is powerful and can change the way one views the world. Swim on.

Trip to Bountiful, Uh, I Mean Branson

During the early 70s, Dick and I took a three-day trip to the Ozarks for Labor Day weekend. Our friends Joanie and Bonnie went with us. We left Memphis on the Friday afternoon before the holiday. Half of the citizens of Memphis left at the same time. Because of the heavy traffic, it took us an hour to get across the Mississippi River Bridge into Arkansas.

We drove for several hours before arriving in Branson, Missouri. We had not called ahead to make motel reservations. When we arrived in the "Country Music City of Mid-America," there were no vacancies to be found. We had no choice but to sleep in my 1959 Chevy Impala. We pulled into the parking lot of the Branson Walmart, where we spent the night. The ladies slept inside the car. Dick and I bedded down in the trunk. We left the trunk lid open. The next morning Dick and I awoke very stiff, cold, and covered in dew. Dick had the serial number from the spare tire embedded into his face. He had used the spare for a pillow.

After a day in Branson, we ventured south for our first trip to Eureka Springs, Arkansas. I immediately fell in love with the charming village. We had better luck acquiring lodging there. We found very reasonably priced accommodations at the Basin Park Hotel. The price was ten dollars a night per room. Dick and I had a room on the fifth floor. It was decorated with funky wallpaper and had a sink in the room. There was a toilet in a small adjoining room. However, there was no bathtub or shower in the room.

We discovered there was only one bathtub per floor. It was located down the hallway. We waited in line the next morning to bathe. Each guest cleaned the tub with a provided brush and Comet before bathing. I hurried through my bath so others didn't have to wait too long. I emerged from the tub "clean enough."

A year later, Dick and I returned to Eureka Springs. We stayed in the Palace Hotel on Spring Street, and once again, the rates were ten dollars per night for two people. The setup in the Palace was about the same: sink and toilet provided with each room but no bathtub. However, the Palace had a men's bathhouse in the basement. We were each provided with a luxurious oversize tub.

From the first time I visited Eureka Springs, I wanted to live there. It took years for my dream to become a reality. My house in Eureka Springs is on the town's historic loop and is more than one hundred years old. I'm happy to report, "My home has a private bathroom, complete with a tub."

Pretty Tree, Ugly Tree

In the early 70s, money was tight, and store-bought Christmas tree ornaments were not in my budget. I decided that I could make ornaments. I strung popcorn and cranberries. I made stained-glass baked dough stars, using a star-shaped cookie cutter to get the shape. I cut out a hole in the middle of the star-shaped dough with a bottle cap. During the last couple of minutes of baking, I melted a Life Saver candy in the opening. I hung each of the stained-glass stars on the tree in front of a light. I was pleased and proud of my tree.

The following December, I had a little money, and I bought some store-bought tinsel and garland. I thought, *This year the tree will be prettier than ever.* Dick and I went to a charity-based Christmas tree lot to buy the tree. For some reason, and I can't recall why, we got into an argument while there. I huffed up and said, "I'm ready to go. Just pick out the ugliest damn tree here and let's go home."

That's exactly what he did. We took it back to my apartment. I was still angry. I put the tree into a stand and decorated it. It looked like a pitiful little shrub. I think the top had been broken out of the tree. It looked so funny that Dick and I started laughing, and we soon forgot what the hell we had been mad about.

Every time that I looked at the tree, I smiled. It was a reminder of how senseless it had been to argue and fight. Although quite ugly, I think it may have been the best Christmas tree I've ever had. It had meaning.

Looking for Elvis

The first song that ever made me cry was "Old Shep." It's a sad ballad about a dog that died, and it was recorded by Elvis Presley in 1957. I was in elementary school when Elvis shot to stardom. My teenage sister became an obsessive fan of Presley. His fan base included women who loved him, men who wanted to be him, and people in all age groups. While hanging out in my mother's beauty shop, I noticed that her customer's conversations would often be about Elvis. His photo graced the covers of magazines that my mother's clients would read while they sat under the hairdryers. I anxiously awaited each issue of the *National Enquirer*. The tabloid newspaper reported the latest news about the rock star in every copy.

After Elvis bought Graceland, Ruby, a neighbor who lived across the street from my family, made a pilgrimage to his new home. When she returned, she had a fruit jar filled with grass that she had pulled from the mansion's lawn by reaching through the fence.

Dick was friends with one of Graceland's decorators. He told Dick that Elvis had informed the decorating team that the ultimate decisions would be made by his mother. They gritted their teeth and let Miss Gladys Presley pick out things for the house. She thought that Sears was the ultimate place to shop, and many of the decorating items she selected came from that store.

One of my cousins met Elvis and had him autograph the top of her breasts. She liked to brag, "He wrote 'Elvis' on the righty, and 'Presley' on the lefty."

For several years, I continued to keep up with Presley's career and buy his music. I saw all of his movies. My favorite was *Blue Hawaii*, and I saw it more than a dozen times. Alas, my interest and loyalty to Elvis faded with the arrival of the British Invasion. I became a devoted fan of the Beatles. I no longer wanted to be a Southern rocker. I wanted to be hip and to be English. I combed my hair forward instead of away from my face. However, when I moved to Memphis in the early 70s, my awareness and interest in Elvis returned. His influence was everywhere.

When he was in the city, everyone seemed to know. The Memphian Theatre was a few blocks from my apartment. If I drove by the theater and it said "closed" on the marquee, I knew that Presley had rented it for a private viewing. If the amusement park at the Fairgrounds was closed for an evening, Elvis had rented it so that he could take his daughter, Lisa Marie, on the rides. If he wanted to shop, his favorite Goldsmith's department store would reopen for him after closing to the public. The entire store staff would remain to wait on him.

His generosity to the people in Memphis was legendary. He was constantly buying cars for people. When my sister was in the hospital on Union Avenue in Memphis, Elvis was a patient on the same floor. He and my sister shared a nurse. The nurse excitedly told my sister, "Elvis told me to go across the street to the Cadillac dealership and pick out a car." She did, and he paid.

I was sitting in a hotel room in San Diego when breaking news came on the television. Elvis had died. The year was 1977.

Two moves and several years later, I was invited to participate in a group art show that was to be held at the Arkansas Arts Center in Little Rock.

The exhibition featured Eureka Springs artists. The theme of the show was *The Shrine*. I didn't want to do a piece that was religion-themed. I decided to pay homage to an entertainer who I thought had been deified. The obvious choice for me was Elvis.

Prior to creating the shrine, Dick and I made a pilgrimage to Graceland for inspiration, and to collect EP items from the many Elvis gift shops that were nearby. I used the purchased items in the creation of my art piece. I enjoyed visiting the Graceland mansion, and I think Miss Gladys did a fine job decorating. However, I don't think that "high kitsch" was what she had in mind when she picked out items from Sears.

I never did meet Elvis. The closest I came was meeting Priscilla Presley. That was almost as good.

Ol' Man River

During my childhood, my family made frequent trips to Memphis, Tennessee. As we approached the river bridge, I would sit up straight to get the best view possible of the Mississippi River. Crossing the bridge was the gateway to visiting the Overton Park Zoo, or to participate in a shopping adventure in the city's downtown.

I would beg my daddy to drive slowly across the bridge. I wanted to relish the view of the river as long as possible. I wanted to see the barges, watch fishermen on the banks, and take note of the width of the river. At times, the river was low with wide expanses of exposed bank, while during the rainy season, the water came close to Riverside Drive, the road that ran alongside it.

I was a geography nerd. I loved maps. My bedroom waste can had a relief map of the USA on it. I studied it, and I knew that the Mississippi River cut a slash through the nation and divided it into east and west. I was glad that Arkansas was bordered by the river on its east side. As the crow flies, the river was about forty-five miles from my house.

When I moved to Memphis to attend the Memphis College of Art, I was just minutes from the river, and I was able to spend time on its banks. One of my college classmates had worked on the river during the summer break. He had been a steward on the steamboat *The Delta Queen*. The big paddleboat often visited Memphis. One time while it was docked there, my friend asked if I would like to go aboard. I jumped at the chance. During the tour, we visited cabins and saw the grand staircase and the ballroom. Because he was friends with the crew, we were able to go below and see the operational parts of the steamboat. The next day we returned to the dock and watched *The Delta Queen* depart. When it left port, colored smoke poured from the boat's large calliope pipes, and Stephen Foster tunes filled the air. I had chill bumps.

After I met Dick, who had lived in Memphis for many years, I learned a great deal more about the river. His father had worked on the Mississippi as a tugboat mechanic. When Dick told me that his father never learned to swim, I thought it strange that he had worked on the river. Even though I knew how to swim, I found the river to be scary.

Dick and I spent several summer afternoons on the river at Engineer's Beach. The beach was an area just across the bridge on the Arkansas side where the Corps of Engineers placed sand that had been dredged from the river channel to accommodate large boat navigation. The long sandy area was frequented by many visitors. Except for an occasional knee-deep wade, no one dared to swim in the Mississippi. It was rough, dangerous, muddy, and filled with sinkholes and whirlpools.

There was a family section on the sandy beach near the point of entry. Further down was a party section for young folks, and near the end of the long sandy beach was the gay area. The last part of the gay section was a designated nude beach. Everyone who visited Engineer's Beach was respectful of each other's favorite place to sunbathe on a hot, sultry Memphis summer afternoon.

In the spring of the year, the annual Cotton Carnival took place in Memphis. There were several Egyptian-themed carnival krewes that were secret societies. Members of the krewes were wealthy Memphians, the city's elite. The most well-attended carnival event was the *Arrival of the Royal Barge.* The decorated barge held the Carnival King and Queen, the Royal Court, and the Maid of Cotton. Additional barges carried debutantes. Cotton Carnival was *the* place to debut in the Mid-South.

Dick and I, and what seemed to be all of Memphis, would go down to the riverbank to watch the barges arrive. The royals and the young women would disembark with great fanfare before getting into limos, heading downtown to ride in the carnival parade, and attending lavish balls. The young women debutantes were splendidly dressed in virginal white, and they were escorted ashore by handsome tux-clad young men.

Dick and I, along with thousands of other "common folk," watched the pageantry from the riverbank. When the sun went down, a massive fireworks exhibition would take place. The fireworks were ignited on Mud Island, which sat in the river. The colorful display was reflected on the water. It was two shows in one with an "up" show in the air and a "down" show on the water. While members of the city's high society attended the balls, the rest of us would enjoy the carnival midway.

My favorite times spent on the Mississippi River were when Dick and I visited the grounds of the Church on the River, a Unitarian church that sat on the river's bank. We would go at night, sit on a blanket, and watch lighted barges slowly pass by the city. We were often alone with only the sounds of the river serenading us. I thought about how the river had passed by that spot for centuries, and I hoped that long after I was gone, it would still be winding its way to the Gulf. While sitting there, I felt at peace. In times of stress, I go back there in my mind and visit my old friend, the Mississippi River. "It just keeps a rollin' along."

The Perfect Model

After completing studies at the Memphis College of Art, I was worried about how I was going to make a living as a fine artist. I was aware that it was difficult to make money as a painter, but I didn't want to return to my previous job as a public school art teacher. I mentioned my concern to my mother. She said, "You know, I've made a good living as a hairdresser. You practically grew up in my beauty shop. You understand the business. Why don't you go to beauty school?" I thought, *Well, why not? Hairdressing is an art.*

I enrolled as a student at the Jett Beauty School, which was not far from my apartment in Memphis. Cosmetology students in Tennessee were required to attend 1,500 hours of class before being eligible to take the licensing exam. A portion of the course took place in the classroom, but most of the time, students were "on the floor" doing hair.

When I started at the school, women were still getting shampoos and sets and having their hair teased to high heaven. After their hair was ratted and combed into place, a large amount of lacquer hair spray was applied.

The heavy coating of spray kept the hair from moving until the customer returned the following week to get another shampoo and set. The school had a special pumping station connected to a vat of lacquer in the back room. Styling stations were connected to the vat with overhead tubing. A sprayer was located at each chair. The lacquer was thick and yellow and stuck like glue to everything. Each day when I got home from school I had to scrub it from my fingernails.

Students had the choice of going to school full-time or part-time. I went full-time, and I did not miss one day of class. I wanted to get through the course as quickly as possible and go to work. School days were eight hours long, except for Thursdays when they were twelve hours long. I opted to work on the floor on Thursdays for the entire twelve hours. I finished the course in a record time of eight months.

Sue was one of my weekly standing appointments at the school, and one of my biggest challenges. She wanted her hair extremely high. When I first started doing Sue's hair, I thought, *I can't do this*. She brought with her two wiglets, popular hairpieces at the time. Following the shampoo, set, and ratting of her hair, I would then put a teased wiglet on top of her "do." On top of that wiglet, I added another wiglet.

After doing her hair a couple of times, I changed my attitude. I began looking at it as if I were doing sculpture. I worked her hair and the wiglets into barrel curls, a popular style so named because the curls were big and round like barrels. One time I counted the number of bobby pins that the style required. The count was forty-seven. Each week, Sue sat in my styling chair, holding a Kleenex to her nose while I ratted away. I didn't know if she had allergies or if she was fearful of inhaling the lacquer that was floating in the air.

Sue was a small woman who weighed about ninety pounds. Her hair added another twelve inches in height to her small frame. Even though I personally thought she looked ridiculous, she often told me that she received many compliments from the women at her church. To them, Sue personified the saying, "The higher the hair, the closer to God."

After completing the required 1,500 hours, I signed up to take the state board cosmetology exam. To prepare for the written part of the test I began to seriously study the previously ignored beauty-school textbook. The practical part of the test that I was going to take required me to do a haircut, a set, a makeup facial, and a partial manicure, and to roll a perm. If I passed all parts of the exam, then I would be granted a Tennessee cosmetology license.

After finishing school and before taking the state board, I was hired by a Glemby Salon that was located in the Memphis Franklin Simon Department Store. It was a relief to know that I had a job waiting for me once I got my license. The New York–based Glemby Company was a nationwide chain of salons that featured the latest in precision haircutting and blow-drying. The trend in hairdressing at the time was moving away from weekly shampoos and sets.

Shortly after being hired, the company sent me to Philadelphia for intensive training to learn the company's latest styling techniques. I was told that once I started work, I would be doing only precision cutting and blow-dry styles, and I would not do shampoos and sets. I was delighted. I thought, *No more yellow fingernails.*

After completing the Glemby course in Philadelphia, I returned to Memphis, and I resumed studying for the state board exam. I had three weeks to prepare. I was required to take a hair model with me to the exam. My mother eagerly agreed to be my model. I began making frequent trips to my mother's house in Arkansas to practice the styling portion of the exam. Because she had a beauty shop attached to her home, we had the perfect place for the practice sessions.

A few requirements included in the exam seemed archaic to me, nothing that I would ever need to know how to do once I started working. One of the exam requirements was to do finger waves. We were not taught how to do the waves in school except for a thirty-minute demonstration given shortly before we finished school.

My mother had finished beauty school in the 30s during a time when many women were wearing finger waves. She still did finger waves on a few of her older customers, including my grandmother. She taught me how to do them by reaching behind her head and doing the waves on her hair. When I practiced the finger waves, my mother could tell by the feel whether I was doing them correctly. She would say, "You need to apply more pressure with your fingers" or "More pressure with the comb." She never complained during the practice sessions, but weeks later she told me that her head had been sore following each finger wave session.

The day before the exam, I drove to Arkansas to get my mother before driving to Nashville, Tennessee, where I was scheduled to take the state board test the next day. We checked into the Hermitage Hotel for the night. I wasn't good company that evening. I was busy studying for the written part of the exam, and I more than once checked the kit I was to take with me the next day. The kit contained test supplies: rollers, perm rods, scissors, nail equipment, and makeup.

The next morning, we arrived early at the exam site. I was extremely nervous. I breezed through the written test before entering a large room where I gave my mother a partial manicure, a makeup facial, and a haircut. I rolled a section of her hair with perm rods. Each step was checked by an examiner. After I removed the perm rods, I sprayed her hair with water. I then started doing the set. Students taking the test had previously been given a pattern diagram for how the set was to be done: rollers, pin curls, and the dreaded finger waves. My hands were shaking. While doing the waves I heard my mother whisper, "Calm down." She also whispered helpful directions while I was doing the finger waves.

As I worked, I noticed more and more students had finished and were leaving the large exam room. I worried that I would not finish before the test was scheduled to end. More than one hundred students had finished the test and left the room. I was the last to finish. The examiners checked my set and the finger waves. One of the examiners said, "This is the best set we've seen today." Another examiner said, "Yes, it is."

I could see my mother beaming. She was proud of me. She knew I was well on my way to sharing her profession, one that she loved. I could not have asked for a better model.

I haven't done a finger wave since that day.

Karma

After finishing beauty school, I managed a hair salon in Memphis. It was a Glemby Salon located in a Franklin Simon Department Store in

Poplar Plaza. Besides managing, I also cut hair in a section of the salon called The Cut Ups. As manager, I was in charge of hiring and firing.

Jean, a Black woman, applied for the position of hairdresser. At the time, Black women were working in the salon, but they did shampoos only. The clientele of the Franklin Simon salon was 95 percent White. I liked Jean and wanted to hire her, but I didn't know if the White salon clients would accept her as a hairdresser. It was during the 70s, and it was the South. I contacted my boss who worked in Glemby corporate in New York and told him that I wanted to hire Jean. I wanted his advice and approval. He said to use my own judgment. I hired Jean. She proved to be a great hairdresser, and she quickly built a large client base. Everyone loved her.

During the 70s, a Memphis radio station, WDIA, was the number one African American station in the nation. It was my favorite station, and we listened to it in the salon. Before work, Jean and I cranked up the radio tuned to WDIA, and we would dance together. If the music lent itself to it, we did the bump, and we were good. We were *very* good.

A few months after hiring her, I was told by corporate that I needed to cut payroll. I had to let someone go. I had hired a couple of people after I hired Jean. The person who I cut was the last hired, a woman who had been employed to do shampoos. The next thing I knew, two NAACP lawyers came to the salon to question me. The woman that I had let go had filed a racial discrimination suit. Jean overheard what was going on and stepped in with finger waving to tell the lawyers, "This man does not have one prejudice bone in his body." And that was that. The lawyers left and never came back. Jean and I hugged and cried a little. I still love Jean, and I miss dancing the "bump" with her. We were good together, and we stood together. Karma does work.

From Rags to Riches, at Least for a Day

While working as a haircutter in Memphis, I was asked to do platform work at the National Hairdressers Association annual convention that was to be held in the Mid-South Coliseum. To do "platform work" a cutter was supposedly one of the best in the field. I don't know if that was the case with me, but I had received training as a precision haircutter in New York

City and in Philadelphia. Precision haircutting with scissors was the latest trend at the time.

I was flattered to be asked to demonstrate my skills as a platform artist, and I said yes. As showtime neared, I thought, *What have I done?* I suddenly realized that the audience of hairdressers would know if I messed up.

The first day of the three-day show finally arrived. I was very nervous. The first couple of days on the platform, I demonstrated cutting and styling techniques on models. I did this in front of hundreds of hairdressers who had come from many Mid-South towns. All went well, and no mistakes were made. My styles came out looking good, and the audience members seemed to be receptive and appreciative.

The third day of the convention was less about education. It was reserved for fun events that included a fashion show. At the time, I was the beauty consultant for the Memphis Modeling Association. When I was asked to be a model in the show, I thought, *Hell, I know how to do this.*

A few days prior to the show, I went to an exclusive men's store to be fitted with my modeling outfits. I arrived for the fitting in my "not-at-work" attire. I had on a ragged tie-dyed T-shirt and ripped bell-bottoms that had been hemmed with safety pins. I wore very nice clothes to work, but on my days off, I liked wearing my comfortable hippie clothes.

The snooty owner of the store was appalled at my attire and made no effort to hide his disdain. He said *out loud* some not so nice things about my clothes. If my mama had heard, she would have grabbed him by the ear and given him a bad scolding for being rude. I didn't say anything; I was embarrassed.

One of the outfits I was to model was a two-piece suit that was imported from Germany. It retailed for two hundred dollars. I didn't know they made suits that cost that much. It fit me perfectly, and I proudly modeled the suit during the show. However, I was very nervous the entire time I had it on. I was so worried about damaging the suit that I didn't dare to even sit while wearing it.

After the show, the expensive German-made suit went back to the store. I never set foot in that exclusive men's shop again. I couldn't forget the comments about my clothes made by the shop's snooty owner during the fitting. No matter what he thought, I thought I looked just fine. At least I was polite enough to know when to keep my mouth shut and to be mannerly. To me, that was much more important.

I Can't Manage

When I managed the Glemby Salon that was located in a Franklin Simon Department Store in Memphis, I was in charge of six employees. My district manager, who lived in New York City, was impressed with my style of management. He offered me the manager's job at the Glemby Salon on Thirty-Fourth Street in Manhattan.

The Glemby Company flew me to New York and put me up in a hotel for a week so that I could visit the salon and consider the position. When I walked into the salon, I immediately noticed that there were six telephones and four receptionists. When introduced to the first receptionist, she asked, "Where are you from?"

I answered, "Memphis."

She asked, "That's somewhere out West, isn't it?"

I wanted to reply, "Don't they teach geography in New York?" but I thought it best to not be a smart aleck. They thought that I talked funny. I thought that they talked funny.

Upon entering the styling area, I saw a beehive of activity with twenty-five stylists, several shampoo girls, and eight or more manicurists. In an adjacent room, there was an exercise spa with six employees. I thought, *They want me, a little Southern boy, to manage all these New Yorkers.*

I spent an interesting week in New York while considering the job opportunity. My district manager invited me to stay over a couple of days as a guest in his apartment in the Village. I said yes because I wanted the extra time to visit the city's art museums. When we got to his walk-up apartment and entered the living room, I noticed how small it was. A door that I thought would go to the rest of the apartment went only to a tiny bathroom. There was not another room. In his one room, there was a roll-up reed screen. Behind it was a small four-burner cookstove, a refrigerator, a sink, a couple of cabinets, and twelve inches of countertop. His coffee table served as the kitchen table, and the sofa folded out into the bed.

He told me that he paid four hundred dollars a month for the tiny space. I thought that was outrageous, as I was paying sixty dollars a month for my apartment in Memphis, a space that was four times larger than his living space.

I decided there was no way I could live in such an expensive and tiny apartment, and there was absolutely no way I could manage all those Northerners at the Glemby Salon in Manhattan.

I returned to Memphis, and I immediately made plans to move to Fayetteville, Arkansas, a town that better suited this Southern boy. At least the folks there spoke the same language.

CHAPTER 7 — FINE TIME IN FAYETTEVILLE

Ozark Bound

After I had worked for two years in the Glemby Salon in Memphis, I was ready for a change of scenery. Memphis was changing, and I no longer felt safe in my Midtown neighborhood. Dick was also ready to move, and we discussed possible places to relocate. We both liked the ocean, and New Orleans was one of our favorite places. We considered all possibilities. Even though I wanted a change of scene, I didn't want to be too far from my family. My parents and my aging grandmother were still living in the town where I grew up in Arkansas. I wanted to be no more than a one-day drive from them.

Dick and I had vacationed in the Ozark Mountains. Towns there were within the one-day driving time to get to my parent's home. We liked the area, and we decided that's where we should move. We decided that Fayetteville, Arkansas, a mountain town, and home to the University of Arkansas, was the perfect place for us, and it was only a six-hour drive away from my parents.

After we had decided on a location, I felt it was time to buy a house. A couple of weeks prior to the move, I boarded a Frontier plane and flew to Fayetteville in search of our first home. Dick stayed behind in Memphis. He trusted me to find the perfect house. I had managed to save $4,400, an ample amount for a down payment.

The first day out with a real estate agent, I spotted a house that had gone on the market that very day. Even though it was little more than a shack, I loved it. The small house sat on two large tree-covered lots, and it had a view all the way to Oklahoma.

Nothing else mattered. I wanted it. I was unaware that the house had no value and was scheduled for demolition. The total price was $8,800, the value of the two lots. I made a full offer right away and beat out several developers who wanted the property. I took out a four-year loan on the remainder, and my house payments were $145.75 a month.

When the time came to leave Memphis, Dick and I rented a U-Haul to move our belongings to Arkansas. We didn't have a lot of furniture to move, and that was a good thing because the house I had purchased was tiny. What we did have were animals. I had a dog, two cats, a dozen finches, a canary, a gerbil, and two aquariums full of fish. We bought a large plastic garbage can, filled it with treated water, and placed the fish in it for the six-hour drive to Fayetteville. I also had lots of house plants that occupied much of the space in the U-Haul. Everything survived the trip.

Dick drove the truck, and I followed in my car. When we got within an hour of our destination, there was snow on the ground. Fortunately, the roads were clear, and we arrived safely. The mountainous town looked like a winter wonderland, quite different from the urban setting that we had been used to in Memphis, where it rarely snowed.

I was excited for Dick to see my real estate purchase. When he saw the house for the first time, he cried, not because he was happy, but because I had bought a shack for us to live in.

The previous owners, who had lived there for many years, were hoarders. They left everything in the house: stacks of newspapers, hundreds of glass jars, broken furniture, dead mice, and tons of trash. They were big drinkers of Pearl beer. There were hundreds of beer cans in the house and in the yard. The brick chimney in the middle of the house was filled with beer cans. The previous occupants were also big consumers of canned ham. There were hundreds of ham tins in the yard. They apparently had taken what remained in the tins out to the dogs.

There was one electrical outlet in the entire house, and a single light bulb hung from the ceiling in each room. The walls were beaded board, and when bumped, the sawdust that had been used as insulation poured out of the cracks. The bathroom window swung out. The first time that I opened it, the entire window, including the frame, fell onto the ground.

Clean up of the property began immediately. We called the city and they agreed to send garbage trucks directly to the home to remove the garbage. It took several loads. Following the cleanup, extensive remodeling began. We paid for the remodeling with hours of "sweat equity."

We were able to transform it into a place that we were proud to call home. Even though it was in the middle of town, I turned the little homestead into a mini-farm complete with a vegetable garden, and I acquired more animals. I added a large dog, two Ragdoll kittens, chickens, and a rabbit to the menagerie. We screened the front porch, and we added a deck where we could "sit a spell," and watch the sun go down in faraway Oklahoma. If it's true that "home is where the heart is," then we were home.

Mr. Toad and Company

Prior to moving to Fayetteville, I subscribed to the town's local newspaper, and I scoured the want ads in search of work. I found an opening in a haircutting salon. Mr. Toad's and Company, which was just off Dickson Street, an area that was home to trendy shops and bars frequented by university students.

A week later I called for an interview, boarded a Frontier airplane at the Memphis airport, and flew to Fayetteville to meet with the salon owner. A man in a chauffeur's hat, driving a long black limo, picked me up at the airport. The limo belonged to the man who owned the salon, and the chauffeur was his assistant.

When introduced to the staff, I immediately liked the employees. They were zany, offbeat, and kindred spirits. I got the job. The salon was named "Mr. Toad and Company" after the stylist who started the business, and he went by the name "Toad." We hit it off immediately.

The haircutting establishment was quite different from the elegant, upscale salon that I had managed in Memphis, Mr. Toad and Company was a funky playhouse. The interior was filled with kitschy items, stuffed toy animals, mismatched furniture, and questionable collectibles. One styling chair had a sign on the back claiming, "Jayne Mansfield sat here." In actuality, she had not.

Weeks before I started working, the salon owner, who went by Dr Johnny, ran ads in the local paper saying, "Zeek is coming." People started asking him, "What's a Zeek?" He enjoyed the suspenseful buildup. The week that I arrived, an ad ran with my photo in it, revealing what a "Zeek" was. I was a little nervous thinking I couldn't live up to the buildup. When I did start to work, I was put at ease from day one and became good friends with my fellow stylists. We worked and played together, dined together, laughed and cried together. We were family.

Sadly, most of the guys who I worked with back then are gone. Some perished due to the AIDS epidemic. I'm still in touch with a couple of my fellow workers from long ago, and some of my clients who came to the salon. The move was a good one for me. I found good times, laughs, joy, and love. I found myself once again.

It is important to be among kindred spirits.

Eggplant Casserole and Frogs

It was not too long after moving to Fayetteville that Dick and I made new friends. I quickly became close with the staff at Mr. Toad and Company, the salon where I worked as a haircutter. We were a tight-knit group, and we often socialized outside of work. We enjoyed meals together, and we traveled together. The salon owner, Dr. Johnny, owned a long black limo that had once belonged to a funeral home. It was large enough to hold the entire staff when we went out on the town and when we traveled to out-of-state hairdressing seminars.

Besides my friends from work, Dick and I hung out with a tribe of gay guys. The number varied but most of the time there were seven of us. We traveled, shopped, dined, and drank together. One year for Halloween we dressed in matching tutus and went out together as a campy ballet troupe to our favorite bar. We were a posse. Sunday nights we met at Pizza Planet for the restaurant's once-a-week smorgasbord. It was rare that one of us did not attend.

I worked half a day on Saturdays and when finished, Dick and I would meet the guys at Wyatt's Cafeteria for lunch. There were a couple of picky eaters in the group, and the cafeteria was a good choice because it offered something for everyone. When we traveled together to shop in Tulsa, we would eat at a Furr's Cafeteria. At Furr's, Billie, the first server in the salad line would look at us and say, "Honey, how 'bout a little fruit salad? You look like a little fruit salad." We would laugh and take her up on the offer.

The first time that Dick and I went to Wyatt's in Fayetteville, it was just the two of us. The cafeteria was different from the Piccadilly Cafeteria that we had frequented while living in Memphis. The Piccadilly was quite fancy. There, the tables were covered with white tablecloths, and the napkins were cloth. After our trays were loaded with food, they were carried to our table by handsome young men wearing short white coats, white shirts, black bowties, white gloves, and black pants. After the young men carefully placed the food on the table, they pulled our chairs out for us. The young Piccadilly servers were rewarded with tips for their good service.

During our first visit to Wyatt's, Dick and I paid for our meals, and we waited by the register for several minutes with our loaded trays. We finally realized that no handsome well-dressed young men were going to appear, and we would have to carry our trays. We laughed about it even though we were embarrassed. I thought, *So much for fancy dining in the Ozarks.*

When we had lunch with the posse at Wyatt's, everyone but our friend Ron would get the cafeteria's most famous dish, the eggplant casserole. Ron didn't like eggplant, and he refused to try a bite. The casserole had a look and taste similar to Southern cornbread dressing. We finally convinced Ron to try it. When he took his first bite, he bit down on a metal washer. The washer had apparently fallen into the ingredients from one of the kitchen's commercial mixers. He didn't break a tooth, and he agreed that the casserole tasted all right, but he would not eat it again.

One of the cafeteria cooks was a heavyset guy with a bad toupee. I often wondered if he may have had the hairpiece on backward. He was very friendly and would often come to our table for a brief chat. During one of the visits to our table, he invited us to his house for a party that he was hosting. He insisted that we would have a good time. He left us a napkin with his address, the date, and time of the party written on it. Dick and I were the only two from our group who ended up going.

The night of the party, we drove to an unfamiliar part of town in search of the cook's home. The neighborhood seemed a little sketchy, and we wondered if maybe we should go back home. Not wanting to disappoint the man from Wyatt's, we kept looking. When we found the street where he lived, it was evident where the action was taking place. There were lots of cars parked on the street, and people were filing into one side of a duplex. The closest place for us to park was more than a block away.

The host greeted us at the door, and he seemed happy to see us. He said it had been a rough couple of weeks for him, and he told us about his recent surgery. He then lifted his shirt to show us some kind of bag attached to a tube in his stomach. I thought, *Okay, I've seen enough. Where's the alcohol?*

We walked into a crowded living room. I was hoping someone we knew would be there. There wasn't. The group was an interesting mixture of folks. There were young people, elderly people, bikers, hippies, people of all colors, street people, gays, and lesbians. There were several teenage boys present who were swilling down lots of beer. There were a couple of hookers present who proudly and openly discussed their chosen profession. Everyone seemed to know them. That is, everyone but us. There was one very good looking blond-haired young man who rarely left the side of the host.

The host said, "Follow me to the kitchen. I want to show you my prize collection, and we will get y'all some beers." When I saw the collection, all I could say was, "Oh my." There were countless items in the kitchen with the image of a cute frog on each one: canisters, mugs, salt and pepper shakers, spoon rests, and a ceramic frog clock. He told us his mother had made most of the items in a local ceramic shop. He opened up the cabinet doors to reveal a vast array of plates, bowls, saucers, serving pieces, and teacups adorned with the cute frog image. Out came another, "Oh my."

Dick and I both told him we thought the collection was very cute. *Cute* was our code word for *bad art*. The blond boy popped the top on a couple of beers and handed one to Dick and one to me.

Dick and I went back into the living room where we stood with our backs to the wall. We were ready to go but we didn't know how to gracefully leave after being there for such a short time. The front door opened, and two people wearing clown costumes entered with great fanfare. The blond boy announced that he was going to go buy some pot and that he would be back soon. He exited the still-open door. Dick and I decided it was the perfect time to escape through the open door while everyone was distracted by the clowns.

Dick had worn a velour pullover shirt to the party. He was leaning against a large velvet painting of dogs playing poker when we made our move toward the door. His pullover stuck to the painting and almost caused it to fall off the wall. Fortunately, it did not, and we escaped unnoticed into the night. We made a beeline for the car. We had just made it to the vehicle when we saw blue lights flashing from two cop cars stopped in front of the duplex. I started my car and we immediately left for home.

It was a long time before we went back to Wyatt's Cafeteria.

Teaching a Chicken to Walk

When I was five years old, my first-grade teacher, Miss Versa Butler, gave me a chicken. One Saturday morning, Miss Versa parked her car in front of my family home. She was there to have her hair done in my mother's beauty shop that was located in the front parlor of our house.

Miss Versa saw me playing in the yard. She called me over to her car before going into the beauty shop. "C'mere, I've got something for you," she yelled. I went running. She took a cardboard box from the back seat of her sedan and placed it on the ground. "Open it."

When I lifted the top of the box, I found a black-and-white speckled hen. I was thrilled. Miss Versa knew that I was an animal lover, and she gave me the gentlest hen from the flock of chickens that she kept as pets on her little farm.

I gave out a whoop, and I hugged Miss Versa. I then picked up the hen and hugged her. Miss Versa asked what I was going to name the chicken, and because the hen was black-and-white speckled, I said, "Polka Dot."

Miss Versa said, "Good name. You can call her Dottie." When my father came home from work, he made a little coop for Dottie to sleep in at night. During the daytime, she was free to roam in our yard.

Not too long after I got Dottie, she started laying eggs in a nest in her coop. When my mother said, "I haven't seen your chicken in a while," I told her that Dottie was busy sitting on some eggs. My mother said, "You should have told me. We could have eaten the eggs." When my mother and I looked at Dottie's nest, there were five or six eggs in it. My mother said the eggs were probably bad. We threw them away. It was evident that Dottie wanted to have baby chicks, but without a rooster around, the eggs were infertile. There would be no babies for my hen.

My mother thought that Dottie having chicks would be a good learning experience for me, and she contacted Miss Versa, who brought some fertile eggs to put into my chicken's nest. I could not wait for the chicks to hatch, and I pestered my mother daily asking, "When are they going to hatch?" The day finally arrived, and ten baby chickens appeared. Nine were yellow, and one was black and speckled like Dottie. The babies lived in our yard for a couple of months, and then they were relocated to Miss Versa's fun farm. Dottie remained with me and lived a good long life. She joined my flock of pet mallard ducks that also lived in our yard. I think Dottie eventually thought that she was a duck.

Decades later, I once again would have pet chickens. When we lived in Fayetteville, Dick worked as an electrician, and he drove a pickup truck for his work. One morning on his way to the job site, he spotted a white chicken in the middle of an intersection at a stoplight. He jumped out of the truck, picked up the chicken, and put her in the bed of his pickup. She remained there the rest of the day before he brought her home to me.

Until we moved to Northwest Arkansas, we had not been around commercial chicken houses, and we had not seen the large trucks that hauled the chickens from the houses to the processing plants. The crates loaded onto the trucks were wooden, and some had broken or missing bars. Often chickens would fall out of the broken crates and end up in the street. Many were run over, and others were snatched up and became dinner. The chickens had been raised inside commercial growing houses that were so crowded there was little space for the fowl to move. They didn't know they could freely walk. When they fell from a truck, they just sat there.

The chicken that Dick brought home was soon joined by another lucky bird that had fallen from one of the transport trucks. I spent time with them, and I taught them to walk. The chickens learned to come to us when we went out with their feed, and they would squat down to be petted before eating. I discovered that chickens were smarter than people thought they were, and I was able to teach them a few simple commands.

I named the first chicken "Elly after Elly May Clampett from *The Beverly Hillbillies* television show. The handle of an old garden hand plow that sat on the rear patio became Ellie's favorite place to perch. The antique plow was by the bathroom window that was covered with a reflective film. The chicken would sit there and look at her reflection in the mirrorlike glass. Surprised guests who used the bathroom would shout out, "There's a chicken looking in the bathroom window." I nonchalantly would say, "Oh, that's just Elly. Don't worry, she's seen one before."

I haven't eaten chicken since 1973.

Strawberry Fields

My favorite childhood Little Golden Book was *The Poky Little Puppy*. At the end of the book, the poky little puppy is the last to arrive home after he and his siblings dug a hole under the fence and spent the afternoon exploring the outside world. By the time he gets back to the house, the other pups have eaten all the strawberry shortcakes their mother made. I felt sorry for the little pup. I hoped it was a lesson learned and that he never missed out on getting strawberry shortcake ever again. Strawberry shortcake was my favorite dessert.

During the strawberry season, my mother made sure I got my fill of the fresh berries. She made several versions of shortcake that included Bisquick shortcake, pie-crust shortcake, and pound-cake shortcake. Sometimes she served berries in the little round store-bought shortcakes. Occasionally she would make a Shoney's knockoff strawberry pie.

When I ate at my grandmother's house, I could count on her to have strawberries on the dessert menu along with an array of other desserts. She kept strawberries in her freezer. Although not as good as fresh, the frozen strawberries satisfied my craving when the berries were not available. My grandmother served them in stainless steel dessert bowls that became cold to the touch when filled with the barely thawed strawberries.

While I was living in Fayetteville, my mother, a niece, and a nephew came for a weekend visit. The guests, along with my sister and her three kids who lived in town, all gathered at my home for an all-day visit. To entertain the nieces and nephews who were teens and preteens, I decided I would take them to a pick-your-own strawberry patch. My mother, my sister, my partner Dick, five kids, and I caravanned to a nearby berry farm. Once we started picking, I foolishly asked, "Who can pick the most strawberries?" The competition was underway, and a picking frenzy began.

After more than an hour of picking, we took the berries to be weighed by the owner of the farm. I gasped when the final tally was almost one hundred pounds. My sister, my oldest niece, my mother, and I spent the rest of the afternoon washing and capping strawberries and placing them in gallon freezer bags. What didn't fit in my large freezer went home with my sister.

I used the frozen berries in many different recipes. I made strawberry bread, strawberry cobbler, and freezer jam. I would get one frozen strawberry out of the freezer and plop it into my chardonnay. I ate lots of strawberries that year. I also drank lots of chardonnay.

The Journey Begins with One Step and Two Long Flights

In 1979 Dick and I decided to take a dream vacation. We put back money each week and managed to save enough for an eight-day visit to Hawaii.

When the day finally arrived to leave for the islands, we drove to the Tulsa airport and boarded a plane for the first leg of the journey. We flew to Dallas to make our connecting flight only to discover that there was a problem with the huge 747 plane that we were to board. Travelers booked on the flight were split into two groups and placed on smaller planes. I thought, *Okay, this is fine. All that matters is getting there.*

Takeoff in Dallas went smoothly. I enjoyed looking out the plane's window as we flew across the continent. When we approached the California coastline, land disappeared and I could see the vast Pacific Ocean. Hours later, we approached Hawaii. We did not land immediately because of a problem at the Honolulu airport. We spent more than an hour circling Oahu. I began to get airsick as we flew around and around. Finally, we were on the ground. I was wobbly, but I was happy when we entered the terminal. A pretty woman greeted me with a welcoming smile and a lei. I was finally on my dream island vacation.

The vacation was everything I had hoped it would be. We visited the islands of Oahu, Maui, and Hawaii, which we visited last. When we arrived at the airport in Hilo to board the Hawaiian Airlines plane for the return to Honolulu, there was once again a delay. We could not get on the escalator to board our plane. A child had sat down on the escalator and his buttocks were caught in the moving steps. I did not look; I felt sick to my stomach. Finally, the poor lad was freed, and we were able to make our flight.

When we arrived at the Honolulu airport, we were not allowed to board the plane. The incoming 747 from Dallas, the plane that was to take us back to the mainland, was stalled on the ground. The incoming flight had been threatened by a call-in bomb threat. The passengers disembarked, left their belongings on the plane, and a bomb squad complete with dogs searched the plane. After an hour-and-a-half search, no bomb was found. We were finally able to board.

We were among the one-quarter of passengers seated before the boarding was halted because a leak was found in the plane's hydraulic landing gear. We were not allowed to get off the plane. The plane's engines were not running, and they were required to run the air conditioners. We were hot. In an effort to keep us cool, not only physically, but in temperament, the flight attendants served free cocktails. By the time the problem was fixed two or three hours later, we were fairly tipsy. The rest of the passengers were allowed to board, and we were finally airborne.

During the showing of the in-flight movie, *Matilda*, we were served supper. We were starving. I didn't receive my vegetarian meal as requested and therefore had very little to eat. I kept drinking. By the time our meal was finished, we had flown eastward into dawn. We had not had a "real" night and therefore no time to sleep.

When we landed in Tulsa, Dick and I were exhausted, and we were famished. We stopped at the first Oklahoma truck stop that we found and ate a late breakfast. Wearing leis and Hawaiian shirts and sporting nice tans, we dined on scrambled eggs and toast while avoiding the stares of curious truck drivers. It was wonderful to have our feet on terra firma.

"A journey is like marriage. The certain way to be wrong is to think you control it."

— *John Steinbeck*

Up on the Roof

In the early 80s, I purchased a small 50s-style house in Fayetteville. It was near the University of Arkansas and across the street from a strip mall. I wanted to convert the house into a beauty salon. Money was tight and the remodeling budget was limited. Dick and I made plans to do the bulk of the work. City code required that the heat and air and the plumbing be done by licensed professionals. Dick had his electrical license, and fortunately he could legally rewire the building.

After scrutinizing the budget and allowing for the cost of building supplies and furnishings, enough funds remained to have a concrete parking lot put in behind the building, and to possibly get a new roof.

After receiving an estimate from a roofer, we learned there was not quite enough money left to have the roof replaced. We were able to work a deal with the man. To lower the cost, we agreed to remove the old roof and put down the tar paper. The roofer would then install the shingles.

Early on a Saturday morning we climbed onto the roof of the building and started removing the shingles. Hours later, after the shingles were removed and placed in a dumpster, we began removing the tar paper. We weren't aware that a thunderstorm located on the other side of a ridge was heading toward us. When a big clap of thunder warned us of the impending storm, we immediately got off the roof. Dick headed to a nearby lumber company to purchase a roll of black plastic to cover the exposed wooden roof decking to keep the rain from getting into the building.

By the time he returned, it was too late. It was pouring, and lightning was flashing. It was too dangerous to get back onto the roof. We decided to take the plastic inside and cover the hardwood floors to protect them from the water that was coming through the cracks in the roof decking.

We quickly covered the oak floor leaving about a foot of the black plastic on all sides of the room to roll up onto the walls. The plastic was stapled in place, and the room looked like a large black wading pool. Water was quickly filling the attic above our heads. To prevent the sheetrock on the ceiling from falling from the weight of the water, Dick started poking holes in the sheetrock with a broom handle.

Water began pouring through the holes and with the water came debris that included black mineral wool insulation from the attic. By the time the rain ended, we were standing in several inches of trash laden water. We were soaking wet and covered with black mineral wool filth.

We had spent a long ten-hour day on the job. Because the storm kept us busy during what would have been our lunch hour, we were famished. There was a grocery store in the shopping center directly across the street from the building. Dick said, "Let's go get something from the store to eat and drink." I was too hungry to object even though we looked a mess. We walked across the street and entered the store. We were soaking wet and filthy with black mineral wool stuck to us. I was aware that people were looking at us, but I was too hungry and too tired to care.

Normally I would not leave my house without dressing up and making sure my hair was perfect. I thought a well-groomed appearance was necessary at all times for someone in my profession. My job as a stylist was to make people beautiful. When I was out and about, I was quick to judge the appearance of others, and I often thought, *Why in the world would someone appear in public looking like that?*

When Dick and I left Dillions grocery store that day, I told him, "Never again will I judge anyone I see in a store who is not dressed up, or who is dirty. They may have just put in a hard day's work." From now on I'll think, *Good for them. I've been there myself.*

The next morning, we went back to the building. Dick opened the front door, and he cut a slit in the black plastic. Water poured out of the building. The floor was saved, and I had learned a lesson.

Rotel and Makeup:

In 1980 I decided it was time to go into business for myself, and I opened a salon near the University of Arkansas. Many of the clients were young professional women and sorority girls. To better serve the salon's customers, I decided to add makeup application to the services I offered. I signed up for a three-day Redken makeup course that was to take place in Cincinnati, Ohio. One of the guys that worked for me also wanted to go to the seminar. We flew to Cincinnati on American Airlines out of Tulsa, Oklahoma.

During the next three days we attended the seminar, where we learned the art of applying makeup. The very last session was Makeup for Men. I was sitting in the front row of the seminar that was attended by approximately one hundred people. Because of my chosen seat, I was an easy target to be selected as a model. Although the makeup was very light— some foundation, a tiny bit of blush, and a light application of mascara—it felt strange on my face. Immediately after the male makeup session, we had to leave via cab for the airport. I didn't have time to wash off the makeup. When we got to the airport, we had to run to catch our plane. I was very self-conscious about the "stuff" on my face. Even though my skin itched like crazy, I didn't dare touch it for fear of smearing the makeup.

Shortly after taking off, the flight attendants came around, and to my surprise I knew them. The two women had attended the University of Arkansas, and they had been clients of mine a couple of years earlier. Their regular route was from New York City to the Bahamas, but that weekend they had traded flights so they could land in Tulsa, visit Fayetteville, and pick up several cans of Rotel. They could not find it in NYC, and they were craving Rotel dip, a delicious mixture of that canned concoction combined with melted Velveeta cheese. The lovely ladies immediately started plying my friend and me with cocktails free of charge. I soon forgot about the makeup on my face. By the time we arrived in Tulsa, my friend and I were plowed.

After we retrieved my car at the airport, we stopped at the first restaurant that we came to, a twenty-four-hour truck stop. I had to eat something and sober up before driving the two hours home to Fayetteville.

Before ordering, I visited the restroom, glanced in the mirror, and wondered, *What the heck is that black stuff that's smeared around one of my eyes?* I scrubbed my face until it was red. After that experience, I decided that I looked just fine with my face "au naturel."

Ice, Ice Baby

While living in Fayetteville, Dick and I enjoyed going to nearby Eureka Springs to celebrate New Year's Eve. Our place of choice was the Center Street Bar. It was *the* place to spend the holiday. Ignoring forecasts for bad weather, one New Year's Eve we drove to Eureka Springs, checked into a cheap motel, and prepared for our night out.

I was excited about a night of dancing, and I couldn't wait to put on my brand-new shirt that was turquoise flannel with black stars. While we were getting ready, the freezing rain began to fall. Young and feeling invincible, we decided to go to the bar anyway. We made it there safely. However, only a handful of others were able to get there.

One group of people seemed a little out of place in the bar— four sanitation workers and their wives who were from Springdale, Arkansas. They were staying the night in the nearby Basin Park Hotel, a location within walking distance to Center Street. The men wore cowboy boots, cowboy hats, and jeans. Their wives had on similar attire.

After a couple of drinks, we ended up sitting with the Springdale group, laughing and having a great time. Every so often Dick and I would dance, and the Springdale couples also danced. They would get excited each time the DJ played a country song. Late in the evening and much to my surprise and to his wife's surprise, the burliest of the sanitation workers pulled me to my feet. Before I knew it, we were doing the Texas two-step to "Looking for Love." Even though I didn't know how to do the two-step, it was fairly easy to follow the big guy who picked me up and put me down where I needed to be. Dick was busy laughing.

That New Year's Eve was one of the most memorable for me. It proved that no matter our differences, by gosh, we can get along and celebrate life with any and all of our fellow human beings. We can have fun.

Talking Slow While Wearing Flannel

Dick and I built a home outside Fayetteville, Arkansas, and moved into it in 1980. I designed the house, borrowing from several designs that I had found in magazines. The two of us did most of the labor even though we were both working full-time. After work, we would drive the few miles to the six-acre building site and work into the night. I was under the impression that if I built a brand-new house, I could have everything just the way I wanted it to be. I soon learned that budget restrictions put a limit on my plans.

Nevertheless, we ended up with a very nice three-story passive solar house that was energy efficient. The home was entered by a forty-foot wooden ramp that went from the street into the top floor where the living room and kitchen were located. The top floor was treetop level. An open, wooden oak staircase led down to the other levels where there were two bedrooms, two baths, and a rec room. Off the front of the rec room on ground level was a sunspace complete with a hot tub and tropical plants. The sunspace served as a solar collector. When heat entered the room, the warm air was moved through an air system to other rooms in the house. The design of the house worked very well. The home was all electric and even during the coldest month the highest electric bill was fifty dollars.

During the early 80s there was a television series on the Arkansas PBS network, titled *Your Energy Dollar*. The director of the show contacted me and asked if they could film the sunspace. I was flattered that he wanted to feature the house on the show, and of course I said yes. For days prior to the filming, I cleaned, scrubbed, washed windows, and did everything I could to make sure the house was perfect.

When the film crew arrived, they began setting up and planning the shots. I was very surprised when they wired me with a mic. I had no idea that I would be on film. The director said he wanted me to explain the workings of the sunspace and explain how heat was collected and transported throughout the house. I was told to ad-lib my part and to do so in a relaxed and casual manner. I was terrified. I also thought, *I wish I had spent more time on my hair, and I wish I had on something that looked better than this old flannel shirt.*

The filming took a while. I felt totally inept during the taping of my television "show biz" debut. I thought I was mumbling and stumbling incoherently. As time neared for the show to air, I again became nervous and apprehensive about the quality of my performance. My friends and family from across the state planned to watch the program. When the show aired, the filming of the house was quite beautiful. However, I was quite shocked to hear myself speak. *Damn*, I thought, *I sound just like Jimmy Carter.* Over the years, I have accepted the way I speak. It is part of who I am. I like listening to Mr. Carter. However, I don't want to be filmed in flannel ever again.

Listening

While living in Fayetteville, I became friends with Nancy Williams. Her husband was John Williams, an American author. He was best known for his novels *Stoner* and *Augustus*. The latter won a US National Book Award. In the literary world, that's like winning an Academy Award.

John and Nancy had moved to Fayetteville from Key West. She wanted to cook Cuban black beans and rice for me. It was a popular dish in Key West, but it was foreign to me. I accepted her invitation to dinner. At the time I suffered from extreme shyness, and I was neurotically nervous about the dinner.

I arrived with a bottle of wine. I was not sure if the wine was appropriate. The clerk at the liquor store took a guess as to what wine should be served with black beans and rice. When I arrived at their home, Nancy introduced me to John and then left the two of us alone in the living room while she finished dinner. Almost immediately he put me at ease. He was very humble and very curious about me, my background, picking cotton, and my general interests. I was flattered and no longer nervous.

That evening I learned a valuable lesson from him. Everyone has a story to tell if we take the time to listen. The best writers are also the best listeners. What I did not learn—What wine goes with black beans and rice?

Going Public

In the late 80s a merchandising representative for The Franklin Company of Chicago thought my artwork would appeal to an international buying market. The rep, who was also a friend, sold the company's limited-edition prints. Her territory was the entire state of Arkansas. She showed my work to corporate headquarters, and they agreed to include my work in their product line.

Besides having reps in each state, The Franklin Company had showrooms in several markets from New York to California with the main locations in Dallas, Atlanta, and High Point, North Carolina. Shortly after my work was added to their line, I was asked to make a guest appearance in the Dallas World Trade Center showroom. I said that I would love to. On the drive to the Dallas Market Center, I started to panic.

During the personal appearance in the showroom I was to create a painting. The artwork would then be given away during a drawing at the close of each day that I was there. I had never performed as an artist in public. Hundreds of people in the Dallas showroom would be stopping to watch me work. I thought, *What if I mess up?* I was quite capable of destroying a painting with one bad brushstroke. I had ruined many a piece in the privacy of my studio.

The night before my first appearance, I did not sleep a wink. At daybreak I seriously considered getting back in my car and returning to Arkansas. However, I had committed to the task ahead, and I felt that I needed to follow through with my obligation. It was my big break, and I didn't want to blow it. My parents had taught me, "If you promise to do something, keep your word and do it."

I arrived early to the showroom, set up the art supplies, and began to paint. My hand was shaking as I applied the first layer of color. After a few brush strokes, everything seemed all right. I began to actually enjoy performing and visiting with potential customers. I breezed through the next couple of days and arrived back in Arkansas with a feeling of accomplishment.

I did a couple of follow-up appearances in Dallas, two in Atlanta, and one in High Point. I also made guest appearances in several Dillard's, a department store chain that carried my work. My work sold well, and limited-edition prints of my paintings ended up in collections around the world.

I'm happy that my parents taught me the importance of fulfilling obligations. I'm glad that I faced my fear of going public, even though how

I felt the first time could best be described by one of my daddy's favorite sayings, "Nervous as a whore in church." Many of life's accomplishments begin with fear.

Put Away Wet

After my artwork was picked up by The Franklin Company, my paintings were sold as limited-edition prints by Dillard's, Neiman Marcus, and other department stores and boutiques worldwide. I continued making personal appearances, representing my work at various venues.

One August the company booked me to appear in the Dillard's store at the Pines Mall in Pine Bluff, Arkansas. I was scheduled to be in the department store to represent my work during the grand opening of the brand-new Pines Mall.

I drove the five hours to Pine Bluff a day before the appearance. It was more than 100 degrees, and the car's air conditioner barely cooled the interior of my vehicle. About an hour into my trip, a truck threw a big rock into the windshield of my car, and it cracked the glass from one side to the other. When I arrived in town, a sign at a bank showed the temperature to be 112 degrees. It had not been a fun trip.

By the time I checked into the motel and unloaded the car, I was drenched from head to toe with sweat. I put on my bathing suit and headed for the pool to cool off. After leaving the pool, I put my damp, sweaty clothes back on. I had not brought a change except for my dress-up duds that I planned to wear the next day. It was too hot to blow-dry my long hair. I was persnickety about my looks when I was representing my artwork, and I usually had my hair styled to perfection. I thought, *Hey, I'm not going to see anyone, and besides, I don't know anyone here, so it doesn't matter. It's too hot to bother with trying to look good.*

That evening I decided to drive to the mall and check it out. Because the mall was not scheduled to open until the next day, I was surprised to see cars in the parking lot. I got out of my car and walked to the main entrance. Two young men dressed in tuxedos opened the door for me. Inside I found lots of people dressed to the nines. Men were in suits and tuxedos, and many women were wearing cocktail dresses. I looked like hell. I had crashed the soiree that was celebrating the opening of the new mall.

Tables lined the long corridor of the mall. Each table was covered with elegant cloths and set with silver service pieces. There were huge mounds of boiled shrimp among a vast array of hors d'oeuvres on the tables. Entertainment included a fashion show complete with runway models, a ballet performance, and music provided by the Pine Bluff Symphony. It was evident that the new mall was an important addition to the community. I was embarrassed that I looked like a field worker while rubbing elbows with the nicely dressed town folk.

The next morning, I put on the nice clothes that I had packed for my public appearance, and I drove to the mall. I was hoping that no one would recognize me from the night before. The parking lot was filled with cars. Hundreds of folks were there for the grand opening, and the Dillard's store had standing room only.

There was a table set up for me in the center of the store, where I created a small painting that was given away during a drawing at the end of the day. Throughout the day, several people who stopped to meet me and to watch me work asked, "Didn't I see you last night?" I answered, "Well, maybe," and I quickly followed with, "Isn't this a nice mall?"

I learned that first impressions don't always hold true. At least I hope that's the case.

7-11 Exposed

When I lived in Fayetteville during the late 70s, private parties dominated social activities. One winter, a friend well-known for his entertaining skills hosted a party with a "silver" theme. All the walls in his apartment were covered with aluminum foil. There were dozens of people attending the event, and most wore silver-colored clothes. Alcohol flowed freely, and folks were dancing and laughing.

One of the party goers, a very inebriated rotund guy, decided he was "a work of art." He removed all his clothing and joined the folks on the dance floor. While dancing, he exclaimed, "It's art, it's art."

Eventually he became tired of dancing and decided it was time to leave. Too drunk to get totally dressed, he put on his shoes and a coat that barely covered what should not be seen. He went out into the cold night air and took off in his car. We should never have let him leave. He ended up spending the night in jail.

On the way home that night, he stopped at a 7-Eleven to buy cigarettes. Before exiting the store, he went to the magazine display, spotted a *Time* magazine on the bottom shelf, and bent over to pick it up. That's when the manager called the police.

He needed a longer coat.

Too Much Isn't Always Good

When I was a child growing up in the Arkansas Delta, the winters were relatively mild. When it did snow, it was gone in a day or two, and the precipitation rarely measured more than two inches. Three inches was considered deep. There were not enough snowy days in the Delta to warrant having a sled. My older sister had a wooden sled that my daddy had made for her. My younger sister and I used a piece of cardboard. The town had few hills, so we mainly slid down ditch banks.

When I was a teenager there was one rare snowfall that was in the eight-to-ten-inch range. When the storm hit, a friend and I were house-sitting for his relatives who lived on a farm in the country. The snow began falling during the afternoon, and by dark, the snow was deeper than either one of us had ever experienced. Even though we didn't have the proper boots for traipsing through the snow, we decided to take a nighttime walk through a nearby graveyard.

It was eerily quiet. I walked closely behind my friend, who was carrying a flashlight. I was scared. I kept my eyes peeled for footprints in the snow and planned a quick retreat if any prints were spotted. Before long, I begin to appreciate the gentle serene landscape. The flakes continued to fall. My friend and I stood still without talking for several minutes. I had never experienced such quiet. When a branch cracked loudly, breaking the silence, we screamed and made a hasty retreat back to the house.

After we thawed out, we decided to make snow ice cream. Neither one of us had made it before. We knew what the recipe called for—PET milk, raw eggs, sugar, and vanilla flavoring—but we didn't know the "how much." We found the needed ingredients in the kitchen cabinet, and we got eggs from the fridge. Still frightened by our graveyard scare, neither one of us wanted to go outside alone to get some snow. We finally agreed to go outside together, and we gathered a large pan of clean snow.

We guessed at how much of each ingredient should be added to the snow. All went well until we added an entire bottle of vanilla flavoring to the mix. We could tell by the color of the mix that something was wrong. No amount of added snow could make it right. We threw the brown batch of ruined snow ice cream out the back door. I later wondered what my friend's relatives thought when they returned home and found brown snow in their yard.

When I returned home, there was still enough snow on the ground for my mother to make a proper batch of snow ice cream for me. While she made it, I wrote down the recipe. She added only one tablespoon of vanilla to the mixture.

While I lived in Memphis, it snowed only once. The city was at a standstill. The slick roads kept most people at home. Memphians did not know how to drive on the snow-covered roads, and the city did not have snowplows. I left my car parked, and I took the slow-moving bus to work. During that one snow event, Dick and I walked all over our neighborhood. Again, I experienced an eerie quiet in what was normally a noisy urban setting. I thought, *Snow is a silencer.*

When Dick and I moved to the Ozarks, we experienced our first real winters. Out of necessity, we learned to drive on slick roads, and I purchased snow tires for the car. I walked to work when necessary while wearing proper boots. I made snow ice cream, and I used the exact measurement of each ingredient as taught to me by my mother. It wasn't quiet in Fayetteville, Arkansas, during a snowstorm. Folks were out walking and sledding, and people were sliding down hillsides on cross-country skis. People were driving cars with clinking chains on their tires.

The street in front of our house in Fayetteville was on a steep incline, and our living room had large windows with a good view of the road. When it snowed, careless drivers would attempt to drive up the hill in front of our house. We suspect that many were University of Arkansas students who were from warmer climates, and who were inexperienced when it came to winter driving. During snowy days, we turned off the television and pulled up a couple of chairs next to the window. We took bets on who would make it over the hill and who would end up in a ditch. We were entertained for hours. It was our guilty pleasure. It's human nature to sometimes find humor in the misfortune of others. It's also human nature to think, *If a little is good, then more is better.* That's not always true, especially when it comes to snow and vanilla flavoring.

Oreos Aren't Always Enough

A near blizzard occurred in North Central Arkansas in the early 80s. Dick and I left Fayetteville by car early in the afternoon on a Wednesday, heading for my mother's house in Marmaduke, Arkansas, where we planned to spend the Thanksgiving holiday. We had planned to be at her house in time for supper, as the trip usually took less than six hours.

About two-thirds of the way there, we stopped in Hardy, Arkansas, to fill up my Oldsmobile Omega with gas, use the restroom, and get a couple of cokes. Heavy snow began to fall. The snow had not been predicted.

We debated what to do and decided to plow on, thinking it would soon stop. A few miles outside Hardy, we came to a standstill. A quarter mile ahead of us, a semitruck had jackknifed and blocked traffic. There were dozens of cars stalled in front of us. Very soon, there were dozens of cars lined up behind us. Nothing moved and the heavy snow kept falling.

Traveling with us were our pets, my little dog, Desiree, and our two cats, Josh and Priscilla. Fortunately, we had plenty of food and water for the animals. Dick and I each had a coke and a package of Oreo cookies. We had enough gas to start the car every so often to run the heater.

The snow kept falling, and it got very dark as nighttime fell. Some folks became impatient. A driver in a four-wheel drive pickup decided he would go for it. He drove around everyone and veered onto the shoulder. His truck slid down a steep hill and stopped only when it hit the tree line. We stayed put. We didn't know it at the time, but there was no snow in

Marmaduke. I did know that my mother would be worried sick. A couple of hours after we should have arrived at her house, she called the state police. They knew nothing about the snowstorm. The police did tell her that they had received no fatality reports and that we were likely still alive.

We spent several hours sitting in the car while thirteen inches of snow piled up. At daylight, wreckers were finally able to move the semi, and the stranded cars ahead of us started to slowly move. By the time we reached the next town thirty minutes down the road, there was absolutely no snow on the ground. We had been trapped overnight in a very small freak blizzard. I stopped at the first phone booth and called my worried mother. She had sat up all night waiting in the kitchen with her radio turned on in case we tragically made the news. Two hours after the call, we finally reached her house.

We ate the supper that my mother had prepared for us the night before. It became our breakfast on that Thanksgiving morn. I was very thankful to be there. I made a mental note to bring more than Oreos with me when traveling in the winter. It's not a bad idea to include the cookies in the survival kit. When stranded, separating the layers helps to pass the time.

Don't Dream It, Be It

In 1975 the film *The Rocky Horror Picture Show* hit the theaters and instantly became a cult classic. I was obsessed with the movie and saw it many times. Before the movie was released on disc, I had received a bootleg copy recorded during a movie screening. As poor as that copy was, I was thrilled to have it and played it over and over.

I didn't think about why I and others were so obsessed with the rather bizarre musical. Granted the songs were top-notch, but I do think the movie's appeal went far beyond the score. Perhaps the movie said to us, "It's quite all right to celebrate who you are and have fun. Don't Dream it, Be It."

In the mid-80s, the movie *Pass the Ammo* was being filmed in Eureka Springs. The film starred Bill Paxton, Annie Potts, Linda Kozlowski, and Tim Curry. Although all the actors were fairly well-known—Annie Potts for *Designing Women*, Linda Kozlowski for *Crocodile Dundee*, and Bill Paxton for many roles, I cared only that Tim Curry was in Arkansas. He had played Dr. Frank-N-Furter in *Rocky Horror*.

I was still living in Fayetteville during the filming. My "stalking" of Mr. Curry required that I drive to Eureka Springs in hopes of spotting Tim. I was determined to meet him. My determination paid off when late one evening, I spotted him in front of the post office in the company of Annie Potts and Linda Kozlowski. I slammed on the brakes, jumped out of the car, and ran toward them with *The Rocky Horror Picture Show Book* in my hand. Unfortunately in my haste, I somewhat pushed the actresses aside in order to get to Mr. Curry.

He was very gracious, and he was pleased that I had the book. He called it "the bloody Rocky Horror bible," and he was nice enough to sign it. I still cherish that autograph, and I still appreciate the effect the movie had on me. It relayed a positive message to me and to many others. We needed to know that it was okay to be different. Annie Potts and Linda Kozlowski, please forgive me for almost knocking you down.

Walk On By

When Dick and I lived in Fayetteville from 1975 to 1987, he worked in the trades as an electrician. He worked on job sites with men who were carpenters, plumbers, concrete finishers, and other types of construction workers. They did not know that Dick was gay, and he wanted that part of who he was to remain a secret for various reasons: scorn, ridicule, rejection, and being fired.

Dick's given name is Oscar Dickerson. To friends and family, he is known as "Dick." When at work, he went by "Oscar." When we were in public together, we had signals. If we were walking together on the street or at the mall and someone said, "Hey, Oscar," I knew it was someone from work greeting him. I would keep on walking, and at that moment, we became strangers. After he finished talking to his fellow workman, we would again link up and go about our business together.

During that time, we had two houses. We lived in one. Dick kept the other one furnished, kept the utilities connected, and stocked the refrigerator with beer. If a man from work wanted to stop by at the end of the day for a beer, Dick met him at the spare house. There were two separate houses and two separate lives that we created because we feared everyone would know that we were gay. We feared.

In 1987 we moved to Eureka Springs, and Dick was working for himself. We felt safe, and we felt comfortable being known as a couple. We felt accepted for who we are, and we decided there would be no more hiding. We would have one house and one life together. My hope is that from this time forward, no one will ever have to live in fear because of who they are or whom they love.

I hope that there will never again be a need to "walk on by."

CHAPTER 8 — EUREKA SPRINGS, I HAVE FOUND IT

Following My Heart

The first time I visited Eureka Springs, Arkansas, I felt the magic. In the early 70s, Dick and I vacationed in the resort town located in the Ozark Mountains. I was drawn to the natural scenic beauty, the Victorian architecture, and particularly the town's funkiness. I was envious of the people who were privileged to live there. I wanted to live there too.

There was a problem. The little town's economy was not too good. Some of the buildings were boarded up. I didn't see the potential for me to earn a living as a haircutter. In 1975, Dick and I moved to Fayetteville, Arkansas, home to the state's largest university. The larger town with a big student population was a ripe market for me to practice the latest trend of hair styling: precision scissor cutting and blow-drying. I had been trained in those styling techniques in classes in Philadelphia and New York City.

I enjoyed living in Fayetteville. I earned a good living there, and I made many good friends in the city. While there I also continued to pursue my other profession, working diligently to become a better artist. I did shows, and I exhibited in galleries. During the late 80s, my art was selling well nationwide, and my income was sufficient enough that I no longer had to work five days a week in the salon.

At the same time, Eureka Springs had boomed, especially the town's art scene. The town had a reputation for being an art colony, and I thought living there could benefit my career. The Ozark village with a population of two thousand was the most freewheeling, funky, accepting town in the state. It long had been described as "the place where misfits fit." An estimated 25 percent of the population were artists, and a sizable gay community lived there. People were drawn to Eureka Springs from all corners of the earth, and I was ready to be there too.

We lived in our first home, a small one-bedroom cottage in Fayetteville, for five years before selling it and building a new house in the woods outside of town. The new house was a three-story passive solar home, and we had lived in it for six years when I put it on the market. It sold to the first people that looked at it.

We loaded our belongings into a U-Haul truck and moved into a rental home in Eureka Springs. After looking at several houses for sale, we bought a Craftsman bungalow that had been built in 1909 and was located on the Upper Historic Loop. We closed on the house on Halloween Day, October 31, 1987.

Dick was unsure about the move, so we decided to maintain a residence in both towns. Besides the house that we had just sold, we also owned another smaller home in Fayetteville. I kept the beauty salon there, and I continued to work four days a week. I spent two nights a week in Fayetteville and five nights a week in Eureka Springs. Dick continued to work five days a week in Fayetteville, and he spent weekends in Eureka Springs. We were on the road a lot.

After living in two places for one year, we decided to sell everything in Fayetteville and live full-time in Eureka Springs. I opened a small one-person salon there, and I worked two days a week cutting hair. The rest of my time was spent painting. Dick opened a business, Alpha Electric, and for the first time in his life, he was self-employed.

I did leave a part of my heart in Fayetteville. Fortunately, the towns are only one hour apart. I consider them to be "hometown one" and "hometown two." As much as I loved living in Fayetteville, the move to Eureka Springs proved to be the right decision. Everything fell into place for me, and my art career blossomed. I was where I needed to be.

It was good luck or perhaps fate that I bought a house on White Street in Eureka Springs. The street is home to many artists. I can walk out onto my front porch, look in any direction, and see the home or the studio of an artist. Two of the artists, Mary Springer and Eleanor Lux, ironically had also gone to the Memphis College of Art, the same school that I had attended. Together we established the "White Street Studio Walk," an annual art show that has been going on for more than a quarter century.

I'm glad I followed my heart, stuck to my dream, and found my tribe. I found "home."

Pretty in Red

A few days after moving into my new home in Eureka Springs, I met my neighbor, Miss Cheatum. She was an elderly woman who lived directly behind me. There was a chain-link fence that separated the properties, and our houses were fairly close. Even though several decades separated us in age, Miss Cheatum and I became close friends. I had planned to erect a privacy fence on the property line between us, but when she told me she enjoyed watching me landscape my backyard, I knew there was no way I would deny her that pleasure. I kept the chain-link fence in place, and she was able to watch me work in the yard.

Miss Cheatum lived in a house that she had built after retiring from a long career with the Sinclair Prairie Oil company in Oklahoma. The home had been designed by the first woman to receive an architect's license in the state of Oklahoma. When entering Miss Cheatum's home, it was evident that she loved the color red. Red was everywhere. Her favorite wingback chair was bright red, and her kitchen appliances had been professionally painted with cardinal-red enamel. There were red throw pillows, red afghans, and red lampshades. She wore lots of red clothing, and her lips were always painted a nice ruby color.

When I worked in my backyard, I could hear Miss Cheatum's television. The volume was set high while she listened to CNN. The news channel played all day long. I, too, was a news junkie, and I enjoyed listening to her television while I worked in the yard.

The Sunday before Thanksgiving, two years after my move, I saw Miss Cheatum walk down the street. She was wearing red shoes and carrying a red purse as she walked the few blocks to the Christian Science Church. She was devout in her beliefs, and they were beliefs that I somewhat shared with her. My beliefs about the healing power of the mind came from studying new age philosophies, while Miss Cheatum's similar beliefs were rooted in the Christian religion.

The next Wednesday before I left for my mother's house to spend Thanksgiving, I called to tell Miss Cheatum that I had baked a pumpkin pie for her. It was her favorite kind of pie.

"I'm not feeling well," she said. "Could you save the pie for me until you get back from your mother's?"

"Of course," I said, and I wrapped the pie in plastic wrap and placed it in my refrigerator.

When I returned home on the Sunday following Thanksgiving, I learned that Miss Cheatum had passed away. When I was away, she had checked into a Christian Science care facility in a nearby town. While there, her health had improved. Feeling good one morning, she stood up, thanked her caregivers for all they had done for her, and then fell back on the bed and was gone. Although shocked, I was glad her end was quick and peaceful.

A few days later, I attended Miss Cheatum's memorial service. It was held in her living room and attended by her many friends. In the middle of the service while looking at her favorite red chair, I became upset, and I had to leave. Even though Miss Cheatum, at the age of eighty-nine, had lived a long life, her time with me had been too short.

The day after her service, I began building the privacy fence.

Where There's Smoke

Eureka Springs has a long history of fires. In 1883, seventy-five structures burned. A little over a century later, one of the town's most beloved buildings, the Old Red Brick Schoolhouse, caught fire. The three-story structure had been built in 1892, and it had served as the city's center of education until 1951. The building had an interesting feature, a two-story metal slide that was attached to the exterior. The slide was a large round metal tube that served as the fire escape from the building. On a hot June day in 1988, the old schoolhouse burned to the ground. Many of the town's citizens thought the fire was arson, and there were several conspiracy theories about why someone would set fire to the old structure. It wasn't arson. I knew the truth.

Late on that June afternoon, a friend and I were sitting in my front porch swing when we saw a large and vivid bolt of lightning shoot downward. The lightning was followed by an ear-splitting boom. We could tell that a building a few blocks away had been struck by the lightning bolt.

We both jumped up from the swing, and my friend said, "Oh God, that hit my house."

I said, "Don't be silly, your house isn't near where it hit."

He insisted that the lightning hit his house. He was in panic mode. To ease his fears, we got in my car and drove the few blocks to his house. We parked on the dead-end street in front of his home. I was right. His house had not been hit. The Old Red Brick Schoolhouse across the alley from my friend's home had been struck. We could see flames dancing through the top-floor windows of the structure, and the air was already saturated with acrid heavy black smoke.

About the time we got out of the car, fire trucks and other emergency vehicles sped down the one-way street followed by vehicles filled with curious town folk. My car was blocked in. While my friend worried about the flames spreading to his house, I jokingly said, "If my car burns, you owe me a new one." I won't tell you what he said to me.

The firemen fought the blaze for several hours. No matter how much water was pumped into the structure, the flames refused to die. Fortunately for my friend the wind was blowing away from his house. Neighbors on the other side of the schoolhouse spent the night hosing down roofs to protect their homes from the hot embers that were falling from the sky.

The schoolhouse was totally destroyed, and the ruins continued to smolder for several days. While little streams of smoke continued to rise from the ashes, old-timers came to pay their respects to a part of their past that had vanished. There were many tears.

The metal slide had attracted the lightning to the building. Even though I witnessed the cause of the fire, many people in town refused to accept what I had seen with my own eyes, and they kept the arson conspiracy theory alive. People believe what they want to believe, even when the "proof is in the pudding," or in this case, witnessed from a porch swing.

Working Fast

There are several things I have vowed to avoid doing: digging post holes for fences, roofing, insulating walls with fiberglass, and especially, pouring concrete. The last time I had roofed, I could barely get onto the ladder while carrying a bundle of asphalt shingles on my shoulder. I broke out in a red rash when I touched fiberglass insulation. As for digging post holes, I just didn't like to dig. Those tasks did not compare to the intense dislike I had for pouring concrete.

When I purchased my house in Eureka Springs, the backyard was a grassy area with a dirt path around the edge of the property where a dog had run the fence line. The driveway was nothing more than two bare ruts covered with a smattering of gravel. My partner Dick and I decided to install a concrete driveway and pour a patio in the backyard.

To save money we decided to do the pour ourselves. It was a do-it-yourself job and one that I hadn't done before. Though inexperienced, I did want to save money, and I was willing to give it a try. After the areas were leveled, and the forms were in place, we anxiously awaited the arrival of the concrete truck. We had the required equipment in hand, and we were wearing the necessary rubber boots.

When I heard the loud concrete truck nearing the property, I started to get nervous. I knew that once the concrete hit the ground there would be no time to waste. The heavy wet material had to be put in place and leveled before it started to set. When it hit the ground, we started doing what needed to be done. There was no time to dally, and there was no time to lean on the hoe. We finished the pour after a couple of fast-paced hours. The job looked good, and I was proud that we had done it ourselves. As satisfied as I felt, I was exhausted. I vowed to never work concrete again.

Several years later we decided to replace the forty-foot-long wooden porch on the front of our house. The Craftsman-style bungalow had been built in 1909. After doing research, we discovered that many Craftsman homes built during that period had concrete porches. If we could use concrete, we would no longer have to replace rotted boards and repaint the constantly peeling porch each spring. First, we needed approval from the Historic District Commission.

Because Eureka Springs had very few Craftsman homes, we drove to nearby towns in search of bungalows with concrete porches, and we took photos of the houses. We took the documented research, the photos, and an architectural rendering of the proposed project before the Historic District Commission. We asked for approval to put the concrete porch on the house, and the commission gave permission for the project to proceed.

We hired a couple of men to do the job. This time, I was not going to be involved in the pour. I made plans to sit nearby with a glass of wine in hand and watch the men work. On the day of the pour, Dick was at work, and I was left at home to oversee the project. The first man arrived plenty early, long before the concrete truck had been scheduled to arrive. The other man didn't show.

The man who was there began to panic because the job was going to be too much for one man to do. A few minutes before the truck arrived, the guy asked me with a desperate look in his eyes, "Do you know how to pour concrete?"

I reluctantly said that I did. He asked if I had rubber boots, and I told him that I did. I downed my glass of wine, ran to the basement, and got my boots.

I barely had them on when the truck arrived. Because the truck could not get the chute to the far end of the porch, we had to drag the material a long way to get it to the other end. We had to hustle to get it done and leveled. We did it, and it looked good. My fellow worker was impressed that I could do the concrete work. I didn't appear to be the type. Although I was exhausted both mentally and physically, when Dick returned home, I proudly puffed my chest out and I told him, "You owe me big time."

Never say never. I threw the boots away.

The Party Has to End Sometime

My friend Lester Armagost loved Halloween. He lived around the corner from me in a turn-of-the-century house. In mid-October, Lester would start turning his house into a haunted castle. For many years, it was the location for the town's most popular and much anticipated Halloween party. The prep involved removing furniture from the lower floor, stapling Visqueen to the walls, putting up decorations, and hauling in bales of hay for seating. For the yearly party, Lester did things to his house that most folks would never consider doing.

On Halloween night, Lester would open his home to the children who were trick-or-treating. Later in the evening at 9 p.m., the house was open to adults. During the Halloween party, the upstairs bathtub served as an iced beer bin. There was a well-stocked bar in his kitchen, and Lester hired bartenders to mix drinks. He did everything necessary to create a good time for his guests.

I knew Lester was ill before we met and became friends. That didn't bother me. I knew several people who had AIDS. I had lost friends to the disease. When I lived in Fayetteville, I hung out with four guys whom I considered my best friends. Of the four, three succumbed to the disease. Although there was a fear among the general population, I knew that AIDS could not be transmitted through casual contact. The stupid disease was not going to keep me from making and loving friends, sick or not.

During March of 1994, a late-season snowstorm dropped several inches of snow on Eureka Springs. Lester called to tell me that we had a friend, Steve, who was in bad shape and was in the ICU at the Eureka Springs hospital. Because the roads were impassable, Steve's nearest relative, a brother living in Oklahoma, could not travel to Eureka Springs to be with Steve. Lester and I donned our snow boots and walked to the hospital. We didn't want our friend to be alone.

Even though we weren't really family, because of the seriousness of Steve's situation, the staff bent the rules. They let us sit in the ICU with him. I don't know if Steve knew we were there, but I like to think that he did know. Lester and I rubbed his arms and legs and held his hand.

As sad and trying as the situation was for Lester and me, the time the two of us spent together at the hospital sitting with Steve was quality time. We cried, we laughed, and we talked about friendship, hopes, and fears. I kept thinking that it could be Lester in that bed. Lester was thinking the same. Steve lived less than twenty-four hours after being admitted. He was thirty-nine years old when he passed. Before leaving the hospital, Lester and I had a good cry, hugged for a long time, and silently walked home in the snow.

The weather in July of 1995 was summertime hot when Lester became bedridden. Unlike Steve, who passed in a hospital, Lester was in a bed in his home and surrounded by many friends who sat with him during his final hours. He lay unconscious with flowers strewn all around him on the bed and pillow. I was very sad. At the same time, I thought that the sight of him on the bed, smothered in flowers like an Indian prince, was beautiful. I knew that Lester was surrounded by love when he left us. He died at the age of forty-one.

The following Halloween, there was one more party in Lester's house. The party was held to honor him, and it was as festive and fun as ever. Lester would have liked that. His ashes were at the party in a beautiful urn, and I know he was there in spirit.

It is good to leave this world while being loved.

Mardi Gras, the Good Times Rolled

In 1995, I attended my first Mardi Gras when Dick and I visited friends who were living on Magazine Street in New Orleans. Their apartment was in easy walking distance to the famous French Quarter and to Canal Street, the location of numerous Mardi Gras parades.

One of our hosts was a regional manager of several McDonald's restaurants in the metro area. Two of the restaurants faced Canal and each had a second-story balcony. The balconies provided perfect viewing spots for parade watching and saved us from being lost in the madness of the crowds on the street. Many of the floats were two stories tall, and because we were watching from a two-story balcony, we were easy targets for bead tossers. We collected lots of beads and trinkets thrown to us on our lofty perch. Actor John Larroquette served as the monarch of the Krewe of Bacchus parade that year, and he easily tossed some gold beads to me.

My New Orleans friend was a member of a daiquiri club. Late each day while we were there, two gallons of frozen daiquiris were delivered to the McDonald's restaurant on the corner of Canal and Royal. We enjoyed sitting on the balcony, sipping cocktails, and watching the revelry below.

The first night after arriving in New Orleans, we spent hours partying in the Quarter. We partied way too much and tried unsuccessfully to keep each other standing. Dick, one of my friends, and I pulled each other down into a nasty gutter. I thought my clothes were ruined. After that fall, I was very careful to remain standing at all costs.

Between parades, we strolled around the Quarter and spent many hours on Bourbon Street. I was shocked at what folks would do to get cheap plastic beads thrown to them. Vendors were selling big cans of beer for one dollar. The beers were cooled in garbage cans filled with ice that were sitting directly on the sidewalk. I thought, *Man, this is living*.

The downside to the consumption of many beers was frequently needing to use a restroom. We kept running back to McDonald's because we knew our friend working there would let us use the restaurant's bathroom. The other option was waiting in line to use one of the portable toilets sitting in urine-soaked mud. Entering required walking a wooden plank that had been placed over the mud pit. Squirming on the way to McDonald's seemed to be the better option.

The day after Mardi Gras ended, Dick and I walked to Payless to buy new shoes and left our "party" shoes on top of a *Times-Picayune* newspaper machine. We hoped a homeless person could clean the shoes and get some use out of them. We didn't dare enter our car wearing the shoes that had walked the streets during Mardi Gras. They had waded through garbage and unspeakable waste created by thousands of revelers.

Years later in 2009, I was honored to be King Krazo during the Eureka Springs Mardi Gras. Although much less decadent than the Mardi Gras in New Orleans, celebrating the holiday in my hometown was just as fun, and I didn't have to throw away my shoes.

Shake, Rattle, and Roll . . . Not

The Arkansas Delta is located in the New Madrid Earthquake Zone. The zone runs approximately 125 miles from Cairo, Illinois, all the way to Marked Tree, Arkansas. The potential quake area includes five states. According to scientists, the area is long overdue for another major quake.

In the winter of 1811-1812 there were three to five major quakes in the area with the epicenter in New Madrid, Missouri. Because there were very few European settlers in the area, few structures were there to be destroyed. It was reported that church bells rang as far away as Boston from the shaking during the quakes. The Mississippi River ran backward for three days, and the backflow created Reelfoot Lake in Northwest Tennessee.

While growing up in the Delta, I felt occasional tremors, and I experienced ground shaking while living in Memphis. While living in Eureka Springs, the only time I thought about earthquakes was when I returned to the Delta. The possibility of the New Madrid Fault becoming active was foremost on my mind each time I was on the bridge spanning the Mississippi River between Arkansas and Memphis.

For the most part, folks living in the zone ignored the possibility that a major quake could occur. That is until climatologist Iben Browning predicted a 50 percent chance of a massive quake occurring on Monday, December 3, 1990. Although no one had ever successfully predicted the date a quake would occur, people living in the area believed him. Widespread concern, almost to the point of panic, took hold.

My mother lived in the quake zone in Marmaduke in Northeast Arkansas. When I visited her for Thanksgiving that year, she was busy preparing for the December quake. Although I didn't believe the prediction, I did secure her gas water heater to the wall with metal straps. The securing of the tank was recommended by "quake experts."

Mama had a list of suggested things to be done to prepare for the disaster. She kept telling me that "they said" to do this or to do that. I asked her who "they" were, and as always when asked that question, she didn't know. She laughed at herself for believing information from an unknown source that for the most part was told to her secondhand from ladies in her beauty shop.

My mother and her friends had collected water in gallon milk jugs. If the quake hit, they would need the water. My mother had several gallons stored underneath the dining room buffet. The nearby Walmart in Paragould was selling earthquake kits that contained survival items that included dried food, candles, a Bic lighter, and a heavy-duty, industrial-grade flashlight. My mother had purchased a kit "just in case."

Mavis, a lady that worked for my mother, was one of the most fearful of my mother's friends about the impending doom. The night of December 3, she moved her car from the carport and loaded it with supplies. Leaving her stubborn husband in the house, Mavis and her dog Tippie slept in the car on the night of great danger. She wasn't going to let her home's roof fall on top of her and the dog.

Ignoring Mavis's warning to vacate her house, my mother refused to sleep in her car that night. However, she did sleep with a pillow covering her head in case the ceiling fell in.

No earthquake occurred that night. Despite massive preparations by thousands of people in the area, most residents were saying, "I knew nothing was going to happen."

My mother said, "Well, at least I got a new flashlight out of it."

Framed

In 1996 I was asked to participate in a benefit art show for the Nerman Museum of Contemporary Art in Johnson County, Kansas. Approximately ninety artists and celebrities from across the United States were asked to participate. I was very flattered to be included in a show with some of the nation's leading artists and entertainers, including actor Martin Mull.

The theme of the show was *Frame of Mind*. Each participant was given a plain wooden frame of unpainted pine, approximately two-foot square with a one-foot square opening in the center. We could do with the frame anything that we felt like doing, even if that meant we totally destroyed it. That's exactly what some of the artists did.

I had participated in an earlier auction for the museum, and I knew the sophisticated buying audience in the area enjoyed artworks that were cutting-edge and a little bit naughty. My finished art piece had a somewhat risqué photo in the center. I adhered cast body parts to the exterior. I was pleased when it sold for a good price.

Included in that show was a piece donated by William Burroughs, who was a major postmodernist author. He is considered "one of the most culturally influential and innovative artists of the twentieth century." Burroughs is probably best known for his book *Naked Lunch*, and he is one of the founders of the Beat Generation. At the time of the show, he was living in Lawrence, Kansas, not too far from Johnson County.

I was very excited about his participation, but alas, the night of the reception, bad health kept him from attending.

Shortly after Labor Day 1951, in Mexico City, Burroughs accidentally killed his second wife, Joan Vollmer, by shooting her in the head in what was apparently a drunken attempt at playing William Tell. For the museum benefit, Burroughs had whitewashed his frame, placed a piece of plywood in the center, and shot a hole in the plywood with a gun. He signed it and titled it *After Labor Day*. The piece brought in more than seven thousand dollars. Although somewhat morbid, I do regret not being able to buy the piece, more for the signature than for any other reason. Burroughs passed away in 1997.

Mr. Burroughs was definitely a "bad boy." There are times that being bad pays off. However, I'm not willing to take that chance.

Just Smile

Dick and I were in Fayetteville eating lunch when one of my crowns came off. At the time, I thought it was just the crown, but when I looked at it, I found the tooth was still inside the cap. One of my lateral incisors, the tooth next to the big tooth, had broken off at the gum line. I had been having what I thought were sinus problems, but as it turned out, the pain on that side of my face was due to the rotten tooth.

It was two days before Halloween, when hundreds of trick-or-treaters would be visiting my home. I also had an art reception to attend that weekend, and I was scheduled to be a poll worker at an election the following Tuesday.

Besides those obligations, I had a reporter and photographer from a national magazine, *The Crafts Report*, coming to my house the following Wednesday to interview me. Not only was the reporter going to interview me, but she was also going to take photographs that would be included in the article.

I called my dentist, who could not see me until the following Wednesday afternoon. I was mortified. My vanity would not allow me to be seen with a tooth missing. I still had the crown. I decided that I would "fix it" myself until I could see my dentist.

I went to Walmart and bought two-part epoxy. I was aware of the material's possible toxic qualities, but I was desperate. I knew that when the two substances in the epoxy were mixed together, they would harden even in a moist situation, like my mouth.

I mixed the epoxy, pressed it into a form that fit my palate, stuck the tooth in it, and made a partial. It seemed to work fairly well, but every now and then, the partial would slip out of place. I went back to Walmart, bought a dental adhesive, and temporarily glued my homemade partial into place.

Because of the strong chemical taste, I decided to only put the partial in my mouth when in public. At home, I refrained from looking in the mirror. I had trouble talking correctly. The homemade partial interfered with my tongue placement. Before meeting the public, I put the partial in my mouth a few times and practiced speaking. I felt like Demosthenes, the ancient Greek orator who practiced speaking with pebbles in his mouth. With practice, I was able to speak clearly.

All went well through each event. And the homemade partial stayed in place. The partial got me through Halloween trick-or-treating, the art reception, and working at the election polls. I was still worried about the upcoming magazine interview and the photo, but it, too, went well.

Immediately following the magazine interview, I called a friend. While talking on the phone, my porcelain crown dislodged from the partial and fell to the kitchen floor. We both laughed. I was quite relieved that the tooth hadn't plopped out during the interview.

That afternoon, I made it to the dentist. He performed a root canal, placed a metal spike in what was left of the tooth, and attached a good-looking false tooth to the spike. My dentist said, "This is a first. I've never had a client make their own partial." I thought, *Yes, necessity really is the mother of invention.*

Man Among Men

Three years after I moved to Eureka Springs, I was invited to join a men's group. The men's group movement had been growing worldwide with the purpose of allowing males to get to know each other and to bond. The groups would meet on a regular basis, and members took vows of confidentiality. Every man was encouraged to express his feelings without the fear of being judged. When invited to attend the local group, I was hesitant. I was concerned about being the only gay man in a group of straight men. The guy who invited me assured me it would be all right. He said, "If members have a problem with your presence due to your sexuality, then that's a problem that needs to be addressed."

Against the advice of gay friends, I decided to venture into the "enemy camp." I told myself that the reason for joining was to educate the men about homosexuality. I hoped by telling my story, I would give insight into what it was like being a gay man, and that we—straights and gays—were more alike than different. Little did I realize what I would learn and what I would gain.

When I started attending the meetings, I was afraid to look at the other men or to hug them. I worried that they would question my actions. My limitations were self-imposed. I also had to combat my natural shyness. It wasn't long before I felt comfortable, and I no longer feared eye contact. I enjoyed the hugs they offered. Each week I looked forward to the social intimacy and the sharing I knew awaited me.

Not long after joining, a weekend retreat was planned. Even though I felt accepted by the group, I still didn't know if they would want me to camp out with them. They encouraged me to attend. The big weekend took place in November. The first day of camping was warm and balmy, until later in the evening when a front came through. It turned bitterly cold, and the wind chill temperature fell below zero.

We were tent camping, and I was miserable. Even though I was freezing, I decided not to pack up and go home. While sitting around the campfire the next day, we shared our life stories. We laughed, and we cried together. The harsh cold only intensified the closeness of the circle of men gathered around the fire.

As cold as it was, I felt warm inside. I was glad that I had attended the outing. I enjoyed the sweat lodge, the drumming, and the sharing of stories. I realized that my sexual preference did not, and should not, limit my participation in the family of man. We are more alike than different, and all life stories ring with familiarity.

All men have hopes and dreams, and we all have fears. My fears lessened. The Eureka Springs men's group continued to meet for several years. I did fulfill my original purpose of giving the group a greater understanding of what it's like to be a gay man. But what I received in return was far greater. I received a gift of trust and brotherhood.

Wasn't Aware That I Wasn't Aware

I first met Gaye Adegbalola when she came to Eureka Springs to perform during the Blues Festival in 1990. She was a member of the very popular blues group Saffire – The Uppity Blues Women. Gaye and I hit it off immediately.

One time while visiting my home, Gaye noticed a picture of Dick and me that we had made in one of the photo studios downtown. In the photo, Dick and I were dressed in Confederate uniforms with a Rebel flag in the background. Being a Southerner, I thought nothing of the setting. I was unaware.

Gaye kindly confronted me about the photo. She explained that for her, an African American woman, the Confederate flag represented racism and oppression. I was heartbroken that I had offended her. I broke down and cried. I loved her so much, and I could not stand the fact that I was insensitive to anything that may have hurt her. She taught me a valuable lesson about sensitivity.

Since that time, I have tried to be aware, stay awake, and always consider what may offend or hurt someone. I thank Gaye for creating that awareness in me. She wrote a song, "It's Alright for a Man to Cry." She told me about the song after I had cried over hurting her.

Tears can be cleansing.

New Bride-to-Be in Hiding

Since 1987, I have lived across the street from the Old Stone Store on White Street in Eureka Springs, Arkansas. The building is divided into four apartments. I have seen dozens and dozens of renters come and go during that time. Some have kept to themselves, and others have been good neighbors who have become friends. The line from the "Tinker, Tailor" nursery rhyme perhaps best describes the diversity of folks who have lived there.

Rich man, poor man, beggar man, thief, doctor, lawyer, Indian chief.

Several years ago, a man who was renting a small apartment in the building called and asked if I would cut his hair and give him a manicure and a pedicure. I said yes to the cut, but I told him he needed to do his own nails. He told me that he needed to look his best because he recently had become engaged to a woman whom he had met online. They had not met in person, and he wanted to look good when she arrived the next week from California. I asked him if he had sent a photo of himself to her. He said, "Yes, it was a recent picture of me, and she liked my looks." I wondered if he had smiled in the photo and if she knew that he was toothless.

Soon after Jayme, the bride-to-be, arrived in Arkansas, she walked across the street to my yard sale. The groom-to-be was with her. When introduced, it was immediately evident that Jayme was a man. She was quite large, shaped like a football player, and had hairy arms. She had on a disheveled large red wig that looked like a bad thrift store find. It was painful to hear Jayme try to elevate her voice to a higher register.

Jayme spent many afternoons that summer strolling up and down White Street. She was often accompanied by a neighbor's teenage daughter who was spending the summer in Eureka Springs. The two were kindred spirits, at least when it came to dress: Daisy Duke cutoffs and halter tops. Their wardrobe did differ when it came to shoes. The young girl wore sandals while Jayme sensibly wore tennis shoes. I think she may have had trouble finding women's sandals in a size fifteen.

One evening an ambulance arrived at the neighbor's apartment. I went across the street, worrying that something could be seriously wrong with one of the tenants. The paramedics were at the engaged couple's apartment. The EMT workers could not maneuver the gurney into the apartment. They had to aid the afflicted out of the apartment onto the porch. They came out with Jayme and placed her on the gurney. She had on a T-shirt, cutoff shorts, and one shoe. I noticed that she wasn't wearing her breasts, and her wig was on sideways. The next morning, I talked with the groom-to-be, and he told me that Jayme was fine. She had suffered a panic attack, and she had stayed overnight in the hospital for observation.

I didn't see her again. I thought that maybe she was staying inside to fully recover from her "bout." A few days later I read in the local paper, "James (name withheld), aka Jayme, a female impersonator, was arrested by the FBI for computer hacking. He was taken into custody while in female attire." As I had suspected all along, Jayme was a man. He was pretending to be a woman to hide his identity in an effort to escape from the law. Jayme was extradited to California. Not too long after the arrest, I noticed that the groom-to-be's scooter was gone. I wondered if he had moved to California to be near Jayme.

When incognito, one should at the least be willing to purchase a good wig.

Purple Muumuu and Big Lashes

Each time Millie rang my doorbell, I knew it was her before opening the door. I could see little else but purple through the frosted panes of the stained glass in my front door. She was a large woman who always wore a purple muumuu. She also sported a dyed-black Cleopatra hairstyle with a couple of inches of white new growth showing. She wore extremely long false eyelashes that touched her eyebrows. The lashes were always crooked. Millie was an antique picker from Neosho, Missouri. In the late 80s and early 90s, she visited Eureka Springs each week to peddle her goods to the town's antique-store owners.

Even though I was not an antique dealer, she stopped by my house to show me each week's "must-have" finds. I think someone told her that I was an easy mark. She always said, "I saw this, thought of you, and just had to bring it to you." I later learned that was her standard spill. Even though I suspected that Millie was working me, I really liked the funny and sweet woman. I sensed a good heart.

Millie drove a large, very old, olive-colored station wagon. She was accompanied by her husband Ern. He was in poor health and never got out of the car. More than once, Millie said, "I've just got to sell something today. We are out of money, and I need to buy Ern an inhaler."

When she told that sad tale, I always bought something. Usually, my purchase was a small item, sometimes chipped and never anything that I needed. One time I did make a big purchase, a very large file cabinet that had belonged to an artist in California. Millie and I wrestled it out of her station wagon and sat it in my driveway. There was no way that the two of us could get it into my art studio. Dick was quite surprised when he came home to find the cabinet sitting in the driveway. I still treasure the file cabinet, and it has an honored place in my studio.

During one visit, Millie informed me that she wanted to sell her home in Neosho and move to Las Vegas. She invited Dick and me to see her home in case we knew someone who might be interested in it. Although I didn't know anyone thinking of relocating to that town, curiosity compelled me to go look. Also, I thought it would be fun to visit Millie in her home environment.

When Dick and I arrived at her home, our jaws dropped. The large brick home was quite grand and sat on a city block. Built in the 20s or 30s, the two-story house had a porte cochere, and the home was just under seven thousand square feet. Upon entering, we were shocked to see the rooms filled with museum-quality antiques. The items included a throne chair, countless grandfather clocks, and a royal liter lift.

If Millie had one set of fine china, she had thirty sets. The bedrooms were filled with exquisite bedroom suites. Dick offered to buy one. Millie thought about the offer, and then said, "No, not for sale." I had been looking for an epergne. Millie had dozens, but none were for sale. She told us to follow her to the basement to see items that could be purchased. The available items were the run of the mill goods that she peddled when in Eureka Springs. We realized that Millie was a hoarder who couldn't bear to let go of her good stuff.

From the large basement we took an elevator to the top floor to look at the ballroom.

We got to see some of Millie's memorabilia. She had photos of herself taken years earlier when she had worked as an exotic dancer in Vegas. She was very beautiful in the pictures.

I was impressed to learn that she had been one of the models for the early Keane paintings that were sold nationwide. I remember as a child seeing the prints of the big-eyed, dark-haired girl that were sold in our local Woolworths. Millie had newspaper articles documenting her role as the black-haired model. She also told us a story about a time when she lived in Tulsa and came home from work to find one of her ex-husbands in bed with a former Miss Oklahoma. We had a good laugh about that story.

Even though Millie and Ern lived in a mansion, they spent most of their waking hours in the home's kitchen with their thirteen cats. In the kitchen there were two green Naugahyde chairs that had been shredded by kitty claws, and a small television.

Even though Millie at times was desperate for money, I understood why she wouldn't sell her priceless antiques that she'd collected over a lifetime. Sometimes it's hard to let go. After the visit, I lost track of Millie. I hope she was able to sell her house and to fulfill her dream of purchasing a double wide in Vegas, and to buy a warehouse to store her collection.

You can't judge a picker by her cover, especially when the cover is a purple muumuu.

Stage Fright

In 2012 a friend of mine was organizing a TEDx event in Bentonville, and she asked me to be one of the speakers. I immediately replied, "No way, I'm not a public speaker."

She said, "I'm not taking no for an answer right now. Please think about it."

Frankly, I didn't know what a TED Talk was. When I mentioned that I'd been issued the invitation, my younger and hipper friends were in awe and very excited that I had been asked. Not wanting to disappoint my friends or miss the honor and opportunity to participate in the TED program, I agreed to give the TEDx Talk.

I had always been somewhat shy, and I suffered from glossophobia, a fear of public speaking. It's estimated that as much as 75 percent of the population struggles with the fear of public speaking to some degree. My fear bordered on severe.

For most of my life, I had found casual conversation to be difficult because I felt my vocabulary to be lacking. I was afraid of making grammatical errors, and that people would think I was stupid. When I attended art receptions, I had a well-rehearsed script loaded in my mind with proper responses to the most asked questions. I could respond to the questions and remarks without thinking because I had my lines memorized.

When I learned that I would have to speak without notes or a teleprompter, and without a lectern, I thought, *What the hell have I done?* I also learned that the talk, approximately ten minutes in length, would take place in front of a live audience and be recorded. Then the video would be put online and available for viewing by a worldwide audience. Agony.

I wrote and rewrote the talk countless times. I rehearsed for hours in front of a mirror, pacing back and forth. My feet were tired, and my voice was hoarse at the end of each rehearsal day. A couple of weeks prior to the event, I was scheduled to give my talk before the organizing committee in a run-through. I had been given the wrong time, and I arrived at the rehearsal site an hour early.

Because I was there early, I was asked to sit quietly and observe while one of the other speakers presented her rehearsal talk. When she had finished, the committee reviewed the notes they had taken and told her to change some things, to rewrite certain parts, and to perhaps change the emphasis. I thought, *Oh no, they are going to be disappointed with my presentation. Why did I say I would do this?*

I stood before the committee and gave my ten-minute talk. When I finished, I looked at the committee with dread. "Perfect," they said. "You did exactly what needed to be done. No changes are needed." I could have yelled a big "hooray" of relief. I smiled all the way home. I was as giddy as an adult man could be. I thought, *Well, well, well. I'm something.*

That "I'm something" feeling didn't last. The night before the actual talk, I was in panic mode. *What if I forget my speech? What if I fall? What if I faint?* The hour-long drive from Eureka Springs to Bentonville seemed longer than usual. The steering wheel became damp from my sweaty palms. I knew that the event had been sold out at fifty dollars a seat, and I didn't want the ticket holders to feel cheated if my talk didn't hold up.

The program began at 10 a.m. There were three speakers ahead of me. I didn't hear a word they said. I was busy rehearsing the talk in my head. Then it was my turn, and I was introduced. When I began, I did remember what I needed to say. I was reassured that I was doing okay when I heard laughter at the appropriate places. At the end of my talk, I was told that there were misty eyes in the audience. The talk ended with hearty applause. I felt that I had survived the ultimate test, and that I could do anything.

During the lunch break, I received many compliments. One of the best came from a high school senior who approached me and said that my talk moved and inspired him. I would have cried happy tears if I had not been in public.

I was physically exhausted during the drive home, but my inner being was energized. I had conquered a fear. Sometimes a pumped-up ego can be a good thing, spurring one on to do difficult things. I consider the TEDx Talk a time that I had my "feet held to the fire." Since that day, I've had many public speaking gigs. I never thought I would be able to say that I enjoy public speaking, but I do. It's never too late to overcome a fear. It can be freeing. It was for me.

Fear of the Little Things

My mother was terrified of mice, and she did everything she possibly could to keep them out of our house. She had my father nail flat canning lids over holes where the rodents had chewed through the baseboards. Despite efforts to keep our home pest free, a mouse would still find its way into our home, and my terrified mother would get on top of the kitchen table. My sister Rhonda and I would join her, and we would all scream in terror. My mother taught me to fear mice. I have kept that fear my entire life even though I think mice are cute, and I know there is no way the little rodents can hurt me.

We did not have cockroaches in my parent's house. The first time I encountered the insects was when I moved to Memphis. For reasons unknown—this fear was not taught to me by my mother—I was terrified of the roaches. The city's warm, moist climate was the perfect environment for the bugs to live and multiply. Many homes in Memphis, mansions included, were infested with the insects. When I would bring groceries home from the Piggly Wiggly store, the bugs would climb out of the brown paper bags. I spent a good part of my budget on roach spray to no avail. Roaches were everywhere, and they were indestructible.

When a friend who lived in the apartment above me was in the process of moving from Memphis to Virginia, Dick and I offered to help him load his belongings into a truck. When we took a large unframed painting off his kitchen wall, we found hundreds of roaches on the back of the canvas. Dick and I dropped the painting, and the roaches scattered. We made a beeline for the door, and on the way out we stepped on dozens of roaches. The sound was like corn popping.

It wasn't long after I had met Dick that I learned he was ophidiophobic. The phobia, a fear of snakes, is a common one and is shared by one-third of adults. When we would visit a zoo, Dick would not go into the reptile house, and if a snake appeared on television, he would recoil, yell, and cover his eyes. I did not share his fear of snakes. Whenever a nonpoisonous snake appeared in our backyard, I picked it up and relocated it to the nearby woods. If poisonous, I shooed it into a plastic bucket, and I would relocate it. One afternoon a large black snake appeared in the yard, and a terrified Dick watched through the kitchen window while I wrangled the critter. I grabbed the reptile by the tail. It wiggled violently with whiplike movements, and I was unable to hold on to it. It escaped and quickly fled into a small opening in the door to Dick's workshop. I told him it was fine and that the snake would more than likely be out of there by morning. Dick would not open the door to the shop for the next two weeks. The experience taught me to pick up a snake by grabbing it behind the head. If I did that, they could not wiggle free.

I received a call late one afternoon while I was attending an Arts Council meeting. It was Dick. He told me there was a snake in our screened-in back porch, and I must come home immediately to remove it. I left in the middle of the meeting. I found Dick looking at the snake through the kitchen window in terror. He had locked the back door in case the snake could somehow figure out how to open it. I put on a long heavy-duty pair of welding gloves to protect my hands. I was prepared for battle, and I bravely entered the back porch. I found a tiny snake not much larger than an earthworm. I didn't laugh, and I didn't make fun of Dick. I understood unreasonable fear. I relocated the little reptile to the woods.

If a snake should ever get into our house, you will not find Dick on the table. He will be several blocks down the street. If it should be a little mouse that gets inside, then I will be on the table. When it comes to phobias, size doesn't matter. Sometimes it's the little things.

Tulsa Time

Along with two of my Eureka Springs artist friends, Barbara and John, I was invited to participate in a group art exhibition at the Dennis R. Neill Equality Center in Tulsa, Oklahoma. On the morning of the day the show was to open, we dropped off our artwork at the exhibition space. We had the rest of the day to run around Tulsa and play tourists before attending the exhibition reception that evening.

It could not have been hotter in Tulsa—it was over 110 degrees. After we toured downtown Tulsa and viewed the city's large number of art deco buildings, Barbara went back to the hotel. John and I continued to pound the hot pavement in search of a bar and a cold beer.

During the search, we were approached by Tony, a homeless man with a crooked leg. He could sense that we were searching for something. When he asked if he could help us find something, we said, "A cold beer." He immediately said, "Follow me. I know a place that has the coldest beer in town." He took us to a nearby bar. Before we entered, Tony said, "This is the most redneck bar downtown." We went in anyway. I have this theory that no matter the situation or place if one acts as if they belong, then they will be okay. I think people are like dogs when it comes to sensing fear. I try not to show fear when I'm in places that may not be safe. My theory may be proven wrong someday, but so far so good.

Tony was right. It was very redneck, and the beer was very cold. We sat at a table and watched burly guys shoot pool on a lone pool table that took up much of the floor space in the small bar. Tony joined us at the table, and we bought him beers. The drinks were a bargain at one dollar a draught. Tony was a fascinating man with a touching hard-luck tale.

A previous visit to Tulsa had proved unpleasant for him. Following a drunken night, Tony woke up in an open field in the company of two policemen. He was booked and put into jail. Shortly after the incident, he left Tulsa for Washington State. He told us that he should have stayed there and not returned to Tulsa. He did have plans to go back to Seattle the very next morning. He somehow had managed to get a bus ticket for the trip. I wanted to give Tony some money, but I was afraid that he would buy more beers, repeat the drunken arrest event, and miss his bus.

I regretted that I couldn't help Tony beyond buying him beers. John and I enjoyed our time with him and our afternoon in the most redneck bar in downtown Tulsa. Everyone has a story worth hearing. Thank you, Tony, for sharing your story. Wherever you are, I hope you are safe and happy.

Karmic Debt Paid

Like most yards in Eureka Springs, mine is very small. There is no room for a pool. I thought, *At least I can have a hot tub.* Dick wasn't keen on the idea, and he thought I would get tired of it in short order. He suggested that I not invest too much money in buying one, and that I should consider a used one. He began checking the ads in the local *Star Shopper*, and he found a hot tub for sale in nearby Centerton, Arkansas, a little over an hour's drive from Eureka Springs. He called the number listed in the ad, and he made arrangements to meet the seller and inspect the hot tub.

I went to the bank and withdrew cash to pay for the hot tub as requested by the seller. With money in hand, Dick and I left Eureka Springs for Centerton. We were pulling a flatbed trailer in hopes of using it to bring the hot tub back home. Following the seller's instructions, we drove down country roads until we eventually came to an old chicken house where the hot tub was being stored. No one was in sight until a young man popped out of the nearby woods and came toward us. He was the seller.

He took us into the chicken house to see the hot tub. It was filthy. It was filled with trash and hay. There was no electricity in the old building, and we could not test the tub to see if it worked. Dick didn't want me to buy it, but I was determined to get it. It was a very good price, and it was a Jacuzzi brand, the best-known spa company. I thought if it didn't work that Dick, who was a master electrician, could fix it. Dick finally gave in, and I gave the young man three one-hundred-dollar bills. Then we loaded the tub on the trailer and headed home.

During the ride to Eureka Springs, Dick asked me, "Do you think the hot tub really belonged to that guy?"

I'm a trusting person and somewhat naive. "Yes, I do," I said. "Why do you think it wasn't his?"

Dick said that the young man was obviously hiding in the woods, and only came out when we showed up. Dick went on to say that the guy seemed somewhat nervous and eager to make a quick transaction.

I said, "Well, maybe it wasn't his, but we don't know for sure." I didn't want to admit that we were possibly hauling stolen goods.

We left the hot tub on the trailer overnight and unloaded it early the next morning. Before installing a permanent electrical outlet for the tub, Dick ran a heavy-duty extension cord to the tub to make sure it ran. When Dick lifted one side of the wooden skirt surrounding the hot tub, he gasped. The area underneath the tub was filled with dried grass, corn, and trash. About that time, a large pack rat came out of the straw and hurriedly came toward me. It was the size of a small rabbit. I yelled and ran in panic. The rat ran across the patio and into the woods. I ran into the house, where I stayed until Dick finished removing the trash from underneath the Jacuzzi. Because of my extreme fear of mice, I waited inside until all the straw had been removed and no other creatures had been found.

Dick rewired and repaired the hot tub, and soon it was in perfect working order. Even though I had likely purchased stolen goods, I felt that I had paid my karmic debt for the illegal transaction when I was terrorized by a giant rat. I enjoyed the hot tub for the next twenty years. I'm still deathly afraid of mice, and I still enjoy a good bargain.

Best Friends Forever Together

I got my first dog when I was four years old. One of my earliest memories is going with my parents to a kennel on Kingshighway in Paragould, Arkansas, to select a pup. I was given full reign to make the selection. I chose a small reddish terrier. I named him Jiggs, after a character in the comic strip "Bringing Up Father."

I was a middle child and the only boy in my family. My sisters had each other as "buds." In my young mind, Jiggs was my "brother," and he was my best friend. I shared my room with him, and I told him everything. The dog was my confidant, and he was my comfort when I was afraid. I could always count on Jiggs.

He was with me all the time while I lived at home, and he was the hardest family member for me to leave when I went away to college. During my sophomore year at Arkansas State University, Jiggs passed away. I was talking with my mother on the phone when she gave me the news. I cried in the phone booth. I had lost my brother.

Through the years, I've had a few dogs including Chelsea, a chocolate poodle; Heather, an Afghan hound; and Desiree, a peekapoo. Desiree was with me in Memphis, Fayetteville, and Eureka Springs. She lived to be eighteen years old and is buried in the backyard in my pet cemetery.

About the same time that I lost her, I also lost her companion Alice, a cat who was also eighteen years old. Within the next few months, I lost my two other cats, Joshua and Priscilla. They were both seventeen years old.

The losses were too close and almost too much for me to deal with. I said, "I can't bear to have another pet and go through this again."

I held out for a few short years before I thought, *I want another pet.* When I told Dick I wanted another one, he said, "You better get one now. You are fifty years old, and the pet may outlive you if you delay, and that wouldn't be fair to the pet." I agreed and decided to get a cat because my yard wasn't really suited for another dog.

I got a Ragdoll kitten and named him Memphis Blue. I spoiled him rotten. I bought an Aliner travel trailer so that he could go on vacation with us. I collected state magnets for him—he had eight. They were on his section of the fridge. The cat had traveled with us to New Orleans, and he had walked on a leash at the beach in Florida. Memphis Blue was with me for more than sixteen years. I still have his ashes.

Besides Memphis, in the past few years, I've had four, Opie, Dixieland, and Glitterbelle that have passed away. They were also cremated, and I have their ashes in nice wooden boxes. I still have one cat, Dutch, and when he passes, I will also have him cremated.

Dick and I have lived in Eureka Springs for a long time. It is home. We want to stay here. A few years ago, as a Christmas present to each other, we pooled money and bought a plot in the Eureka Springs cemetery. We plan to be cremated, and have our remains buried there. We will also have the "cremains" of our pets buried with us. We want to stay together.

Perhaps our tombstone should read, "Merry Christmas to all and to all a good night." And that includes our fur babies.

What I Did for Love

One night I was in the kitchen fixing supper when I heard a commotion. My cats were on the back screened-in porch when the porch door was accidentally pushed open. One of my male cats, Opie, was suddenly outside. The other cats were yowling, telling me that something was wrong. Opie panicked and ran. I made it to the back porch in time to see him scramble underneath the fence.

I turned off the burners, stopped fixing supper, and began searching for the cat. I searched all night long to no avail. The next day, I put up reward posters in the neighborhood, and I posted on social media about my lost cat. I spent the next several days looking for Opie. I walked the entire length of the hollow behind my house. I wanted my cat back, even if it was his lifeless body. I needed to know what had happened to him.

After ten fretful days and sleepless nights, a friend and neighbor who lived a block away called me and said that he had seen Opie behind his house. I immediately went there. Opie was nowhere to be found. I decided to set a live trap. I thought if the cat was hungry and showed up again, he would enter the trap baited with food. The first evening that I checked the trap, I had caught a possum. I carefully released him. The next evening, I put on protective welder's gloves to protect my hands in case I had caught another critter. I had. It was another possum. I released the animal, and I went back home.

On the evening of the thirteenth day following Opie's disappearance, I went back to check the trap. No Opie. I removed the gloves and sat on a nearby stone wall, and I cried. Then I heard a faint meow. Opie came out from under a nearby shed, and he came to me. I picked him up, and I immediately started walking home. I left the live trap and gloves behind.

Everything was fine until we were in front of my house, and a loud motorbike went by and spooked Opie. He panicked and started biting my hand. After thirteen days of searching for him, I endured the pain, and I refused to put him down. He bit me more than thirty times. I got to the backyard, and I put the cat inside my art showroom by the patio. I ran inside the kitchen, sat on the floor, and held my hand over the kitchen sink. Blood was gushing from the many wounds. I yelled for Dick, who ran into the kitchen in a panic.

It took a while, but we eventually stopped the bleeding. The bites were on my index finger, thumb, and the area below my thumb on my left hand. I thought, *Thank goodness, I'm right-handed.*

After treating and applying bandages to my hand, I went to my showroom to retrieve Opie. He was thin and he stunk. When I carried him into the house and put him down, he acted as if nothing had happened.

I didn't blame Opie for biting me. I knew he was terrified when it happened. My finger did swell to three times its normal size, and it turned black. My doctor said that I had almost lost it. Still today I can only bend my index finger so far, and the area below my thumb is partially numb from nerve damage. I don't care. I would do it all again to save my kitty.

What I did for love.

Wildfire on the Set

After several months of delays that were partially caused by the COVID-19 pandemic of 2020, a movie scene that I was to appear in was finally rescheduled. Based on the Native American legend about a ghost horse combined with elements from the 70s hit song, "Wildfire," the movie was scheduled to be filmed in Tahlequah, Oklahoma. Although I knew I would have very little screen time speaking my two lines, I was excited about being in a feature-length film, one that was going to have widespread distribution.

I did have a little film experience. I had appeared in a commercial for a national yarn company, and I had been in one short comedic movie. I worried that my limited experience had in no way prepared me for being in a feature-length film. The movie, titled *Wildfire: The Legend of the Cherokee Ghost Horse*, was being directed by Eric Parkinson, and was to star Chevel Shepherd in the lead. Chevel had previously been a winner of the television singing competition *The Voice*. Veteran actor Anne Heche also had a part in the movie. I knew that there would be a sizable crew on set, and I was nervous about my small part in the movie's final scene. What if I flubbed up my two lines in front of a large group of professional movie people?

I had received the scene schedule and a copy of my two lines a couple of weeks before the shoot was to take place. I was instructed to bring two sets of clothes because I was to appear in two scenes that in the movie took place on different days. I was also asked to bring a cowboy hat. The character I was going to play was a photographer who worked for the *Tahlequah Daily Press*. I was going to be paid SAG (Screen Actors Guild) wages for my movie role.

The director contacted me and said they needed someone to act as my assistant, and he asked if Dick would be interested in the role. Dick said yes. He was to receive payment as an extra, and he, too, was asked to wear a cowboy hat. The next day, we went to a Tractor Supply store that had a Western wear section, and we bought the hats.

Several days before the shoot, I rehearsed my two lines over and over. I knew them forward and backward. I woke up each morning silently rehearsing the lines in my head before I got out of bed. I'd recite them out loud while preparing lunch or while watering the garden. I could say the lines perfectly, but every once in a while, I would mess up. I would say, "It's for the *Tahlequah Daily News*" instead of saying the correct line, "It's for the *Tahlequah Daily Press.*" I thought, *One little damn wrong word could cause me a lifetime of embarrassment.* Dick assured me that I would be able to do my part perfectly. I wasn't so sure.

We left Eureka Springs early on a Saturday to make the two-and-a-half-hour drive to the rodeo grounds in Tahlequah, where the scene was to be shot. The first scene we were to be in was scheduled to shoot at 1:30 p.m. The director greeted us and told us they were running about an hour behind schedule. I had an extra hour to rehearse my lines and to be nervous. Finally, it was time for the scene, and after only two takes the director said, "Good job. No need to do it again." A day later on social media, he said that I had nailed my performance.

I was in additional scenes that night that were filmed around a massive bonfire. By then I was at ease on set, and there were no nerves on my part. The rest of my speaking lines were ad-libbed and required no memorization. I was relaxed, and I was having fun.

Both Dick and I enjoyed our time on set. I left Tahlequah feeling good about my tiny part in the movie, but I also left knowing I was not a threat to Brad Pitt.

Happily, Ever After

Dick and I had been together forty-three years when Circuit Judge Chris Piazza ruled the Arkansas ban on same-sex marriage invalid on May

9, 2014. The ruling came late on a Friday, after courthouses in the state had closed. I was attending an art reception when I heard the news.

I immediately called Dick, told him about the ruling, and said, "Do you want to get married in the morning?"

He asked, "Is this a proposal?"

I laughed and said, "Hell yes."

"Yes," he answered. "I will marry you."

The Eureka Springs's courthouse was the only one in Arkansas that would be open the next day, a Saturday. The resort town is a marriage destination. Our courthouse opens for four hours on Saturdays to accommodate tourists wanting a license. I knew that folks from all over the state would be flocking to town the next day to obtain one. I told Dick that we would get to the courthouse bright and early the next morning.

The evening before our big day, a representative from the Human Rights Campaign called and asked if one of their reporters could follow us through the licensing process and the marriage ceremony. I liked the idea that our wedding would be recorded. I had not thought about or had enough time to hire a photographer. As it turned out, that would not be necessary. There were plenty of press photographers present.

I planned for us to get the license and have a nice luncheon, followed by an outdoor wedding on our patio. Before I had planned much, I was notified that a stay would probably be issued that could put the judge's ruling on hold. I called former mayor Beau Satori, who was to conduct the ceremony, and asked him to be at the courthouse early the next morning. I told him *if* we were able to secure the license, we would be wed immediately and have the marriage recorded on the spot.

We got to the courthouse early the next morning. There were two female couples in line ahead of us. Soon many more couples arrived, and the line grew very long. The Human Rights Campaign reporter and cameraperson found us. We waited for the clerk to arrive. Word spread that the county clerk was "out of town," and a deputy clerk would be issuing the marriage licenses.

When the deputy clerk arrived at 9 a.m., she refused to issue licenses to same-sex couples. She said she did not have the proper authority. Knowing this was a possibility, I had come prepared. I had printed out the judge's fourteen-page ruling, and I showed it to her. She still refused. The female couples were crying. I was angry that we were having our rights denied.

When the deputy clerk opened the door, I told everyone to get in line. We filed in and lined up at the window to get our licenses. The clerk still refused. She called the police. Several police officers arrived. The clerk shut the window in our face. The police told us to leave or be arrested.

The Human Rights Campaign's camera continued to roll, and the reporter continued to interview me. Dick, my friends, and I were the last ones standing our ground inside the courthouse, but eventually we too were forced to leave. Dick and a friend of mine, Cyd King, went to our home to take care of the food and drink that Cyd had brought with her from Fayetteville for our wedding feast.

As I walked to my nearby car, someone yelled, "Zeek, come back." Upon my return, the police informed us that the courthouse would reopen in ten minutes. Another deputy clerk who was at the courthouse to register early voters had kindly stepped forward to issue the licenses.

I called Dick and told him to come back to the courthouse. We got back in line directly behind the two female couples. We were issued the license.

We immediately walked down a hallway to a bay window, joined by several of our close friends. The HRC cameras were still rolling. Our friend Beau conducted a beautiful ceremony. There were many tears. We immediately had the license recorded. We were legally married.

On that Saturday morning, May 10, 2014, we were not thinking about the historical significance of two men being legally united in the South. We just wanted to get married. We had been together for forty-two years, and we wanted to have the same legal and financial protections that marriage afforded straight couples. These were protections that had previously been denied to us even though we had been in a long-term, loving relationship.

Dick and I are honored to have been the first male couple to be married in the South.

The afternoon following the wedding, the phone began ringing. It was the press. During the following days and weeks, we were interviewed on camera by more than one television station, and we were interviewed by several newspapers, including the *Washington Post* and the *New York Times*. News of our wedding was in publications around the world. A reporter for the largest wire service in Asia came from Tokyo, Japan, to our home to conduct an in-person interview. We appeared twice via Skype on *Huffington Post Live*. One of the segments was with actor John Lithgow.

After being pushed into the worldwide spotlight, Dick said, "Well, if people don't know I'm gay by now, they never will." That's for sure. Since that day, I've had more than one person ask, "Don't you wish you had waited and had a nice formal ceremony, followed by a beautiful reception?" My reply is, "No, I wouldn't change a thing about our wedding day." What we did that day was exciting, and important. It was a drama-filled roller coaster of a day. We made history. We were married. Our loving, committed relationship is recognized as "equal." We knew it all along.

Love wins in the end.

Teenage Angst

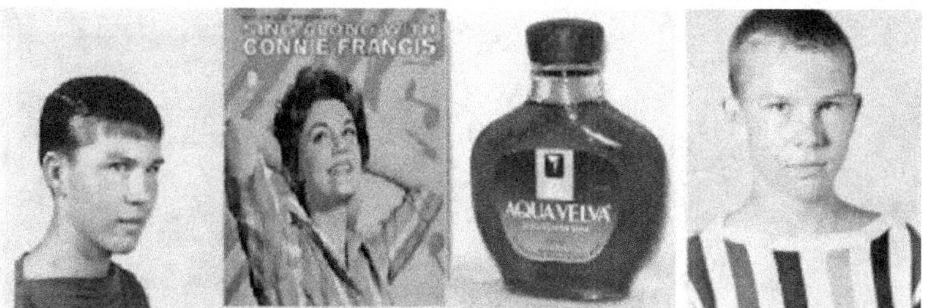

A little dab will do you   My first album   There's something about an Aqua Velva man

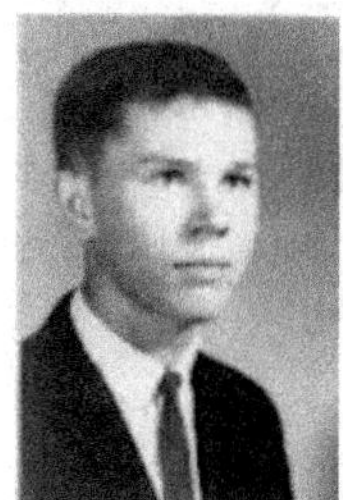

Senior photo

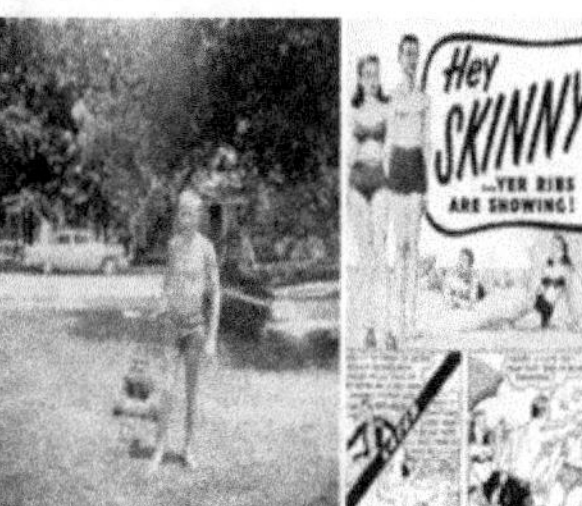

Prime candidate for this Charles Atlas ad

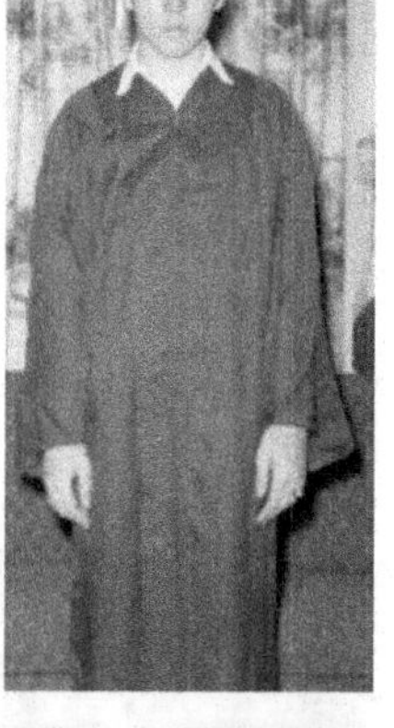

At Right – Graduation
Day 1966

At Left – Looking for
Kim Novak at the Sunset
Drive-in movie

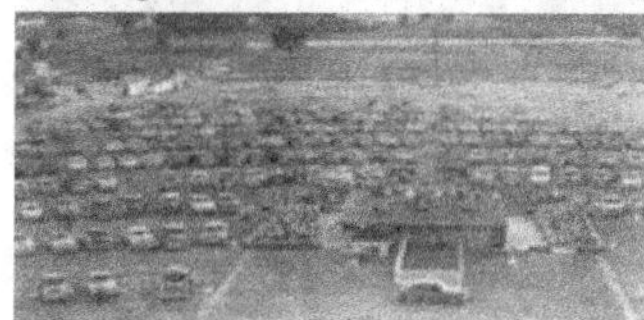

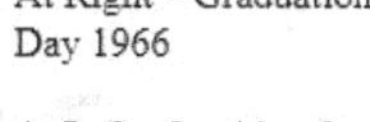

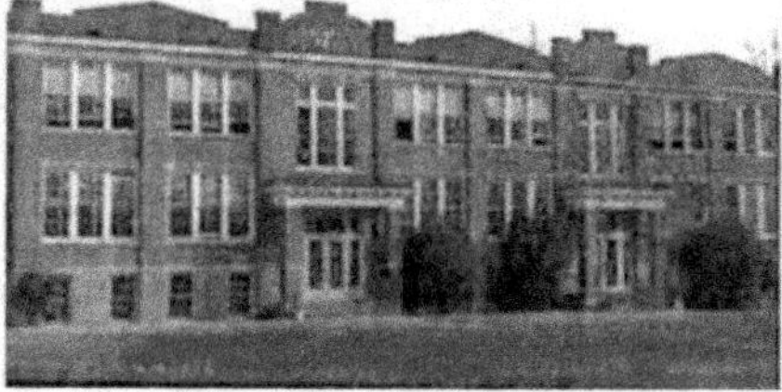

Marmaduke High School

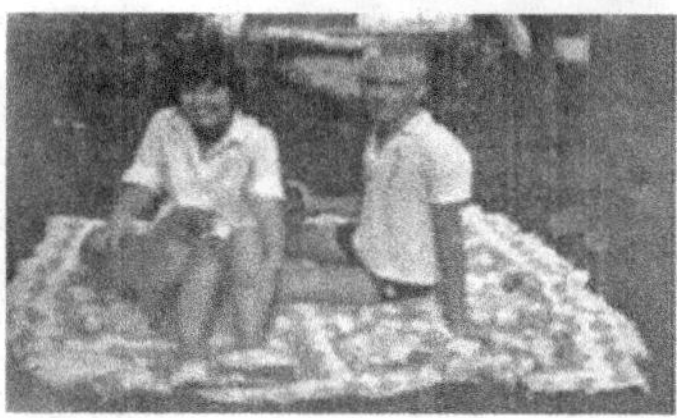

About to catch some rays with a friend

Off to College

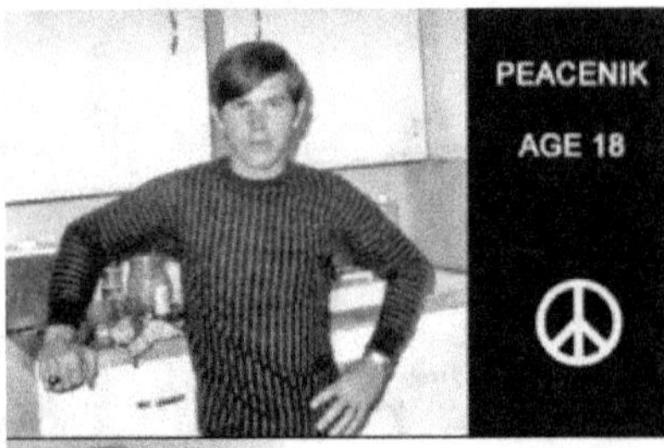

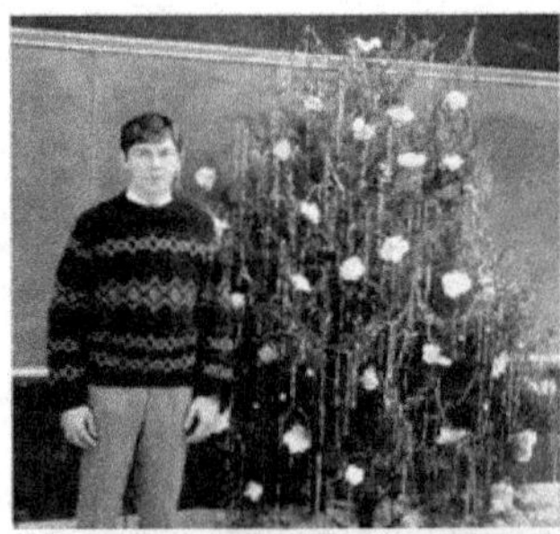

Top Left- Off to college
Top Right – Home for the holidays

Left – Barefoot hippie
Right – Memphis Academy of Arts

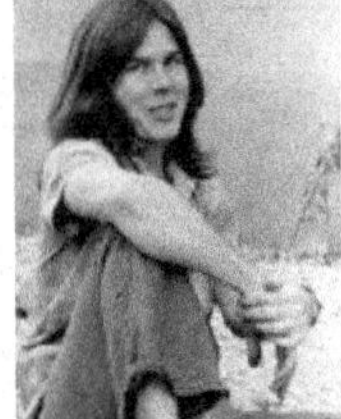

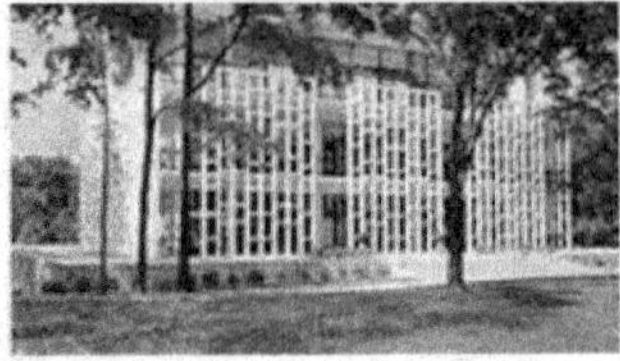

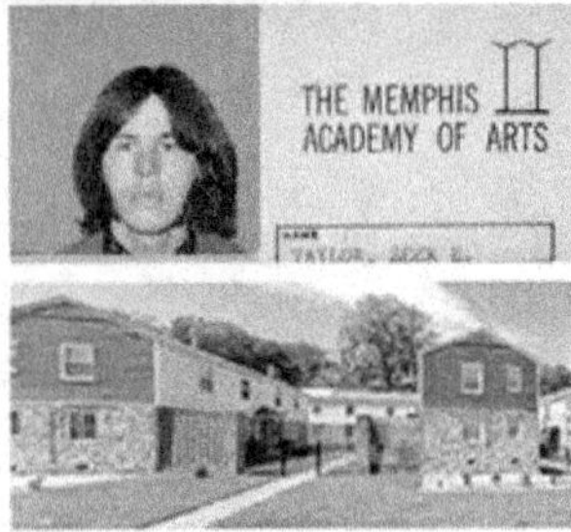

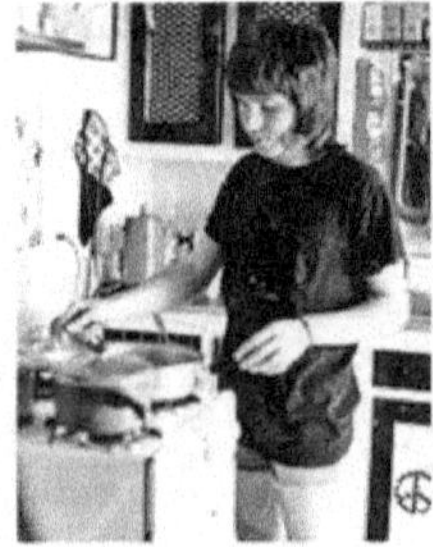

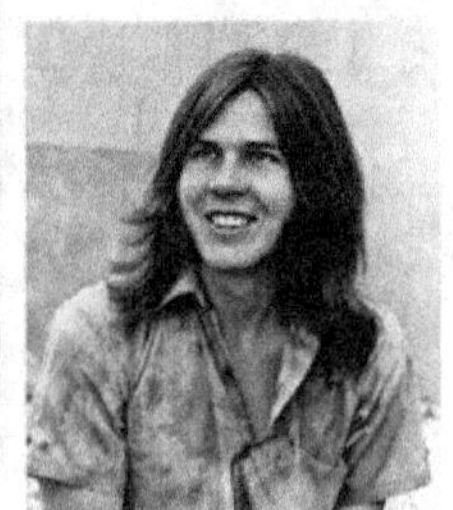

College ID and Living Quarters   Making beans and rice   Happy to be on my way

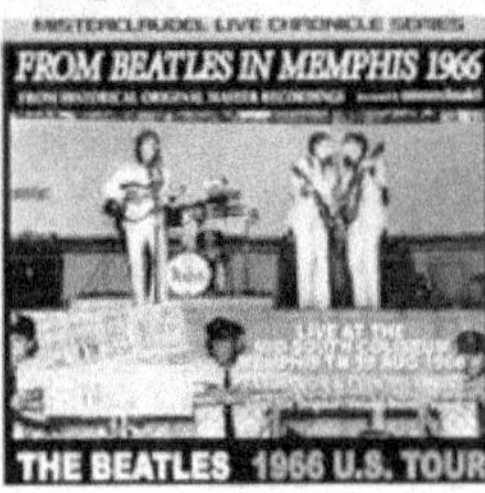

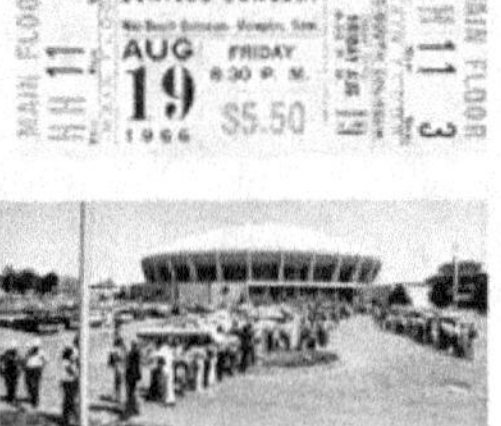

Imagine seeing the Beatles for just five dollars and fifty cents. On the left is the proof. Memphis, August 19th, 1966. It was amazing!

Keeping Body and Soul Together

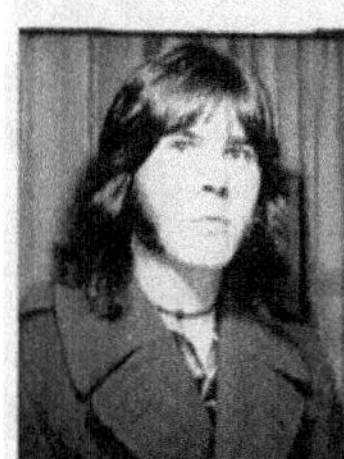

Zeek Taylor

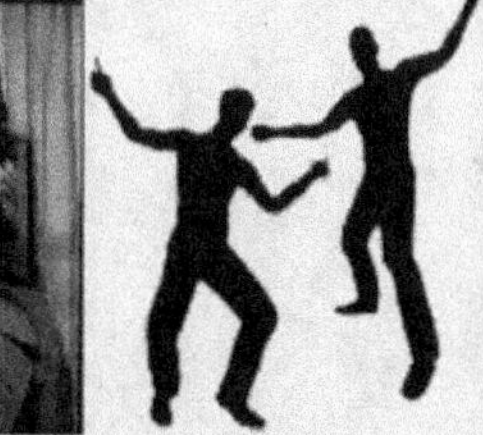

The Way We Were

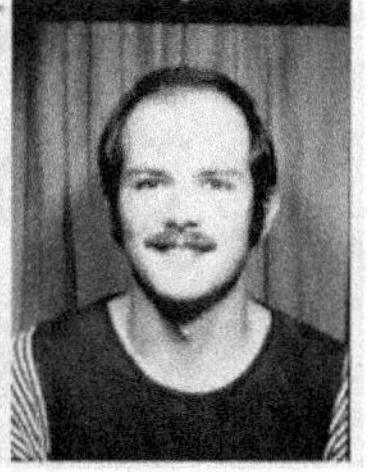

Dick Titus

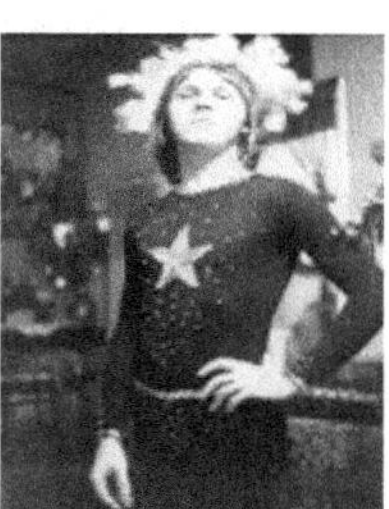

Ballet South

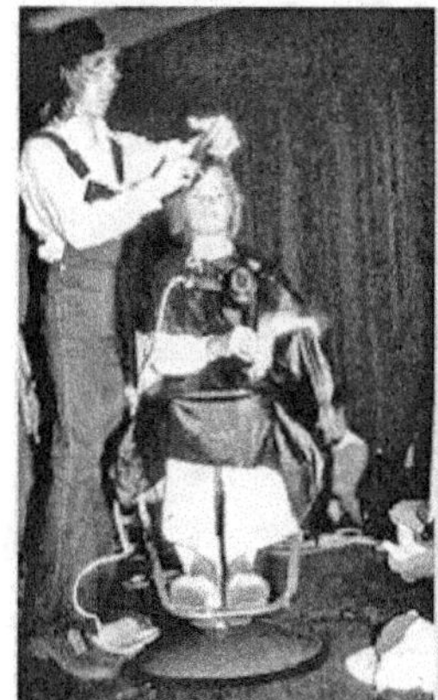

Platform work

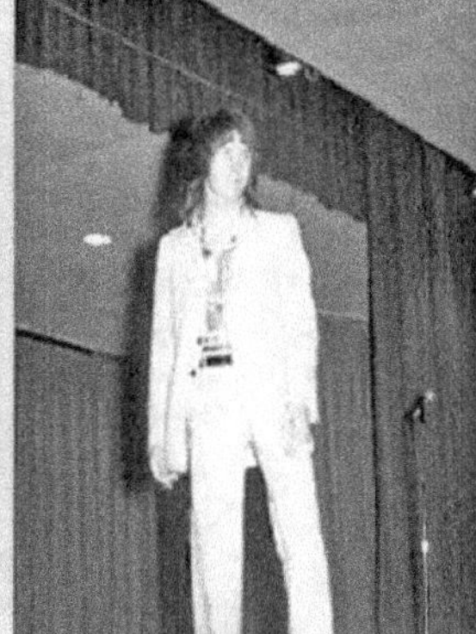

Modeling the $200 suit

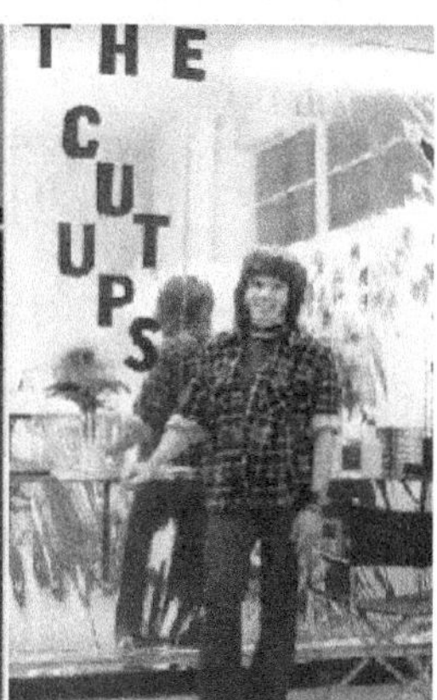

Just stylin'

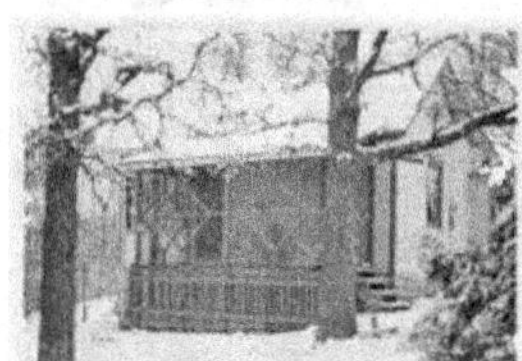

Our First House

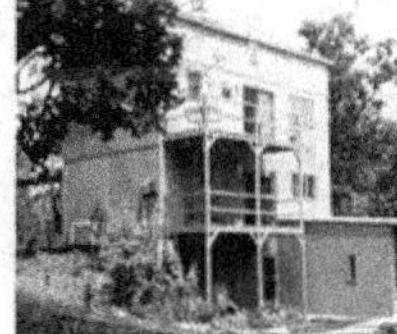

The energy house on PBS

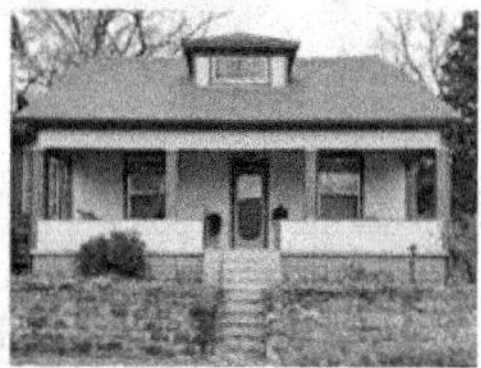

Our house in Eureka Springs

Making Friends and Memories Along the Way

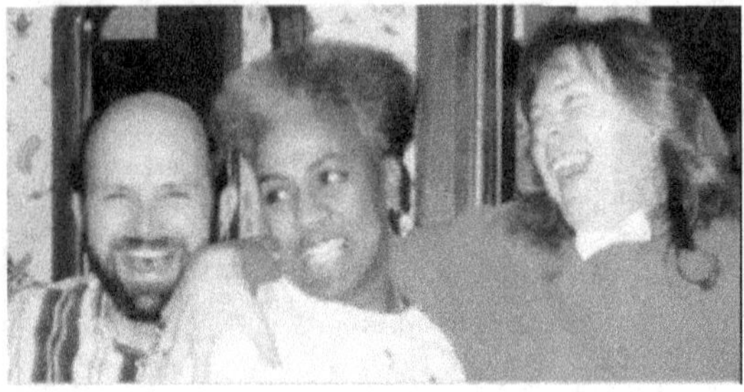

Dick, Gaye and Zeek having a ball

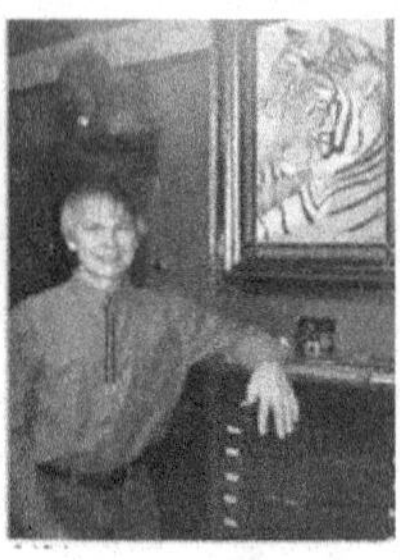

Zeek is featured in the
Crafts Report Magazine

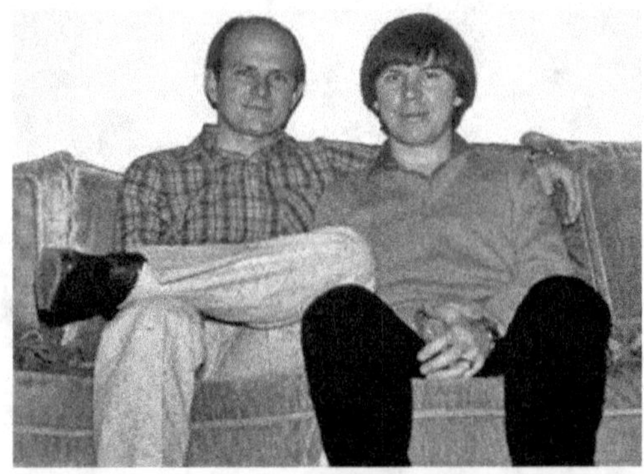

At Left – Dick and Zeek
"approaching" middle age

At Bottom – National
recognition as an artist

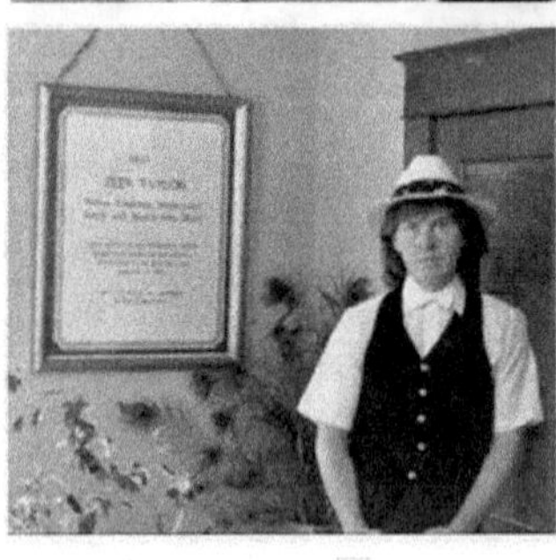

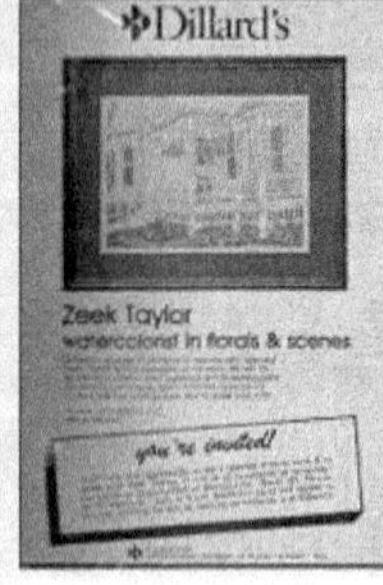

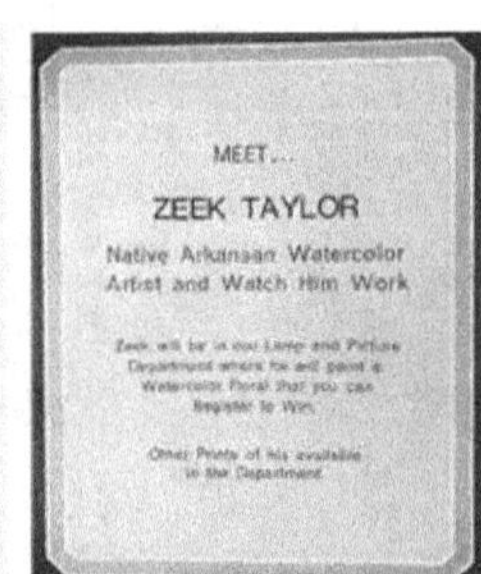

Much Ado

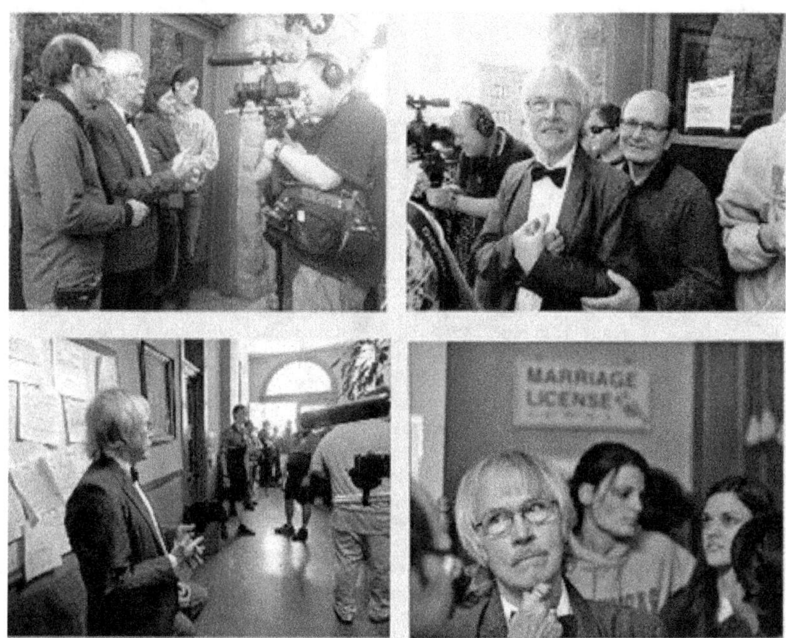

The battle at the courthouse, the uncertainty of the day, the media attention and wondering if finally, our rights will be recognized or if we will be turned away again.

Love Conquers All

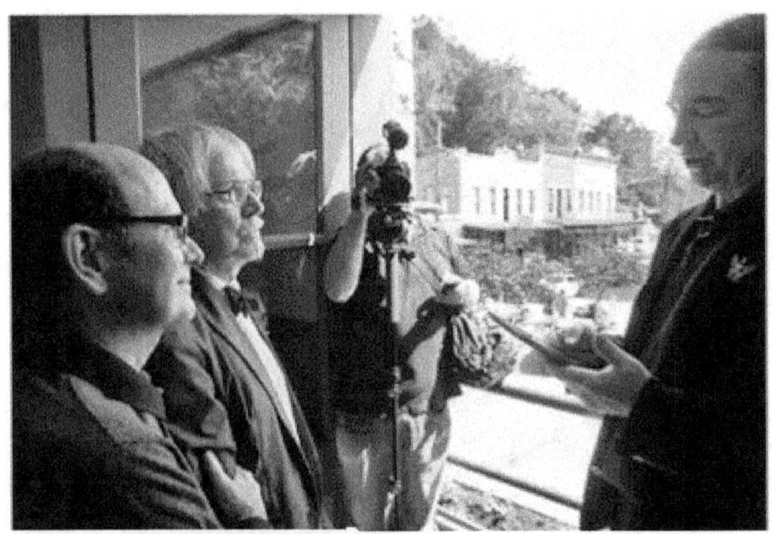

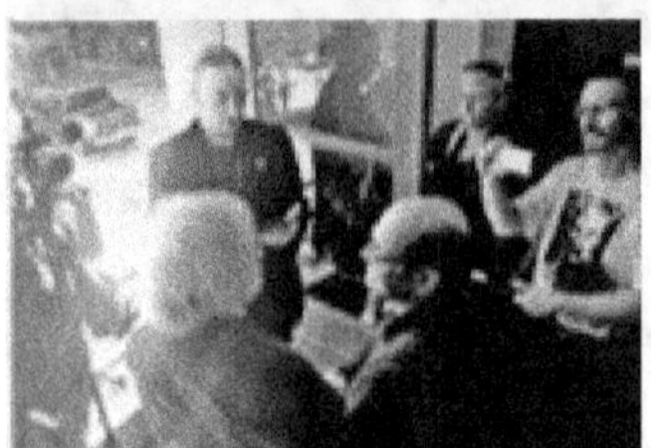

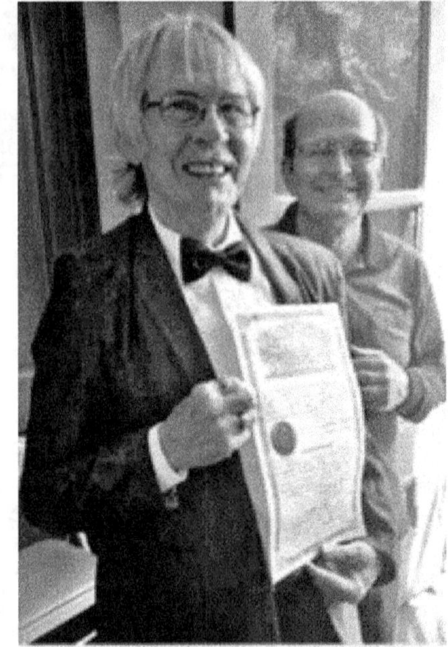

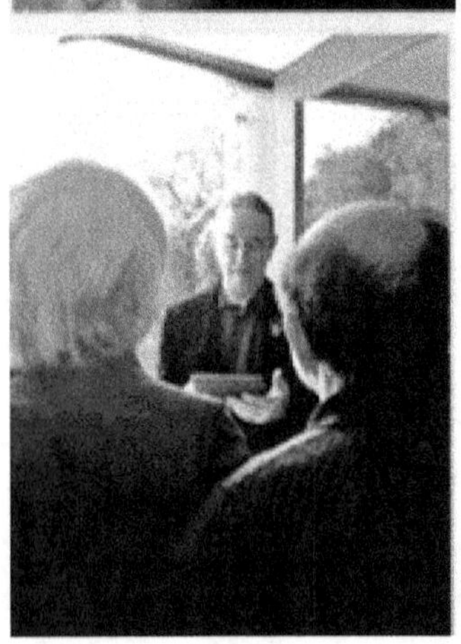

Eureka, I've Found It

~ 279 ~

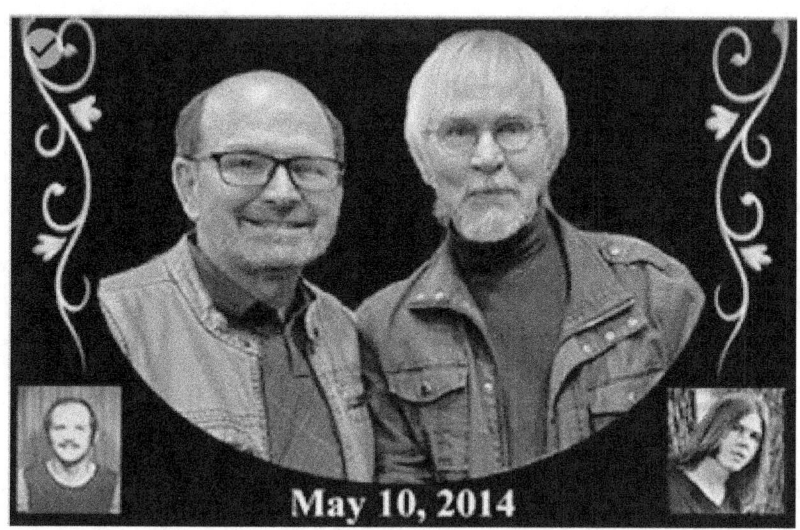

ACKNOWLEDGEMENTS

I had wonderful parents, Z.W. and Allene Taylor, who loved me and encouraged me from an early age to "go for it." I would also like to thank my biggest fan and my life partner, Dick Titus for his unwavering support and for his love. He made me believe in myself. I also thank my best friend and biggest cheerleader John Rankine who has encouraged me in every endeavor I've undertaken. I thank Paula Martin, producer of the NPR show Tales from the South. She encouraged me to write and to share my stories with the public. And last I would like to thank the fine folks of Eureka Springs, Arkansas, who nurtured my desire to create, propped me up when needed, and applauded my successes.